D1178164

"AN EXTREMELY IMPORTANT

Saturday Review

"WOMEN AND MADNESS details the damage that psychiatry has done to women and offers valuable documentation and new insights. But it goes much further than that. This book challenges the definition of madness itself.

Gloria Steinem

"Phyllis Chesler brings to life and interprets the enslavement of women, and particularly the role of psychiatry and psychiatrists in enforcing this enslavement. She offers some deeply personal and very political alternatives for women who want to change their lives and the society."

Peter Roger Breggin, M.D.

"The right book at the right time by the right person . . . As a practicing psychoanalyst, I can validate most of what [Phyllis Chesler] says."

Robert Seidenberg, M.D.

"True—and helpful . . . open, vulnerable, honest book."

Susan Sontag

WOMEN & MADNESS

Phyllis Chesler

▲ AVON
PUBLISHERS OF BARD, CAMELOT AND DISCUS BOOKS

Some of the material from Chapters Two, Three and Four has appeared in different form in:
"Women and Psychotherapy," THE RADICAL THERAPIST, September, 1970. "Patient and Patriarch; Women in the Psychotherapeutic Relationship," WOMEN IN A SEXIST SOCIETY: STUDIES IN POWER AND POWERLESSNESS, edited by Vivian Gornick and Barbara K. Moran, Basic Books, 1971. "Stimulus/Response: Men Drive Women Crazy," PSYCHOLOGY TODAY, July, 1971. "Women as Psychotherapeutic Patients," WOMEN'S STUDIES, Summer, 1972.

AVON BOOKS
A division of
The Hearst Corporation
959 Eighth Avenue
New York, New York 10019

Copyright © 1972 by Phyllis Chesler
Published by arrangement with Doubleday and Company, Inc.
Library of Congress Catalog Card Number: 72-76136
ISBN: 0-380-50559-2

First Avon Printing, October, 1973
Ninth Printing

AVON TRADEMARK REG. U.S. PAT. OFF. AND
FOREIGN COUNTRIES, REGISTERED TRADEMARK—
MARCA REGISTRADA, HECHO EN CHICAGO, U.S.A.

Printed in the U.S.A.

They all looked half drugged or half asleep, dull, as if the creatures had been hypnotized or poisoned, for these people walked in their fouled and disgusting streets full of ordure and bits of refuse and paper as if they were not conscious of their existence here, were somewhere else: and they were somewhere else . . . each was occupied in imagining how it, he, she, was triumphing in an altercation with the landlord or the grocer or a colleague, or how it was making love. . . . It was painful in a way she had never known pain, an affliction of shameful grief, to walk here today, among her own kind, looking at them as they were, seeing them, us, the human race, as visitors from a space ship might see them. . . .

But the most frightening thing about them was this: that they walked and moved and went about their lives in a condition of sleepwalking: they were not aware of themselves, of other people, of what went on around them . . . they were essentially isolated, shut in, enclosed inside their hideously defective bodies, behind their dreaming drugged eyes, above all, inside a net of wants and needs that made it impossible for them to think of anything else.

Doris Lessing
The Four-Gated City

Acknowledgments

I thank Lillian, my mother, for giving birth to me, and for taking care of me long before I could write such a book—and for whatever dreams, whatever wisdom she and Leon, my father, whispered or sang to me while I slept.

I thank my friends for their love and support, and for certain evenings, weekends, and conversations: especially, Vivian Gornick, Ruth Jody, Judy Kuppersmith, Jim Pelletier, Michael Pessah, and Marjorie Portnow.

I thank the women I "interviewed" for surviving—and for sharing their experiences with me.

I thank the members of the Association for Women in Psychology, especially those in the Chicago collective, and those feminists without whose existence, encouragement, and examples this book may not have been written just now.

I thank Natalie Braverman, Louise Brown, Lillian Chesler, Catherine Clowery, Bici Forbes, Mary Shartle, Martha Hicks, and Angie Waltermath for their secretarial assistance.

I thank my students for their interest and for their help in various phases of the data-collection and statistical analysis: Elizabeth Friedman, Doris Fielding, Delsinea Jamison, George Sideris,

Marina Rivas, and Roland Watts. I especially thank my colleagues in the Department of Psychology at Richmond College, and George Fischer and Larry Mitchell for their loyalty and support during the winter of 1971.

I thank Betty Prashker and Diane Matthews of Doubleday for their invaluable help in seeing this book through to publication.

Much appreciation is due the MacDowell Colony for housing and feeding me during most of the summer of 1971; to Shirley Willner of the Biometrics Branch of the National Institute of Mental Health for answering all my questions promptly and sympathetically, and for sending me all the necessary data; to Laura Murra of the Women's History Research Library in Berkeley, California, for sharing the files with me; to Sylvia Price of the New School for Social Research for getting me many of the books I needed—and for her help when I needed them still longer; to Stuart Kahan of the Downstate Medical Center in Brooklyn for his review of the statistical analyses; and to Sara Whitworth of the Whitney Museum for her suggestions about Amazons and goddesses in Greek art.

Contents

DEMETER REVISITED—
AN INTRODUCTION

In the beginning, if there ever was such a time, Demeter, the goddess of life, gave birth to four daughters, whom she named Persephone, Psyche, Athena and Artemis. The world's first children were unremarkably happy. To amuse their mother—with whom they were all passionately in love—they invented language, music, laughter—and many more useful and boisterous activities.

One morning Persephone menstruated. That afternoon, Demeter's daughters gathered flowers to celebrate the loveliness of the event. A chariot thundered, then clattered into their midst. It was Hades, the middle-aged god of death, come to rape Persephone, come to carry her off to be his queen, to sit beside him in the realm of non-being below the earth, come to commit the first act of violence earth's children had ever known.

Afterwards, the three sisters agreed that he was old enough to be Persephone's father. Perhaps he was: who else could he be? There were no known male parents . . . and thus they each discovered that in shame and sorrow childhood ends, and that nothing remains the same.

Persephone's sisters came home without her. Demeter raged and wept. Her bones seemed to shrink, her cheeks became wrinkled. She bound up her hair and turned wanderer, but could not find her eldest daughter anywhere on earth. Finally the sun spoke and told Demeter what had happened, that her daughter was married and a queen. He counseled her:

"Why mourn the natural fate of daughters—to leave their mothers' home, to lose their virginity, to marry, and to give birth to children"?

Demeter was grieved beyond and before reasoning. Remembering an oracle's prophecy of a splitting, a scattering, and an exile, she said to the sun:

"Yea, if that be the natural fate of daughters, let all mankind perish. Let there be no crops, no grain, no corn, if this maiden is not returned to me."

Because Demeter was a powerful goddess, her wishes were commands and Persephone returned. Persephone still had to visit her husband once each year (in winter, when no crops could grow), but her union with him remained a barren one. Persephone was childless. Neither husband nor child—*no stranger* would ever claim her as his own. Persephone belonged to her mother. That was Demeter's gift to herself. (In those days, goddesses were still able to perform the miracle of "not choosing." They were both virgins and mothers, mortal and immortal, forever the same and forever changing.)

But "oh" and "oh" and "oh" sighed Persephone's sisters after they had seen everything: the maiden's helplessness and rape, the young bride's childlessness, the mother's suffering—the terrifying simplicity and repetition of it all.

"Yes," they said of the maiden and the mother, "yes, she rules both beneath and above the earth, but she cannot keep us here any longer."

Psyche was the first to speak. "I am beautiful—some say more beautiful than all my sisters, and still no man claims me as his wife." (Actually, Psyche and Persephone looked quite alike: you could not tell them apart.) "Sisters! I am longing for love. I am lonely and frightened in our mother's house. I wish a husband—with strong and handsome eyes—and I wish to have a child."

Athena spoke next: "I am not beautiful—and care not for such things. (She was in fact exceedingly beautiful, but was very tall—even for the daughter of a goddess.) "Sisters! My childhood is over and must be relived. I wish to be born again—and of man. I wish to plot the clash of heroes from afar, dressed in the finest armor, moved by the finest wisdom. I wish for my own wholeness and not for children or a husband."

Artemis spoke last. (She too was tall, and of a darker complexion than her sisters.) "Sisters! Perhaps I wish for the impossible and will have to wander even farther than our mother did in search of it. I, too, want heroic clashes and great deeds. But I also want love and children. My head aches with visions of swords and altars, dazzling cities, and beautiful maidens. There is a music in my ears strange to our mother's house."

Well, as this conversation is common knowledge among schoolgirls, we know what each sister arranged for herself.

Psyche went home to plead for a husband. Demeter and Persephone were astounded by such a strange desire, yet they knew it must be satisfied. In secrecy, for such a thing had never before happened, Psyche was married to Eros—to Love himself, to Cupid, Aphrodite's son. Psyche lived alone with her husband, in a splendid palace, set high on a nameless mountain. Silent, invisible servants brought her whatever she wished. At night, and only at night, Love came to visit: Psyche's husband—but she didn't know who he was or what he looked like. Love had warned her never to look at him, but to love him in darkness. One midnight, after he had fallen asleep, Psyche lit a small oil lamp for a single, guilty look—and woke Love, who fled the palace. Miserable and frightened, Psyche set out to find him. After many near perilous failures, Love finally rescued his unhappy wife. He brought her to Heaven to live in an even more splendid palace. There, surrounded by the immortals, Psyche, Love, and their daughter, Pleasure, lived happily forever after—the first heavenly Holy Family.

Athena never returned to her mother's house. Instead, she went straight to Zeus, the god of gods, and proposed a bargain much to his vain and clever liking: to be re-born of him. She asked him to become her mother. And so Athena became twice-born, the second time of man. She emerged fully grown from Zeus's head, wearing the armor she so desired. Like Persephone, Athena remained childless and fiercely loyal to her one parent. Unlike Persephone, Athena was never raped, abducted, or made a king's unwilling queen. She needed no rescuing. If there was rescuing to do, Athena herself would do it. Indeed, she rescued many a male hero, helped him slay hideous monsters, capture unobtainable prizes, win great wars, and destroy ancient cities. This stately daughter of Demeter seemed to have no memory of her earthly and female origins. She never understood why certain men still insisted on sacrificing to her before planting and after harvesting. She smiled to herself. Didn't they know it was a strange tribute to one who had chosen her own parent—and, in so doing, had stopped turning on the wheel of repetition?

Artemis, the youngest of Demeter's daughters, returned to her mother's house. First she had Demeter consecrate her to the moon, so that no matter how far she'd have to wander, she would never forget, never betray her origins. That done, Artemis quickly perfected the arts of hunting and riding and warfare, of plant healing and midwifery. Then, with the moon for guide, she left to found a city—no, it was a tribe—no, it was a culture, the likes of which the world had never known. Every woman in it was a soldier and a mother, tears were as common as physical bravery, marriage was scorned, rape unthinkable, and the love of young girls praised in poems written by even the most hardened war veterans. Artemis herself had many female lovers, and many daughters, each of whom founded other Amazon cities in Africa, in South America, and elsewhere in Asia.

Goddesses never die. They slip in and out of the world's cities, in and out of our dreams, century after century, answering to different names, dressed differently, perhaps even disguised, perhaps idle and unemployed, their official altars abandoned, their temples feared or simply forgotten. What of Demeter and her four daughters?

Demeter, the goddess of life, and Persephone, her ghostly, embryonic maiden-daughter, were for a long time celebrated in elaborate secret ceremonies by the most sophisticated of the ancients, and more openly by everyone else. But somehow—no one really knows why—such celebrations of mothers and daughters certainly ceased. That which had gone before could no longer be worshiped. Fierce prophets proclaimed martial law against the past. Even fiercer prophets proclaimed martial law against the present. Monotheism changed the fate of mortals and immortals alike.

Still, not everything changed. Mother worship shifted, ever so subtly, ever so keenly, from Demeter to her daughter Psyche. Gentle Psyche, in love with Love, in love with marriage, was soon enshrined as the gentle Virgin Mother Mary, her daughter, Pleasure, became a son named Jesus. And it happened as quickly as this. Demeter was stripped of her powers, torn from her maidenhood, and exiled into history as a wretched, fearful wanderer. No longer was she a mother-goddess. Now Demeter appeared only as a stepmother, often a cruel one, or as a witch, often an evil one, come to haunt children in their fairy tales and nightmares. Children cried at the sight of her. Their fathers tortured and burned her many times at the stake.

And what of Persephone and Psyche and the Virgin Mary? Why, they became Cinderella, Snow White, the Sleeping Beauty, struck dumbly domestic by a Demeter turned stepmother. They all turned to princes and white knights to rescue them from this rather incomprehensible turn of events.

In our time, Psyche has three children but is very depressed. Lately, she never gets up before noon. The Virgin Mary is an alcoholic, hiding behind drawn shades. Persephone is frigid—and worries about it. Cinderella is anxious, paces back and forth a great deal, and has twice tried to kill herself.

In our time, the stepmothers wander still—exiles, with no memory of what has gone before. Demeter has been known to curse at passing airplanes, to dress in shapeless mourning costumes, to talk to herself, to talk nonsense. . . . Often these days, when Demeter gives birth to a child, she abandons her then and there, turning her own face to the hospital wall. Sometimes, as in a trance, Demeter tries to keep her daughter at home with her again forever.

What of Artemis and Athena? Some say that Artemis and her daughters drowned in a flood—or, like angels, left earth in sorrow, before their work was done. Others say that after losing some very great battle, they killed themselves. Still others claim to have heard them decide to retreat, break up, and wait for better times. Even Athena, that most exceptional woman, had eventually to put away her shield and helmet, and take up books, rosaries, knitting needles, and gossip—and occasionally a royal crown or a university post.

Today both Artemis and Athena have increasingly been caught at violence—at crimes of passion, greed, even of honor. Most often, they do whatever is required of them, these proud and lonely two, do their jobs well, too well. Sometimes Athena, sometimes Artemis, is well known for some accomplishment—envied, admired, misunderstood—until she turns on the gas, poisons herself, drowns—and is done with it once more.

This is a book about female psychology—or, if you will, about the many faces of Demeter and her four daughters, about what has happened to them in the twentieth century, and how it has been viewed and treated in psychiatric settings: certain myths reveal a great deal about the origins and models of contemporary female personality. I draw upon them often, as I describe the relationship between the female condition and what we call madness—that divinely menacing behavior from whose eloquence and exhausting demands society protects itself through "reason" and force.

This is a book about the dramatically increasing numbers of American women of all classes and races, who are seen, or who see themselves, as "neurotic" or "psychotic," and who seek psychotherapeutic help and/or are psychiatrically hospitalized. This is a book about the many "whys" of such help-seeking behavior; about "what" is experienced and viewed as in need of help; and about "how" these women are—or aren't—helped.

Chapters One and Ten discuss the basic psychological dimensions of female personality in our culture. Chapter One presents the lives and "psychiatric" histories of four women, based on autobiographical, biographical, and "case history" material. These, and modern women in general, are viewed in terms of what growing up female in the family means. The mother-daughter relationship is analyzed, as is the role played by mythological or historical heroines, such as the Virgin Mary or Joan of Arc, in female experiences of "normality" and "abnormality." Chapter One describes how female reproductive biology, patriarchal culture, and the modern parent-daughter relationship have so combined as to insure such characteristically female behaviors—and ideals—as self-sacrifice, masochism, reproductive narcissism, compassionate "maternality," dependency, sexual timidity and unhappiness, father-worship—and the overwhelming dislike and devaluation of women.

Chapters Two and Three view both the mental asylum and private therapy as recapitulations or mirrors of the female experience in the family. Clinicians, most of whom are men, all too often treat their patients, most of whom are women, as "wives" and "daughters," rather than as people: treat them as if female misery, by biological definition, exists outside the realm of what is considered human or adult. A double standard of mental health—and humanity—one for women, another for men, seems to good-naturedly and unscientifically dominate most theories—and treatments—of women and men. Traditional and contemporary clinical theories and practices are reviewed in Chapter Three. A new definition or, rather, a different way of understanding female "psychiatric" symptoms (such as depression or frigidity), male "psychiatric" symptoms (such as alcohol and drug addiction, or sociopathic personality), and what we call madness (or schizophrenia) is presented in Chapter Two. The types of behaviors that are *hospitalized* in America are also related to caste (sex and race), age, class, and marital status.

Chapter Four and the Appendix present an analysis of our nation's "mental illness" statistics from 1950 to 1969. These chapters document the extent to which women, more than men, and in greater numbers than their existence in the general population would predict, are involved in "careers" as psychiatric patients: women who are having "nervous breakdowns," crying fits, temper tantrums, paranoid delusions; women who attempt suicide, who take unknown quantities of drugs to smother their anxieties, their hostilities, their ambitions, their panics, their sexual unhappiness—and their visions. In 1968, American women comprised 62 per cent of the adult (ages eighteen to sixty-four) population in outpatient clinics, 61 per cent of the adults in private hospitals, and 60 per cent of the adults in general psychiatric wards. Women of all ages comprised 50 per cent of the adults in state and county hospitals—where they returned more frequently and were detained for longer periods than their male counterparts. Adult women currently compose two thirds of the patients in Community Mental Health Centers and in private psychotherapeutic treatment. And most "patients" over sixty-five, in asylums or in old-age homes, are, of course, women. (Our society does not overly like old age— or women.)

Chapters Four through Nine describe the patient "careers" of sixty women whom I interviewed about their experiences in psychiatric hospitals and private or clinic outpatient therapy— experiences which took place from 1945 to 1971 in America and England. The women I spoke with were of European, Latin-American, and African descent. Their ages ranged from seventeen to seventy. Their sexual, marital, maternal, and "political" involvements were as far-ranging. Only a minority of these women experienced what I would call genuine states of madness. Most were simply unhappy and self-destructive in typically (and approved) female ways. Their experiences made it very clear to me that help-seeking or help-needing behavior is not particularly valued or understood in our culture. Help-seekers are pitied, mistrusted, tranquilized, physically beaten, given shock therapy, lied to, yelled at, and ultimately neglected—and all "for their own good." Many women in American state mental asylums participated in sex-role-typed slave labor, i.e., they worked as domestics for no or token payment. Many were also medically abused—or neglected; sexually repressed—or exploited; ridiculed and abandoned—by family and professional establishments alike; and given very little "therapy," verbal or otherwise. Many women who were lucky or rich enough to buy the best verbal treatment therapists could offer were not always or often understood or helped.

It has never been my intention to romanticize madness, or to confuse it with political or cultural revolution: certainly because of the pain our mistreatment of it insures, certainly because of the pain that it may intrinsically involve. (Such pain is to be understood and respected—but never romanticized.) Most weeping, depressed women, most anxious and terrified women are neither about to seize the means of production and reproduction, nor are they any more creatively involved with problems of cosmic powerlessness, evil, and love than is the rest of the human race.

I speak in many voices throughout this book: as a psychological researcher, theoretician, and clinician—*and* as a literary and philosophical person, a lover of poetry and myths.

In bringing you this book, I feel like a time-traveler turned messenger, a bearer of bad news. I wonder how you will receive it, I wonder what will you do?

MADNESS

Chapter One

WHY MADNESS?

ATHENA:

For I did not have a mother who bore me.
No, all my heart praises the male.

Aeschylus, *The Oreisteia*

Sigh no more, ladies
          Time is male
and in his cups drinks to the fair.
Bemused by gallantry, we hear
our mediocrities over-praised,
indolence read as abnegation,
slattern thought styled intuition,
every lapse forgiven, our crime
only to cast too bold a shadow
or smash the mould straight off.

For that, solitary confinement,
tear gas, attrition shelling.
Few applicants for that honor.

Adrienne Rich[1]

CHARLOTTE CORDAY:
Now I know what it is
like when the head is
cut off the body. . . .

In my room in Caen on
the table under the
open window lies open
the Book of Judith.
Dressed in her legendary beauty
she entered the tent of the enemy
and with a single blow,
slew him.

Peter Weiss[2]

"The first time a boy hurt me" said Lillian to Djuna "it was in school. I don't remember what he did. But I wept. And he laughed at me. Do you know what I did? I went home and dressed in my brother's suit. I tried to feel as the boy felt. Naturally as I put on the suit I felt I was putting on a costume of strength. . . . I thought that to be a boy meant one did not suffer. That it was being a girl that was responsible for the suffering. . . . Then there was another thing. . . . I discovered one relief, and that was action. . . . I felt if only I could join the war, participate, I wouldn't feel the anguish and the fear . . . if only they would let me be Joan of Arc. Joan of Arc wore a suit of armor, she sat on a horse, she fought side by side with the men. She must have gained their strength."

Anais Nin[3]

The surprising thing about the myths of Demeter . . . is her restless search for her [raped and abducted] daughter [Persephone] . . . a great Goddess could . . . in a single figure which was at once Mother and Daughter . . . represent the motifs that recur in *all* mothers and daughters.

C. Kerenyi[4]

Perhaps the angry and weeping women in mental asylums are Amazons returned to earth these many centuries later, each conducting a private and half-remembered search for her Motherland—a search we call madness. Or perhaps they are failed Goddess-Mothers, Demeters, eternally and miserably unable to find their daughters or their powers. . . .

(A romantic thought of my own)

There is nothing wrong with me—except I was born at least two thousand years too late. Ladies of Amazonian proportions and Berserker propensities have passed quite out of vogue and have no place in this too damned civilized world . . . here I sit—mad as the hatter—with nothing to do but either become madder and madder or else recover enough of my sanity to be allowed to go back to the life which drove me mad.

Lara Jefferson[5]

WOMEN IN ASYLUMS: FOUR LIVES

Mrs. Elizabeth Packard   (1816 – c.1890)
Mrs. Ellen West   (c.1890 – c.1926)
Mrs. Zelda Fitzgerald   (1900 – 1948)
Mrs. Sylvia Plath Hughes   (1932 – 1963)

During the nineteenth and twentieth centuries these four women were hospitalized for various psychiatric "symptoms." All were uncommonly stubborn, talented, and aggressive. Some became socially withdrawn: they no longer cared how they "looked," they refused to eat, they became sexually disinterested in their husbands. One woman "heard" things. Two others repeatedly attempted to kill themselves. Ellen West and Sylvia Plath finally committed suicide when they were in their early thirties. Zelda Fitzgerald burned to death in a mental asylum fire. Elizabeth Packard managed to escape after three years in an Illinois asylum. She published an account of her hospital experience and fought for the legal rights of mental patients and married women.

These four women share a rather fatal allegiance to their own uniqueness. For years they denied themselves—or were denied—the duties and privileges of talent and conscience. Like many women, they buried their own destinies in romantically extravagant marriages, in motherhood, and in approved female pleasure. However, their repressed energies eventually struggled free, demanding long overdue and therefore heavier prices: marital and maternal "disloyalty," social ostracism, imprisonment, madness, and death.

There is at least one important difference between Elizabeth Packard and the other three women. Packard was a devout believer in both Christianity and Motherhood. Romantic passion, doubt, creative egoism, and anguish were either flawlessly subdued or never part of her grandly practical sensibility. Her sins of individuality concerned religious freedom. Packard's husband literally forbade her to express her own opinions on theological matters. Her conscience did not allow her to obey him. Unlike Packard, Fitzgerald, West and Plath were not churchgoers. They were impractical and romantic. And unlike Packard, these three women were as dangerously wedded to Eros—to love—as was his first and mythological wife Psyche.* Like Psyche's, their marriages were consecrated in darkness. Unlike Psyche, however, they failed —or refused—to complete the maiden's pilgrimage toward divine marriage and motherhood. Plath's heroine, Esther Greenwood, in her autobiographical novel *The Bell Jar,* says:

> . . . one of the reasons I never wanted to get married [was that] the last thing I wanted was intimate security and to be the place an arrow shoots off from. I wanted change and excitement and to shoot off in all directions myself . . . the trouble was, I hated the idea of serving men in any way. I wanted to dictate my own thrilling letters . . . maybe [marriage and children] was like being brainwashed and afterwards you went about numb as a slave in some private totalitarian state. . . .[7]

Ellen West was a wealthy, sensitive, and suicidal young married woman, whose fear of eating was so great that she even-

---

* According to myth, Psyche remains unmarried despite (or because) of her great physical beauty. Finally, in desperation, her parents consult an oracle. They are advised to abandon their daughter on a mountain crag. Symbolically speaking, they abandon her to the inevitable Virgin's death (in marriage), and to an unknown, possibly bestial husband. But Psyche's husband is none other than Eros (Amor), Aphrodite's son. Psyche is ecstatically happy: she is also very lonely. Her husband visits her only at night, under cover of darkness, and she is warned against "seeing" him. When Psyche finally violates this wifely taboo, Eros flees. Psyche must then perform a series of "Hero's" tasks in order to be reunited with Eros, bear their child, and constitute a Holy Family in heaven.[6]

tually refused to eat at all.† She is presented to us as having preferred "trousers" and "lively, boyish games" until she was sixteen. Her childhood motto was "Either Caesar or nothing." In a poem written when she was seventeen, she expressed the desire "to be a soldier, fear no foe, and die joyously, sword in hand." She became an ardent horsewoman, diarist, and poet. After feverishly and competently performing a variety of approved female activities (doing volunteer work with children, taking non-matriculated university courses, engaging in serious love affairs), she grew suicidal and stopped eating. She said:

> . . . something in me rebels against becoming fat. Rebels against becoming healthy, getting plump red cheeks, becoming a simple, robust woman, as corresponds to my true nature. . . . For what purpose did nature give me health and ambition? . . . it is really sad that I must translate all this force and urge to action into unheard words [in her diary], instead of powerful deeds. . . . I am twenty-one years old and am supposed to be silent and grin like a puppet. I am no puppet. I am a human being with red blood and a woman with quivering heart. . . . Oh, what shall I do, how shall I manage it? . . . I am not thinking of the liberation of the soul; I mean the real, tangible liberation of people from the chains of their oppressors. . . . I want a revolution, a great uprising to spread over the entire world and overthrow the whole social order. I should like to forsake home and parents like a Russian nihilist, to live among the poorest of the poor and make propaganda for the great cause. Not for the love of adventure! No, no! Call it the unsatisfied urge to action. . . .[9]

Zelda Fitzgerald's husband was a famous writer who was (therefore) incapable of understanding or nurturing his wife's

---

† This sympton is psychiatrically interpreted as a fear of becoming pregnant. Ludwig Binswanger, her "anthropological case historian" records her life and psychiatric history.[8]

talents. Scott Fitzgerald experienced Zelda's dancing lessons as pathetic and foolish. Nancy Milford, in her excellent biography of Zelda Fitzgerald,[10] quotes Scott's letter to Dr. Forel, one of Zelda's psychiatrists, in which Scott complains that for the last six months, Zelda had taken no interest in their child.‡ He pointed out that before Zelda had become "devoted" to the ballet, she had devoted herself to her tasks as a wife and mother. He described her increasing absorption with dancing, dancers and with *herself* as distressingly egoistic and boring. Scott explains his own alcoholism in terms of Zelda's growing individuality and "madness." He told the doctor that he had to fortify himself with wine in order to put up with a woman whose tastes were different or "diverging" from his own. Although he describes her behavior—or its effects on him—as embarrassing and "maddening" he still recognized a certain boldness and honesty in Zelda's actions. In describing her, Scott's tone ranges from self-pity and impatience with Zelda's stubborn childishness to a sense of real loss and concern for her.

Scott was extremely jealous and threatened by Zelda's considerable literary talent. He reacted with fury when Zelda completed an autobiographical novel before Scott had finished his own novel—a "story" of Zelda's life and psychiatric confinement. In a letter to Dr. Meyer, another of Zelda's many male psychiatrists, Scott admitted that perhaps Zelda could have developed into a genius if they had never met. But the fact was that they did meet and marry, and her insistence on a career as an author was hurting Scott and their daughter. Zelda was being entranced, practically "possessed" by dreams of success and recognition dangerously like his own. Zelda's "genius," an adolescent and demonic inconvenience, really, was hurting him and their marriage. Cer-

‡ I was unable to obtain permission to quote directly from Scott and Zelda Fitzgerald's letters and conversations with each other and with Zelda's various psychiatrists. However, the material is completely available in Nancy Milford's book.

tainly, Zelda experienced and was broken by this very conflict.
Milford quotes from the stenographic transcription of a conversation between Zelda, Scott, and Dr. Rennie, Zelda's psychiatrist in
1933. Scott accuses Zelda, rather hysterically, of being a "writer of
limited talent" and reminds her of his world-wide literary reputation. Milford notes that "Scott had some very fixed ideas of what
a woman's place should be in a marriage." He thought of himself
as being in charge. Something like a pilot charting the course. He
was firm in his resolve that Zelda halt her efforts to write fiction.**
Zelda says she does not want to be "dependent" on Scott, either
financially or psychologically. She wants to be a "creative artist":
she wants "work." Only if she does "good work" can she defend
herself against Scott's slighting comments. She says she is tired of
being forced into accepting Scott's opinions and decisions about
everything. In fact, she would not do so, she would rather be hospitalized. She feels that their marriage has been nothing but a
struggle from the beginning. Scott's reply to this was that as a
couple they were envied by the world. She suggested that they
had put on a very good show.††

In 1860 Elizabeth Packard's husband psychiatrically imprisoned her because she dared to engage in "free religious in-
quiry."[12] (She insisted on teaching her Bible class that human
beings are born "good" and "not evil."‡‡ Her husband, a clergy-

---

** When monkeys and serving wenches begin to write, can the Eumeni-
des be far behind?

†† Jessie Bernard in her paper entitled, "The Paradox of the Happy
Marriage" has shown that men, in general, have different (more positive)
opinions about their marriages than their wives do. Many husbands expect less
from marriage than their wives and gain more in terms of domestic and sexual
convenience and in emotional support.[11]

‡‡ In Christian times women have systematically been murdered, not only
as "witches" but as "religious heretics" who espoused more sexual and compassionate creeds than their male counterparts. For example, in the sixteenth
century, during the reign of England's Henry VIII (the royal Bluebeard), Anne
Askew was accused of heresy and sentenced to death. She reminded the Lord
Chancellor that, according to the Scriptures, neither Christ nor his disciples had

man, kidnaped her against her will (although he was within his legal rights to do so) and removed her to an asylum at Jacksonville, Illinois. He forbade her children, whose ages ranged from eighteen months to eighteen years, to communicate with or talk about her. He kept her own (inherited) income from her. He deprived her of her clothes, books, and personal papers and misrepresented her situation to her parents. Dr. MacFarland, the psychiatrist-director of the asylum, remaindered her outgoing mail and seized her few books and smuggled-in writing paper. Despite these events, Mrs. Packard never lost her "wits." She always referred to the asylum as a "prison"—and never as a "hospital." She began a secret diary of asylum events and ministered to the other inmates, most of whom she regarded as sister victims of the patriarchy. However, she still believed in marriage and in male chivalry; she never wanted a divorce. She was thoroughly devoted to her children, and to a (male) Godhead. She "forgave" Dr. MacFarland his "sins"—until, in a moment of fury, he nearly strangled her normally docile roommate, Bridget. (Bridget had refused to do some domestic dirty work for him, and the doctor became enraged.) After this, Mrs. Packard was

> . . . converted from the theological error of vicarious suffering. I have never since asked my Father to let me bear the punishment of any other brother or sister, due them for their own sins; neither have I asked any other intelligence to bear punishment due me for my own sins.

ever put anyone to death. She argued religious doctrine for two hours after being submitted to the rack, and was burned to death later that year. In America, in the seventeenth century, Anne Hutchinson was excommunicated from the Church and exiled from Boston for being a powerful "preacher woman." Interestingly enough, she too emphasized more love, gentleness, mercy and peace—within this lifetime—than did the male Puritan authorities. Mrs. Anne Yale, Lady Deborah Moody, Mrs. King, and Mrs. Tilton were all excommunicated in New Haven for publicly opposing the "baptism of infants" (male churchly maternity). Mary Dyer was exiled from Boston and eventually hanged there for Quakerism; she had supported Anne Hutchinson.[13]

Her account of asylum abuses is lucid and at times brilliant. She describes many female asylum suicides as due to constant harassment, loneliness, and despair. She condemns the "torture" of women who *she* felt were really "witless." It is Elizabeth Packard who first makes the analogy of Institutional Psychiatry and the Inquisition.

Sylvia Plath's life is known to us through her own writing, through various biographical materials, and, increasingly, through new facts and writings her recent "death-cult" popularity has made available.* Plath grew up in Massachusetts and began writing poems and stories when she was very young. Her poems and her autobiographical novel, *The Bell Jar,* describe her battle as an *artist* with the female condition—a battle she did not necessarily see in feminist terms. Before she was thirty, Plath attempted suicide, was psychiatrically hospitalized, finished college, published her work, got married, moved to England, and became the mother of two children. A. Alvarez, in a memoir of Plath,[14] says that

> . . . in those [English] days, Sylvia seemed effaced: the poet taking a back seat to the young mother and housewife. . . . Considering the conditions in which she worked, her productivity was phenomenal. She was a full-time mother with a two-year-old daughter, a baby of ten months, and a house to look after. By the time the children were in bed at night she was too tired for anything more strenuous than "music and brandy and water." So she got up very early each morning and worked until the children woke. . . . In those dead hours between night and day, she was able to gather herself into herself in silence and isolation, almost as though she were reclaiming some past innocence and

* Many of Plath's contemporary admirers are, of course, women. Their admiration is rooted in their recognition of her fine poetry and, especially, in how finely it speaks to the female condition. Plath is also an excellent Christ-figure: and women, like men, have never had any trouble worshiping a victim "they" have destroyed or, more particularly, in "forgiving" a talented woman her talent—after her death.

freedom before life got a grip on her. Then she could write. For the rest of the day she was shared among the children, the house-work, the shopping, efficient, bustling, harassed, like every other housewife.

Of course, "housework" and "motherhood" are not nec-essarily more time-consuming or degrading than a fifteen-hour day in an office, factory, or coal mine. But then, most male poets do not work in coal mines, and for such long hours. Some-how, once recognized, they gain some sort of acceptance, how-ever seedy, however limited, by the male literary brotherhood. Not so for Plath. Alvarez notes that he was at first shocked that Sylvia *Plath* was Mrs. Sylvia *Hughes*. He reacted to her as to a "bright young housewife." Although he came to respect her work enormously, he became Ted's and not Sylvia's drinking mate and occasional friend.† Plath was lonely and isolated. Her genius did not earn for her certain reprieves and comforts tendered the male artist. No one, and especially men of culture, felt "responsible" for her plight or felt responsible to honor the poet by "saving" the woman. After separating from her husband, Plath continued to write and keep house for her children. On the night of February 10, or the morning of February 11, 1963, she killed herself.

These four women were treated and/or imprisoned by male psychiatrists—most of whom were, quite literally, agents for their husbands' "will."‡ Dr. MacFarland knew that Elizabeth Packard was not "mentally ill." After sexually approaching her and being rebuffed, he abandoned her to the brutality and anonymity of

---

† With great honesty, he retells his early reactions to such strongly feminist poems as *Daddy* and *Lady Lazarus:* he was "appalled . . . at first hearing, the things [poems] seemed to be not so much poetry as assault and battery." Many later critics, including female critics, have felt the same way.

‡ Packard's psychiatrist-jailer offered to testify for her husband at her insanity hearing. Only Plath's heroine, Esther Greenwood, is unmarried in the novel.

the "back wards." She clearly saw that Dr. MacFarland's "cure" was the "subjection of the wife to the husband's will." Her "therapy" consisted of imprisonment and domestic servitude to the other women. She washed them, prayed with them, comforted them, and tried to shield them from beatings. She also freely "chose" to participate in slave labor.

> By sewing for the State, as its imprisoned slave, I can buy the privilege of exchanging the putrid, loathsome air of the ward, for the more wholesome purer atmosphere of the sewing room for half a day. [The male inmates could choose to work on Dr. MacFarland's private farm.]**

Zelda Fitzgerald's psychiatrists, in Milford's words, tried to "re-educate her in terms of her role as wife to Scott." When Zelda said she wanted to be an artist, her male psychiatrist asked her whether being a famous writer would be more important to her than her life with Scott. Holding up the specter of old age and lovelessness, he asked her whether that would be enough for her when she was over sixty. All of Zelda's psychiatrists consulted with Scott about his wife's "condition" and about what was "good" for her. In 1931, when Zelda was released after a year and three months of treatment, her "case" was summarized as an inferiority complex—particularly toward Scott. The psychiatrists declared her ambitions to be forms of self-deceptions, which had deeply troubled their marriage. Over the years, despite Zelda's pitiful requests for freedom, her obedient confessions of self-blame, and her promises of "good behavior," the men decided if and when she could spend "vacations" outside the asylum.

Plath's autobiographical heroine, Esther Greenwood, is sent to a male psychiatrist named Dr. Gordon. He sits, happily en-

----

** Such slave labor still exists in most American state mental asylums: the jobs are neatly parceled out along sex-role lines.

throned at his polished desk, surrounded by books and family photographs. Esther wonders:

> How could this Dr. Gordon help me anyway, with a beautiful wife and beautiful children and a beautiful dog haloing him like the angels on a Christmas card?

He intones the standard "suppose you try and tell me what you think is wrong" and Esther

> . . . turned the words over suspiciously like round, sea-polished pebbles that might suddenly put out a claw and change into something else. What did I *think* was wrong? I only thought it was wrong.

Dr. Gordon recommends shock therapy for her. Plath's description of this treatment of choice for "manic-depressives," most of whom are women, is as follows:

> Doctor Gordon was fitting two metal plates on either side of my head. He buckled them into place with a strap that dented my forehead, and gave me a wire to bite.
> I shut my eyes.
> There was a brief silence, like an indrawn breath. Then something bent down and took hold of me and shook me like the end of the world. Whee-ee-ee-ee, it shrilled, through an air crackling with blue light and with each flash a great jolt struck me till I thought my bones would break and the sap fly out of me like a split plant.
> I wondered what terrible thing it was that I had done.

One of Ellen West's psychiatrists, thought she was getting better because

> . . . whereas during the summer she was repulsively ugly, since then she has grown more and more feminine and almost pretty.

During one of her asylum periods she, like Esther Greenwood, developed a "homo-erotic" attachment—which, of course, was certainly not encouraged. West's last letter before fatally poisoning herself was written to this woman.

Fitzgerald, West, and Plath were desperately and defiantly at odds with the female role. They attempted to escape its half-life by "going crazy." There, as "helpless" and "self-destructive" children,†† they were superficially freed from their female roles as private social losers, as wives and mothers.‡‡ However, neither "madness" nor mental asylums offered them "asylum" or "freedom."

Plath correctly saw that there was nothing very different about

> . . . us in Belsize and the girls playing Bridge and gossiping in the college to which I would return. Those girls, too, sat under bell jars of a sort.

Uncannily, Ellen West also referred to her condition as being in a "glass ball."

> I feel myself excluded from all real life. I am quite isolated. I sit in a glass ball. I see people through a glass wall, their voices come to me muffled. . . . I stretch out my arms toward them; but my hands merely beat against the walls of my glass ball.

All four women existed under a "bell jar"—both inside and outside the asylum. For them, madness and confinement were both

†† Plath describes the asylum inmates as "blank and stopped as a dead baby."

‡‡ Zelda tells Scott that she is so unhappy she would rather be in an asylum. His response is cold and defensive: he doesn't care to hear such things. Zelda, in heroically and tragically self-destructive fashion, sees that there is no difference between being hospitalized and being married. She would rather be open about it; she would rather stop the social lie. Let her dependency, helplessness, abandonment and unhappiness be seen for what it was. Of course, Zelda remains a financial and psychological burden to Scott— one that he bears—as long as she is willing to isolate herself and view herself as "sick" or "bad."

an expression of female powerlessness and an unsuccessful attempt to reject and overcome this state. Madness and asylums generally function as mirror images of the female experience, and as penalties for *being* "female," as well as for desiring or daring *not* to be. If the dare is enacted deeply or dramatically enough, death (through slow or fast suicide) ensues. I. J. Singer portrays this in "The Dead Fiddler," a story about a young girl's possession by a dybbuk or demon.[15] The girl, Liebe Yentl, is reared in an orthodox Jewish household in which her father "paid little attention to her (and) prayed to God to send her the right husband." Despite this, she spends most of her time alone, reading. She "complained that the girls of the town were common and backward: as soon as they were married they became careless and slovenly." A marriage is arranged, but the groom dies before the wedding. A second betrothal is arranged, but unconsummated, as Liebe Yentl is "invaded" by a dybbuk—with a male voice. The dybbuk is a boisterous adventurer —a fiddler—who demands liquor, laughingly insults the townspeople, both quotes and mocks the Torah—and all in singsong rhyme. Soon the fiddler has the village dancing in Liebe Yentl's bedroom, as he-she

> . . . told each one exactly what he was: a miser or a swindler, a sycophant or a beggar, a slattern or a snob . . . most of the time he heaped mud and ashes upon the respected leaders of the community and their wives . . . his jests provoked both astonishment and laughter.

Suddenly, Liebe Yentl is invaded by a second, and female, dybbuk, who is a barmaid and whore. Beyle Tslove, for that is her name, sings "ribald songs and soldiers' ditties." She calls Liebe Yentl's father a "short Friday—nothing but bone and beard."

Liebe Yentl is able to avoid an unwanted husband through her "madness"—it is the only way she can. Only in "madness" can she also tyrannize her parents, inspire fear and respect, "name" reality as she sees it, criticize the community's hypocrisy, and engage in some very "unfeminine" behavior: drinking, boasting, and dirty-joke telling.* After the two dybbuks depart her body, Liebe Yentl still refuses to marry her parents' bridegroom choice. Isolation, poverty, neglect, and death are her fate. She is discovered dead, one day

> . . . among piles of garbage, in a long shift, barefoot, her red hair loose. It was obvious that she had not been among the living for many days.

MOTHERS AND DAUGHTERS: A MYTHOLOGICAL COMMENTARY ON THE LIVES

Women in modern Judeo-Christian societies are motherless children. Painting after painting, sculpture after sculpture in the Christian world portray Madonnas comforting and worshiping their infant sons. Catholic mythology symbolizes the enforced splitting of Woman into either Mother or Whore—both of whom nurture and ultimately worship a dead man and/or a "divine" male child. The fierce bond of love, continuity, and pride between the pagan Demeter (the Earth Mother)and her daughter Persephone (the Kore-Maiden) does not exist between women in Catholic mythology or culture.† It cannot. Mothers have neither land nor

---

* It is important to note that she doesn't become a rabbi or a highway-woman; she remains in a feminine reclining position.

† Demeter is the goddess of life, corn or grain. Her daughter Persephone is abducted, raped, and married by Pluto (Hades), god of the underworld (or by Zeus or Dionysius, either of whom may have been Persephone's own father), while she is playing in a field of poppies. Demeter seeks her daughter and remains inconsolable at her absence. Finally, in anger, she refuses to let any crops grow if Persephone is not returned to her. Eventually a compromise is reached: Persephone will remain with her mother for most of the year (spring, summer, and autumn) and with her husband during winter (when no seed or crops can grow). This tale, which incorporates many features of matriarchal and early agricultural societies, also comprised the heart of the Eleusinian mysteries—a Mother-Daughter religion in later—and patriarchal—Greek society.[16]

money to cede to their daughters. Their legacy is one of capitulation, via frivolity or drudgery. For example, poor and black mothers in America may be employed outside the home—but as drudges, whose labor does not result in economic, military, or political power. Middle- and upper-class mothers who are not employed outside the home, or whose employment is "frivolous" or non-paid, cannot provide their daughters with legacies of dignity and self. It is true that women are more cooperative and sympathetic to each other where "male" and "female" roles are sharply and traditionally defined and segregated, as in non-Western Islamic societies, or in rural and ghetto subcultures within the Western world. However, such cooperation is based on unindividuated uniformity, discontent, and powerlessness. Neither mother nor daughter can redeem the other from certain harsh realities that define the female as "mother" and "loser" under bio-patriarchal rule.‡

Female children are quite literally starved for matrimony: not for marriage, but for physical nurturance and a legacy of power and humanity from adults of their own sex ("mothers"). Most mothers prefer sons to daughters[17] and are more physically and domestically nurturant to them. Within modern society, woman's "dependent" and "incestuous" personality probably stems from not being experienced as "divine" by the mother (and father). Most women are glassed into infancy, and perhaps into some forms of madness, by an unmet need for maternal nurturance.** Thus,

‡ As we shall see, this is really true of Demeter and Persephone also—but in an era where maternity and biology are more highly valued than today.
** I say "maternal" because the hourly care of infants and children in most families is entrusted to biological women and rarely shared by biological men. It can certainly be argued that infant males are emotionally scarred by being deprived of "maternal" (Dionysiac) nurturance from their fathers and "paternal" (Apollonian) nurturance from their mothers. Perhaps the "male" fear and hatred of women, as well as "male" violence and ego-greediness, stems from sex-role stereotyped families: perhaps it stems from the male biological presence in the universe—and the way in which culture has used it.
I am using the word "nurturance" somewhat loosely. I mean the consistent and readily available gift of physical, domestic, and emotional support

female children turn to their fathers for physical affection, nurturance, or pleasurable emotional intensity—a turning that is experienced as "sexual" by the adult male, precisely because it is predicated on the female's (his daughter's) innocence, helplessness, youthfulness, and monogamous idolatry. This essentially satyric and incestuous model of sexuality is almost universal. It is reflected in marriage laws and practices, and in the rarity with which rapists, child molesters and frequenters of prostitutes are legally prosecuted. This model of sexuality is mythologically Olympian in origin: Zeus, the Father, made a habit of seducing, raping, and impregnating as many Virgin Maidens as possible. The Catholic Father apparently preferred virgins for his divine offspring also.

Daughters don't turn to their mothers for "sexual" initiation, or, as Freud would have it (but couldn't explain it), they specifically turn away from them, for a number of reasons. "Mothers" are conditioned not to like women and/or the female body. They are phobic about lesbianism; they are jealous of their daughters' youth—rendered so by their own increasing "expendability." Also, "mothers" must be harsh in training their daughters to be "feminine" in order that they learn how to serve in order to survive.††

The way in which female children grow up—or learn how not to grow up—is initiated by the early withdrawal or relative ab-

in childhood, together with the added gift of compassion and respect in adulthood. "Nurturance" or, mythologically speaking, "protection," "guidance" and "intervention," is depicted most often by pagan gods and goddesses helping mortal *men* on their pilgrimages to heroism. For example, Athena helps Odysseus and Perseus to either escape from or slay female powers as embodied by Circe and Medusa. It is interesting to note that Psyche, one of the few mortal heroines in pagan culture, is helped on her pilgrimage toward an essentially "feminine" destiny only by *non-human* objects. No wise or powerful goddess or god (save her husband Eros) intervenes for her. Her "protectors" are an ant, a reed, water, an eagle, and a tower.

†† This harshness traditionally characterizes fathers' training their sons to be "masculine." Any society with sex-role stereotypes implies an often crippling harshness between adults and children of the same sex. However, biopatriarchal culture is still essentially a male homosexual one—in spirit and/or in practice. It is neither lesbian nor bisexual in spirit or practice.

sence of the female and/or nurturant body from their lives. Nur-
turance-deprivation, and the sexual abuse of female children are
possibly the two most important factors involved in making female
children receptive to "submission" conditioning—at a very early
age. Female children move from a childhood dominated or peopled
by members of their own sex to a foreign "grown-up" world dominated, quite literally, by members of the opposite sex. Male children graduate from a childhood dominated or peopled by members
of the opposite sex (women) to a "grown-up" world dominated
by members of their own sex. Unlike women, they can safely go
home again by marrying "wives," who will perform the rites of
maternal domestic and emotional nurturance, but who are usually
younger, economically poorer, and physically weaker than themselves. In patriarchal society, the basic incest taboo (between mother
and son and father and daughter) is *psychologically* obeyed by
men and disobeyed by women.‡‡ Psychologically, women do not
have initiation rites to help them break their incestuous ties. While
most women do not commit incest with their biological fathers,
patriarchal marriage, prostitution, and mass "romantic" love are
psychologically predicated on sexual union between Daughter and
Father figures. In a matriarchal or Amazonian society, the incest
taboo would have another purpose entirely, and *women* would
not violate it. The taboo would function as a way of keeping sons
and husbands away from daughters—who are their mothers' only
heiresses. This particular distance is precisely what is breached by
patriarchal mores: the breach immediately tells us which sex is
dominant, i.e., which sex controls the means of production and
reproduction.

What would female sexuality be like if women did not violate
the incest taboo, did not willingly marry Father figures, or were
not unwittingly raped by them? How would women know pleasure,

‡‡ Many female children are raped or molested by their fathers or by
adult male relatives in our culture. Maternal incest is a far rarer occurrence.

love, and economic security? How would they reproduce themselves when and if they wished to? And how would they raise "their" children?

> The institution of marriage makes a parasite of woman, an absolute dependent. It *incapacitates* her for life's struggle, *annihilates* her social consciousness, paralyzes her imagination, and then imposes its gracious protection, which is in reality a snare, a travesty on human character. . . . If motherhood is the highest fulfillment of woman's nature, what other protection does it need save *love* and *freedom*? Marriage but defiles, outrages, and corrupts her fulfillment. Does it not say to woman, Only when you follow me shall you bring forth life? Does it not condemn her to the block, does it not degrade and shame her if she refuses to buy her right to motherhood by selling herself? Does not marriage only sanction motherhood, even though conceived in hatred, in compulsion? Yet, if motherhood be of free choice, of love, of ecstasy, of defiant passion, does it not place a crown of thorns upon an innocent head and carve in letters of blood the hideous epithet, Bastard? Were marriage to contain all the virtues claimed for it, its crimes against motherhood would exclude it forever from the realm of love.
>
> Emma Goldman[18]

Female biology obviously includes the capacity for sexual pleasure, physical prowess, and childbearing. Whether or not human childbearing constitutes the "greatest pleasure" for women,[19] whether or not it is a "natural" or a "learned" activity[20] is irrelevant. What is relevant is the price modern women are forced to pay for this pleasure, and the overwhelming lack of other available pleasures and duties. Women are forced to choose between reproduction and (hetero) sexual pleasure; reproduction and physical prowess; reproduction and worldly or spiritual power.

Today, women are still choosing maternity for traditional and male-imposed reasons: in order to survive economically and psychologically, and because contraception and abortion are still inadequate, illegal, expensive, dangerous, and morally censured for most women. The twentieth-century phenomenon of "romantic" love also accounts for—or justifies—the traditionally *inevitable* female destiny of marriage and children. Contemporary women are "free" slaves: they choose their servitude for "love."[21] Women are trained to be those creatures who are supposed to get so "carried away" emotionally that they cannot think clearly, if at all. Pluto (Zeus, Dionysius) had to *carry* the Daughter-Maiden Persephone away from her mother Demeter; for centuries families have *arranged* this leave-taking for their daughters; today, contemporary women carry *themselves* headlong down the same path to the Underworld.

Maternity has been glorified and feared, by ancient and modern people, as *the* most eloquent and effective human response to the fact of biological death. Mothers have been eulogized—and I use the word advisedly—as more powerful than kings and soldiers who, in turn, have defended motherhood in speeches and destroyed its labors in battle. Poets, scientists, and philosophers have sighed over the time-bound vanity of male accomplishment and have continued their creative work.

Modern businessmen envy the female maternal "out"—often to the point of disease—but remain involved with the accumulation and circulation of money, an activity best done without children underfoot. Despite the numerous ways in which men have attempted to mimic or colonize the "gloriousness" of biological maternity (and consequently, to devalue or punish it in women), men, particularly in Christian culture, are not very "maternal" to their children, their wives, their mistresses, their prostitutes, their secretaries, their housekeepers—or to each other.

> A heart attack can be harder on the wife than the husband-patient. . . . They [the wives] grew angry at times over their husbands' demands, then developed guilt over the anger. . . . The husbands were more relaxed. . . . They [the husbands] openly discussed sexual difficulties and hostility toward their loved one. But their tension and anxiety were relieved by shared feelings, by joking, by profane language and by rationalizing that a heart attack is beneficial because it makes one face up to one's self. The women, on the other hand, made little use of humor or uninhibited expression. . . . There was mild depression among the men but no severely depressed mood as among the wives.
>
> New York *Post*, January 16, 1971

In patriarchal culture, Mother-Women, as deified by the Catholic Madonna, are as removed from (hetero) sexual pleasure as are Daughter-Women, as deified by the pagan Athena. Athena is the archetype of a motherless daughter: Zeus's forehead is her "mother." (Interestingly, Aphrodite, the goddess who persecutes Psyche, is also motherless. According to myth, she was "created from the severed phallus of Uranus which had fallen into the sea."[22] It is Athena who casts the deciding vote in Orestes' favor and proclaims matricide to be of lesser importance than patricide.* Athena, despite her warlike trappings, is an original "Daddy's girl": she does not get sexually involved with men—or women. Athena pays for her wisdom and power by giving up reproductive

---

* Orestes' mother kills her husband Agamemnon for sacrificing their daughter Iphigenia. Orestes avenges his father's death by killing his mother and is acquitted of the crime. In Aeschylus' trilogy Athena says:

> "My task it is to render the last verdict,
> And I cast this stone for Orestes,
> For I did not have a mother who bore me;
> No, all my heart praises the male,
> May Orestes win over your tied vote."

sexuality and (hetero) sexual pleasure. Mary, mother of Jesus, pays for her maternity by giving up her body, almost entirely: she foregoes both (hetero) sexual pleasure (Christ's birth is a virgin and "spiritual" birth) and physical prowess. She has no direct worldly power but, like her crucified son, is easily identified with by many people, especially women, as a powerless figure. Mary symbolizes power achieved through receptivity, compassion, and a uterus. (There is nothing intrinsically wrong with a consciously willed "receptivity" to the universe; on the contrary, it is highly desirable, and should certainly include "receptivity" to many things other than holy sperm and suffering.)

A more feminist (or rather, matriarchal) interpretation of the Catholic Virgin birth certainly exists: it symbolizes the unique and "miraculous" ability of women to conceive and bear children. Childbearing—the union of body and spirit that overcomes death —resides in the female principle. Men do not enter this realm, either socially or biologically. Thus it is just as we all thought as children: all our mothers immaculately conceived us and we are all divine.

In many pagan and Catholic "downfall" myths, the male god is usually stripped of his full former powers by being sent "earthward," the female, by being sent "skyward." For example, Poseidon was sent to the sea; Pluto, as well as the Judeo-Christian Lucifer, beneath the earth. Mythologically, one expression of power loss for men is to be returned to the earth, to the concrete. Often for women, the expression of power loss is to be removed from the earth, or from their (heterosexual) bodies. Goddesses such as Athena, Diana, or the Catholic Madonna are virgins.† Virginity,

† I.e., Either unmarried or childless, (hetero) sexually uninvolved or "innocent" of experience. In Amazon society, a "virgin" was not chaste, but unmarried; in Catholic mythology a "virgin" is married and chaste. The pagan Artemis (Diana), the Virgin-Huntress, is not motherless. She is raised together with her brother Apollo and, unlike Athena, is probably a lesbian goddess of Amazon origin. She requested—and received from Zeus—sixty ocean nymphs

one form of mind-body splitting, is the price that women are made to pay in order to keep whatever other "fearful" powers they have: childbearing, wisdom, hunting prowess, maternal compassion.‡

HEROINES AND MADNESS:
JOAN OF ARC AND THE VIRGIN MARY

> The invalidation of women like Zelda [Fitzgerald] who 'break through' by the most perilous explorations in the world [schizophrenia], the voyage back in time in consciousness to recover the paradise of lost dimensions of being is extensive. . . . Egorova [Zelda's ballet teacher] was a new mother or the Demeter or the Hera appearing as in a vision to the lost daughter.
>
> Jill Johnston, *The Village Voice*.

How do mythological figures such as Athena or the Catholic Madonna, or historical heroines such as Joan of Arc, relate to what we call madness?** On one level, not at all. Most twentieth-century women who are psychiatrically labeled, privately treated, and publicly hospitalized are not mad. Like Plath, West, Fitzgerald, and Packard, they may be deeply unhappy, self-destructive, economically powerless, and sexually impotent—but as women they're supposed to be.

---

and twenty river nymphs as companions. According to one myth, she *rescues* Iphigenia from being sacrificed by her father Agamemnon. According to another myth, one of her lovers is the woman Callisto—whom Artemis' father Zeus seduces—*only by taking Artemis' form*.[23]

‡ Of course, de-virginization via heterosexual *rape* is as maddening a split in female mind-body continuity.

** Mythology may be viewed as the psychology of modern history. It seems to represent the interaction of biology with early culture, just as history represents the interaction of biology with later culture. Myths may also refer to actual historical events of personages.

There are very few genuinely (or purely) mad women in our culture. Their madness usually lasts a short time, or is short-circuited by psychiatric intervention altogether. Society generally banishes such experiences from understanding, respect—and from plain view. Madness is shut away from sight, shamed, brutalized, denied, and feared. Contemporary men, politics, science—the rational mode itself—does not consult or is not in touch with the irrational, i.e., with the events of the unconscious, or with the meaning of collective history.

Such madness is best understood within a mythological context. For example, mad women in our culture experience certain specific transformations of self, or incorporate the meaning of certain heroines such as Joan of Arc and the Catholic Madonna.†† Both these figures involve the sacrifice of the Maiden (Persephone-Kore) for purposes of male renewal. In the Madonna's case the renewal is achieved through classic patriarchal rape-incest; in Joan's case, first through military victories and then through patriarchal crucifixion, guilt, and expiation.

†† Some women also experience themselves as female Christs or as Dionysus. Dionysus is essentially androgynous but is most often depicted as a male. The male Dionysus is the mirror image of Persephone's, or the passive Maiden's sacrifice. Dionysus is killed by women—by women whom he has driven mad. I wonder if Dionysus is not really her mother's female Maiden (or Kore) whose incestual rape drives her mother mad, and often drives her to destroy her real daughter, as she herself was destroyed. Phillip E. Slater, in *The Glory of Hera*, sees Dionysus as a male child, forever envied, loved, hated, and seduced by his cruelly imprisoned and crippled mother. In understanding Dionysus, he also says that: "Dionysus' characteristic attribute of boundary-violator is symbolized by the Orphic myth of his serpent birth—a myth whose great antiquity is alleged by Kerenyi (cf. also Euripides: The Bacchae 100ff.). Demeter is said to have hidden Persephone in a cave in Sicily, guarded by two serpents. While the maiden was engaged in weaving, however, Zeus came to her in the shape of a serpent and copulated with her, Dionysus being the fruit of this union (Kerenyi, 1960, pp. 252–53). His ability to shatter cognitive boundaries is thus intrinsic, and does not depend upon any external power. He is in fact born with it—it is the child itself which drives the mother mad by its very existence. Just as the child has twice violated the physical boundaries of the mother by its conception and birth, so it drives her to raving infanticide by its having ceased to be a psychological part of her. In the child-murdering myths of Dionysus one can easily discern some of the underlying ideation of the postpartum psychosis."[24]

Joan of Arc is the only Persephone-Kore Maiden in modern history who is not raped or impregnated by her father—be it by her biological father or her psychological-religious representation of her biological father. Joan remains a "Daughter" figure. As such, she is one of Christianity's prime remembrances of Amazonian cultures. Joan, like earlier mythological heroines, such as Athena, is a virgin-warrior who helps men.‡‡ Although, like all Kore-Maidens, she serves as a source of male renewal, she does so through her military victories and her subsequent political persecution. Her identity, as such, is a crucial one for women. Although she is doomed (and women might identify with her on this ground alone), she is also physically and spiritually bold; she is a leader of men; she is not sexually raped and consequently does not become a Mother. She embodies the *avoidance* of both the Demeter-Mother fate and the Persephone-Daughter fate. As such, she begins to step completely outside the realm of patriarchal culture. For this, she is killed in her own lifetime—and re-experienced by those women who are mad enough to wish to "step outside" culture also —but who do not wish to be crucified for doing so.* It is as tragic as it is inevitable that female warriors in patriarchal mythology are necessarily denied that part of their sexuality that includes biological maternity. What this always signifies is grief at not having been

---

‡‡ It is important, however, that Joan herself, at her trial of condemnation, said that she bore her banner or standard aloft "when we went forward against the enemy, I held the banner aloft to avoid killing anyone. I have killed no one."25

* It is frightening to read the account of Joan's imprisonment by Aeneas Sylvius Piccolomini (the future Pope Pius II), quoted by Régine Pernoud: "It is known that, taken in the war, the Maid was sold to the English for ten thousand gold crowns and conveyed to Rouen. In that place she was diligently examined to discover whether she used sortilèges (spells) or diabolical aid or whether she erred in any way in her religion. Nothing worthy to be censured was found in her, excepting the male attire which she wore. And that was not judged deserving of the extreme penalty. Taken back to her prison she was threatened with death if she resumed the wearing of man's clothes . . . her gaolers brought none but male attire."26

born male—because of the nurturance deprivation being female implies.†

After women grasp the meaning—and limitations—of Joan of Arc, they seek protection and redemption—from the Catholic Mary, the compassionate and powerful mother. Unfortunately, Mary is no Demeter. Catholic mythology has not granted Mary either a daughter or Demeter's bartering power with men and gods. Nevertheless, women in madness wish to give birth to the world (and to themselves) anew. They wish to avoid Joan's crucifixion and can do so only by becoming Virgin-Mothers. They also wish to become their own much-needed mothers.‡

Alas: the reality of parthenogenesis under biological patriarchy is less than glorious. Mary avoids crucifixion, but she is condemned to asexuality and sorrow.

Joan and Mary are very painful experiences for those women who incorporate their meaning. They are the modified (and tragic) Christian equivalents of the pagan Demeter and her daughter Persephone. However, Joan and Mary are separated in time and biology. Joan, unlike Persephone, is not raped, and Mary, unlike Demeter, gives birth to a son and not a daughter. Neither of these Christian figures gives rise to or symbolizes a Mother-Daughter religion. C. G. Jung understood the effect of this. He says:

> It is immediately clear to the psychologist what cathartic and at the same time rejuvenating effects must flow from the Demeter

---

† For example, Phillip Slater, describing the mythological Atalanta, says: ". . . like Artemis, she is a virgin huntress, and punishes the attentions of would-be suitors with cruel death. Furthermore, her own history reveals the origin of this attitude, for it is said (Apollodorus: iii 9.2) that her father had wished for a boy, and had exposed her on a mountain top, where she was suckled by a bear which the goddess sent to her aid. In her refusal to marry, in her competitions with men (beating them at racing and at wrestling), and in her general masculine demeanor, Atalanta both complies with this wish and expresses her resentment of it."[27]

‡ The women whom I spoke with who *did* have Virgin Birth experiences all gave birth to sons. However, some experienced their *own* rebirth at the same time.

cult into the feminine psyche, and what a lack of psychic hygiene characterizes our culture, which no longer knows the kind of wholesome experience afforded by the Eleusinian emotions.[28]

However, it is important to realize that the "Eleusinian emotions" are rooted in an acceptance of nature and biology's supremacy. Demeter's world is one in which women, despite their awesome fecundity, do not even initiate *sexual* contact with either men or women. Only heterosexual rape exists—and only for procreative purposes. Neither Demeter nor Persephone *acts*. They *react*—to rape or to the loss of a daughter or virgin self. Demeter and Persephone are not Amazon figures. Their cult is essentially one of Earth-Mother-worship: mothers who produce more mothers to nurture and sustain mankind with their "miraculous" biological gifts of crops and daughters. The inevitable sacrifice of self that biology demands of women in most societies is at the heart of the Demetrian myth. Even so, or precisely because this is so, modern women, deprived of both maternal nurturance and dignity, would be very comforted by Eleusinian rituals: after all, we live in a culture in which science and Christianity have increasingly devalued female biology, without yet freeing women from being defined solely in biological terms.

While it is true that Demeter rescues Persephone from isolation in a male world, she also condemns her to a universally female fate: an identity no different from her mother's. As Kerenyi notes:

To enter into the figure of Demeter means to be robbed, raped, to fail to understand, to rage and grieve, but then to get everything back and be born again. And what does all this mean, save to realize the universal principle of life, the fate of everything mortal? What, then, is left over for the figure of Persephone? Beyond question, that which constitutes the structure of the living creature *apart from* this endlessly repeated drama of coming-to-be and passing-away, namely the *uniqueness* of the individual and its *enthralment to non*-being.[29]

This "uniqueness" and "heroism" are precisely what define Persephone's male mythological counterpart—the divine male child and male adult hero.

Persephone does not wish to be raped, nor do women today. Neither do they wish to recapitulate their mother's identity. But the modern Persephone still has no other place to go but into marriage and motherhood. Her father (men in general) still conforms to a rape-incest model of sexuality. And her mother has not taught her to be a warrior, i.e., to take difficult roads to unknown and unique destinations—gladly. Her mother and father neither prepare her for this task nor rejoice in her success. They do not mourn or comfort her in crucifixion, be it as a warrior (as Joan of Arc) *or* as a mother (as the Virgin Mary).

> Any woman born with a great gift in the 16th Century would certainly have gone crazed, shot herself, or ended her days in some lonely cottage outside the village, half witch, half wizard, feared and mocked at. For it needs little skill in psychology to be sure that a highly gifted girl who had tried to use her gift for poetry would have been so thwarted and hindered by other people, so tortured and pulled asunder by her own contrary instincts, that she must have lost her health and sanity to a certainty.
>
> Virginia Woolf[30]

Zelda Fitzgerald, Sylvia Plath, and Ellen West, for example, want and need mother love—but not at the price of "uniqueness" or glory. They are probably as maddened by the absence of maternality in their lives as they would be by the demands it would eventually place upon their freedom. The combination of nurturance deprivation *and* restrictions upon their uniqueness or heroism is deadly. They cannot survive as just "women," and they are not allowed to survive as human or as creative beings.**

All women who bear children are committing, literally and symbolically, a blood sacrifice for the perpetuation of the species. (Only certain men actually shed blood for the redemption or immortality of other people.) In this sense, female sacrifice in patriarchal and prescientific culture is concretely rooted in female biology. To the extent to which the interaction of human biology and culture produces myths that shape our personalities, just so will female sacrifice (and psychological self-sacrifice) continue to exist. Perhaps the myth and reality of female (and male) sacrifice will cease when intrauterine biological reproduction ceases—or when the function is not assigned to one sex only.††

Women are impaled on the cross of self-sacrifice. Unlike men, they are categorically denied the experience of cultural supremacy, humanity, and renewal based on their sexual identity—and on the blood sacrifice, in some way, of a member of the opposite sex. In different ways, some women are driven mad by this fact.‡‡ Such madness is essentially an intense experience of female biological, sexual, and cultural castration, and a doomed search for potency. The search often involves "delusions" or displays of physical aggression, grandeur, sexuality, and emotionality—all traits which would probably be more acceptable in female-dominated cultures. Such traits in women are feared and punished in patriarchal mental asylums.

** *Male* creativity is usually so valued that eccentricities, cruelties and emotional infantilism are usually overlooked, forgiven, or "expected."

†† *Perhaps* either of these events would occur more quickly if women were to control the means of production and reproduction—in this case, the scientific investigation of contraception, extrauterine birth, and uterus implantation; the economic means to insure the eventual success of such research; and the political, legal, and religious authority to publicize and enforce the research findings.

‡‡ Their madness is *treated* in such a way as to turn it into another form of self-sacrifice.

Chapter Two

ASYLUMS

> The entire existence of madness, in the world now being prepared
> for it, was enveloped in what we may call, in anticipation,
> a "parental complex." The prestige of patriarchy is revived
> around madness . . . henceforth . . . the discourse of unreason
> will be linked with . . . the dialectic of the Family . . . the
> madman remains a minor and for a long time reason will
> retain for him the aspect of the Father. . . . He [Tuke, a
> psychiatrist] isolated the social structure of the bourgeois family,
> reconstituted it symbolically in the [mental] asylum, and set it
> adrift in history.
>
> Michel Foucault[1]

THE MENTAL ASYLUM

As early as the sixteenth century women were "shut up" in
madhouses (as well as in royal towers) by their husbands.[2] By
the seventeenth century, special wards were reserved for prostitutes,
pregnant women, poor women, and young girls in France's first
mental asylum, the Salpêtrière.[3] By the end of the nineteenth
and throughout the twentieth century, the portraits of madness,
executed by both psychiatrists and novelists were primarily of
women.

Today, more women are seeking psychiatric help and being hospitalized than at any other time in history.* In 1964, the number of American women being psychiatrically "serviced" began to suddenly or at least measurably increase. Adult female patients rapidly exceeded the number of adult male patients. There were significantly more women being "helped" than their existence in the population at large would allow us to predict.

This increase may be understood, not only in the context of the "help-seeking" nature of the female role, or the objective oppression of women, but in the context of at least three recent social trends. Traditionally, most women performed both the rites of madness and childbirth more invisibly—at home—where, despite their tears and hostility, they were still needed. While women live longer than ever before, and longer than men, there is less and less use, and literally no place, for them in the only place they "belong"—within the family. Many newly useless women are emerging more publicly into insanity. Their visibility is also greater, due to our society's relatively successful segregation of violence (into ghettos and jails) and "madness" (into hospitals and

* We must not forget: (1) that more men are too; (2) that both the number of clinicians and mental asylums have increased; (3) that we keep better records of hospital stays than ever before.

doctors' offices). Finally, the prevalence of female mental patients is related to our society's atheism, or worship of the tangible: no longer are women sacrificed as voluntary or involuntary witches. They are, instead, taught to sacrifice themselves for newly named heresies.[4]

The patriarchal nature of psychiatric hospitals has been documented by M. Foucault, T. Szasz, E. Goffman, and T. Scheff.[5] Journalists, social scientists, and novelists have described, deplored, and philosophized about the prevalence of overcrowding, understaffing, and brutality in America's public mental asylums, jails, and medical hospitals.† It is obvious that *state* mental asylums are the "Indian reservations" for America's non-criminally labeled poor, old, black, Latin, and female populations. It is also obvious that the state hospital, much like the poor or workhouse of old, functions as a warning specter, particularly to those women involved in earlier or more part-time phases of their "careers" as psychiatric patients.

Mental asylums rarely offer asylum. Both their calculated and their haphazard brutality mirrors the brutality of "outside" society. The "scandals" about them that periodically surface in the media are like all atrocities—only everyday events, writ large. Madness —as a label or reality—is not conceived of as divine, prophetic, or useful. It is perceived as (and often further shaped into) a shameful and menacing disease, from whose spiteful and exhausting eloquence society must be protected. At their best, mental asylums are special hotels or collegelike dormitories for white and wealthy Americans, where the temporary descent into "unreality" (or sobriety) is accorded the dignity of optimism, short internments, and a relatively earnest bedside manner. At their worst, mental asylums are families bureaucratized: the degradation and disenfranchisement of self, experienced by the biologically owned

† No changes have occurred. Avoidance, denial, and tokenism continue.

child (patient, woman), takes place in the anonymous and therefore guiltless embrace of strange fathers and mothers. In general
psychiatric wards and state hospitals, "therapy," privacy, and self-
determination are all either minimal or forbidden.‡ Experimental
or traditional medication, surgery, shock, and insulin coma treatment, isolation, physical and sexual violence, medical neglect, and
slave labor are routinely enforced.** Mental patients are somehow
less "human" than either medical patients or criminals. They
are, after all, "crazy"; they have been abandoned by (or have
abandoned dialogue with) their "own" families. As such, they
have no way—and no one—to "tell" what is happening to them.

The mental asylum closely approximates the female rather
than the male experience within the family. This is probably one of
the reasons why Erving Goffman, in *Asylums*, considered psychiatric
hospitalization more destructive of self than criminal incarceration.
Like most people, he is primarily thinking of the debilitating effect
—*on men*—of being treated like a woman (as helpless, dependent, sexless, unreasonable—as "crazy"). But what about the
effect of being treated like a woman when you *are* a woman?
And perhaps a woman who is already ambivalent or angry about
just such treatment?

Perhaps one of the reasons women embark and re-embark on
"psychiatric careers" more than men do is because they feel, quite
horribly, at "home" within them. Also, to the extent to which *all*
women have been poorly nurtured as female children, and are
refused "mothering" by men as female adults, they might be
eager for, or at least willing to settle for, periodic bouts of ersatz
"mothering," which they receive as "patients." Those women

‡ In such settings, I have heard legitimate and pitiful patient requests
for cigarettes or spending money, or complaints about bureaucratic red tape,
"interpreted" psychodynamically by student psychiatrists, psychologists, social
workers, nurses, and orderlies.
** Legally, all medication and treatment can be refused if the patient
has not been legally declared "incompetent" as well as "insane."

who are more ambivalent about or rejecting of the female role are often eager to be punished for such dangerous boldness—in order to be saved from its ultimate consequences. Many mental asylum procedures *do* threaten, punish, or misunderstand such women into a real or wily submission. Some of these women react to such punishment (or to a dependency-producing environment) with increased and higher levels of anger and sex-role alienation. If such anger or aggressiveness persists, the women are isolated, strait-jacketed, sedated, and given shock therapy.†† One study published by four male professionals in 1969 in the *Journal of Nervous and Mental Diseases*[6] describes how they attempted to reduce the aggressive behavior of a thirty-one-year-old "schizophrenic" woman by shocking her with a cattle prod whenever she "made accusations of being persecuted and abused; made verbal threats; or committed aggressive acts." They labeled their treatment a "punishment program" and note that the "procedure was administered against the expressed will of the patient."

Celibacy is the official order of the asylum day. Patients are made to inhabit an eternal American adolescence, where sexuality and aggression are as feared, mocked, and punished as they are within the Family. Traditionally, mental hospital wards are sex-segregated; homosexuality, lesbiansim, and masturbation are discouraged or forcibly interrupted.‡‡ The heterosexual dances sponsored in the late 1950s and 1960s were like high school proms, replete with chaperones, curfews, and frustration.

The female-"dominated" atmosphere of hospitals means a (shameful) return to childhood, for both men and women. However, the effect of sexual repression, for example, is probably dif-

†† They certainly aren't recruited by the Marines—or by an Olympic committee.

‡‡ Although homosexual, lesbian and heterosexual seduction and rape of the patients by the staff are not unknown, I think they occur less frequently than in criminal institutions.

ferent for female than for male patients.* Women have already
been bitterly and totally repressed sexually; many may be reacting
to or trying to escape from just such repression, and the powerlessness it signifies, by "going mad." Many male patients may be
escaping the demands of a compulsive and aggressive heterosexuality by "going mad." Its absence is *perhaps* not as psychologically or physiologically devastating as it is for women.

Female patients, like female children, are closely supervised by
other women (nurses, attendants) who, like mothers, are relatively
powerless in terms of the hospital hierarchy and who, like mothers,
don't really "like" their (wayward) daughters. Such supervision,
however, doesn't protect the female as patient-child from rape,
prostitution, pregnancy, and the blame for all three—any more
than similar "motherly" supervision protects the female as female
child in the "real" world, either within or outside the family.
From 1968 to 1970 there were numerous newspaper accounts of
the prostitution, rape, and impregnation of female mental patients
by the professional and non-professional staff, and by male inmates.†

Both sexual repression and sexual abuse still haunt women
in their "asylums." They do not escape enforced maternity either.
A study published in 1968 in the *American Journal of Orthopsychiatry*[7] documented a 366 per cent increase in the *recorded*

---

* We must remember that in state hospitals approximately 50 per cent of
the male patients are drug addicts and alcoholics—groups which are already
somewhat withdrawn from heterosexual activity, for any number of reasons
(lack of money, lack of desire for family "responsibilities," passivity, anxiety,
physiological incapacity, misogyny, etc.).

† For example: the New York *Times,* June 1968, regarding Chicago
State Hospital and an "unnamed hospital in suburban Tinley Park"; the New
York *Times,* June 1969, regarding Fairfield Hills Hospital in Newtown, Con-
necticut; the New York *Daily News,* November 1969, regarding Modesto State
Hospital in California; *Newsday,* January 1970, regarding Pilgrim State Hospital in New York; the New York *Daily News,* February 1970, regarding Grey-
stone State Hospital in New Jersey.

pregnancy and delivery rate among psychiatrically hospitalized women in Michigan state hospitals from 1936 to 1964.‡ Sixty per cent of the responding mental asylums in this study did not and/or would not prescribe contraceptives or perform abortions.

THE FEMALE SOCIAL ROLE AND PSYCHIATRIC SYMPTOMS: DEPRESSION, FRIGIDITY, AND SUICIDE ATTEMPTS

Why are women psychiatrically "disturbed" and hospitalized? Why do they seek private therapy? What is "schizophrenia" or madness like, or about, in contemporary women?

Two researchers recently stated that men are really as "psychologically disturbed" as women are:

> There is no greater magnitude of social stress impinging on one or the other sex. Rather [each sex] tends to learn a different style with which it reacts to whatever fact has produced the psychological disorder.[8]

I would not so much disagree with this statement as qualify it in several important ways. Many men *are* severely "disturbed"— but the form their "disturbance" takes is either not seen as "neurotic" or is not treated by psychiatric incarceration. Theoretically, all men, but especially white, wealthy, and older men, can act out many "disturbed" (and non-"disturbed") drives more

‡ This is not a "true" maternity rate; it is true only for those women who were considered "severely ill or those women who were financially restricted and who actually delivered within the state hospital." Their children's "fate" was as follows: 38 per cent were placed in adoptive or foster homes; 29 per cent were taken by "relatives"; 4 per cent died before leaving the hospital and the data is "unknown" for 29 per cent. The United States rate for 1964 was 23 *unmarried* mothers per 1000.

easily than women can.** The greater social tolerance for female "help-seeking" behavior, or displays of emotional distress, does not mean that such conditioned behavior is either valued or treated with kindness. On the contrary. Both husbands and clinicians experience and judge such female behavior as annoying, inconvenient, stubborn, childish, and tyrannical. Beyond a certain point, such behavior is "managed," rather than rewarded: it is treated with disbelief and pity, emotional distance, physical brutality, economic and sexual deprivation, drugs, shock therapy, and long-term psychiatric confinements.

Given the custodial nature of asylums and the anti-female biases of most clinicians, women who seek "help," women who have "symptoms," are actually being punished for their conditioned and socially approved self-destructive behavior. Typically "female" and "male" symptomatology appear early in life. Studies of childhood behavior problems have indicated that boys are most often referred to child guidance clinics for aggressive, destructive (anti-social), and competitive behavior; girls are referred (if they are referred at all), for personality problems, such as excessive fears and worries, shyness, timidity, lack of self-confidence, and feelings of inferiority.††[9] Similar, sex-typed symptoms exist in adults also:

> . . . the symptoms of men are also much more likely to reflect a destructive hostility toward others, as well as a pathological self-indulgence. . . . Women's symptoms, on the other hand, ex-

** Men are generally allowed a greater range of "acceptable" behaviors than are women. It can be argued that psychiatric hospitalization or labeling relates to what society considers "unacceptable" behavior. Thus, since women are allowed fewer total behaviors *and are more strictly confined to their role-sphere than men are,* women, more than men, will commit more behaviors that are seen as "ill" or "unacceptable."

†† Self-destructive or "loser" behavior, from suicide attempts to a fearful narrowing of life experience, is only fully punished as the female grows older. The female child is usually praised for the "maturity" of her submissiveness, obedience, and unadventurousness.

press a harsh, self-critical, self-depriving and often self-destructive set of attitudes.[10]

A study by E. Zigler and L. Phillips, comparing the symptoms of male and female mental hospital patients, found male patients significantly more assaultive than females and more prone to indulge their impulses in socially deviant ways like "robbery, rape, drinking, and homosexuality."[11] Female patients were often found to be "self-deprecatory, depressed, perplexed, suffering from suicidal thoughts, or making actual suicidal attempts."

Most women display "female" psychiatric symptoms such as depression, frigidity, paranoia, psychoneurosis, suicide attempts, and anxiety. Men display "male" diseases such as alcoholism, drug addiction, personality disorders, and brain diseases (see Table 1).‡‡ Typically female symptoms all share a "dread of happiness" —a phrase coined by Thomas Szasz to describe the "indirect forms of communication" that characterize "slave psychology."

In general, the open acknowledgement of satisfaction is feared only in situations of relative oppression (e.g. all suffering wife vis-a-vis domineering husband). The experiences of satisfaction (joy, contentment) are inhibited lest they lead to an augmentation of one's burden . . . *the fear of acknowledging satisfaction is a characteristic feature of slave psychology.* The "properly exploited" slave is forced to labor until he shows signs of fatigue or exhaustion. Completion of his task does not signify that his work is finished and that he may rest. At the same time, even though his task is unfinished, he may be able to influence his master to stop driving him—and to let him rest—if he exhibits signs of imminent collapse. Such signs may be genuine or contrived. Exhibiting signs of fatigue or exhaustion—irrespective of

‡‡ There are still fewer men hospitalized for "male" diseases than women hospitalized for "female" diseases.

whether they are genuine or contrived (e.g. "being on strike" against one's boss)—is likely to induce a feeling of fatigue or exhaustion in the actor. I believe that this is the mechanism responsible for the great majority of so-called chronic fatigue states. Most of these were formerly called "neurasthenia," a term rarely used nowadays. Chronic fatigue or a feeling of lifelessness and exhaustion are still frequently encountered in clinical practice.

Psychoanalytically, they are considered "character symptoms." Many of these patients are unconsciously "on strike" against persons (actual or internal) to whom they relate with subservience and against whom they wage an unending and unsuccessful covert rebellion.[12]

The analogy between "slave" and "woman" is by no means a perfect one. However, there is some theoretical justification for viewing women, or the sex-caste system, as the *prototype* for all subsequent class and race slavery.[13] Women were probably the first group of human beings to be enslaved by another group. In a sense, "woman's work," or woman's psychological identity, consists in exhibiting the signs and "symptoms" of slavery—as well as, or instead of, working around the clock in the kitchen, the nursery, the bedroom, and the factory.[14]

Depression

Women become "depressed" long before menopausal chemistry becomes the standard explanation for the disease. National statistics and research studies all document a much higher female to male ratio of depression or manic-depression at all ages.[15] Perhaps more women *do* get "depressed" as they grow older—when their already limited opportunities for sexual, emotional, and in-

TABLE 1:
PERCENTAGE INCIDENCE OF DIAGNOSTIC CLASSIFICATION

DIAGNOSTIC CLASSIFICATION	GENERAL HOSPITALS			OUTPATIENT CLINICS		
	TOTAL NO. OF PATIENTS	WOMEN	MEN	TOTAL NO. OF PATIENTS	WOMEN	MEN
The "Female Diseases"						
Psychotic Depressive	30,743	69%	31%	5,453	73%	27%
Manic Depressive	28,232	64%	36%	8,411	67%	33%
Psychoneurotic	378,289	70%	30%	156,525	68%	32%
Psychophysiological	27,562	67%	33%	5,317	59%	41%
Psychotic	262,961	64%	36%	143,092	62%	38%
Schizophrenic	158,689	61%	39%	116,088	60%	40%
Paranoid	59,718	57%	43%	38,030	57%	43%
Drug Intoxication (Poison)	20,229	60%	40%	831	56%	44%
The "Male Diseases"						
Alcohol Addiction	69,183	25%	75%	20,564	22%	78%
Alcohol Intoxication	52,087	27%	73%	3,907	30%	70%
Drug Addiction	11,004	36%	64%	3,622	24%	76%
Personality Disorders	143,142	40%	60%	169,239	44%	56%

N PSYCHIATRIC FACILITIES BY SEX: 1966–1968

PRIVATE HOSPITALS			STATE AND COUNTY HOSPITALS		
TOTAL NO. OF PATIENTS	WOMEN	MEN	TOTAL NO. OF PATIENTS	WOMEN	MEN
7,140	73%	27%	6,058	68%	32%
7,579	66%	34%	36,694	69%	31%
61,241	66%	34%	20,159	64%	36%
858	64%	36%	547	63%	37%
57,882	66%	34%	636,195	54%	46%
32,548	63%	37%	546,237	51%	49%
10,418	67%	33%	191,309	53%	47%
1,103	58%	42%	1,508	48%	52%
9,487	29%	71%	18,168	18%	82%
6,054	27%	73%	37,943	25%	75%
1,643	45%	55%	3,081	23%	77%
21,717	41%	59%	44,064	23%	77%

SOURCE: Reference Tables on Patients in Mental Health Facilities. U. S. Department of Health, Education and Welfare. Public Health Service. Health Services and Mental Health Administration. National Institute of Mental Health: 1966, 1967, 1968 (combined).

tellectual growth decrease even further. Dr. Pauline Bart studied depression in middle-aged women[16] and found that such women had completely accepted their "feminine" role—and were "depressed" because that role was no longer possible or needed.*

Traditionally, depression has been conceived of as the response to—or expression of—loss, either of an ambivalently loved other, of the "ideal" self, or of "meaning" in one's life. The hostility that should or could be directed outward in response to loss is turned inwards toward the self. "Depression" rather than "aggression" is the female response to disappointment or loss. The research and clinical evidence for any or all of these views is controversial. We may note that most women have "lost"—or have never really "had"—their mothers; nor is the maternal object replaced for them by husbands or lovers. Few women ever develop strong socially approved "ideal" selves. Few women are allowed, no less encouraged, to concern themselves with life's "meaning."† (Women lose their jobs as "women," rather than any existential hold on life's meaning.) In a sense, women can't "lose" what they've never had. Also, as I'll discuss in Chapter Ten, women are conditioned to "lose" in order to "win."

Women are in a continual state of mourning—for what they never had—or had too briefly, and for what they can't have in the present, be it Prince Charming or direct worldly power. It is not very easy for most women to temper, idle, or philosophize away their mourning with sexual, physical, or intellectual exercises. When female depression swells to clinical proportions, it unfortunately doesn't function as a role-release or respite. For example,

---

* As we shall see in Appendix, however, the more children a married woman has, the greater her chances are of being psychiatrically committed—when compared to her husband, to childless married women, or to married women with fewer children.[17]

† While this may *also* be true for many men, it is certainly not *untrue* for most women.

according to one recent study, published by Dr. Alfred Friedman in 1970,[18] "depressed" women are even *less* verbally "hostile" and "aggressive" than non-depressed women; their "depression" may serve as a way of keeping a deadly faith with their "feminine" role. "Depressed" patients were actually *less* verbally hostile than "normal" control patients—and their verbal hostility and "resentment" decreased even further as they "improved"—i.e., became less "depressed" according to clinical and self-rating.‡ (Depressed male patients were more verbally hostile than their female counterparts.) Dr. Friedman's interpretation of this finding is as follows: he hypothesizes that the "depressive" *usually* expresses very little verbal hostility (or other forms of) hostility, and become "depressed" only when the "usual defenses break down":

> It may be that it is their [the depressives'] inability to verbalize the hostility spontaneously to the person for whom they feel it at the time when it is appropriate [that] is part of their predisposition to become depressed. The tendency to deny the "bad" in significant others and to perceive them selectively so they do not consciously become angry or depressed may be one of the ways to ward off a disturbed or depressive reaction.

It is important to note that "depressed" women are (like women in general) only *verbally* hostile; unlike most men, they do not express their hostility physically—either directly, to the "significant others" in their lives, or indirectly, through physical and athletic prowess. It is safer for women to become "depressed" than physically violent. Physically violent women usually lose physical battles with male intimates; are abandoned by them as "crazy" as well as "unfeminine"; are frequently psychiatrically or (less frequently)

‡ This study's sample consisted of 534 white patients, hospitalized in Philadelphia. Seventy-one per cent were women, with a median age of forty-two, who attended but did not complete high school; 89 per cent of the female patients were or had been married.

criminally incarcerated. Further, physically strong and/or potentially assaultive women would gain fewer secondary rewards than
"depressed" women; their families would fear, hate, and abandon
them, rather than pity, sympathize, or "protect" them. Psychiatrists and asylums would behave similarly: hostile or potentially
violent women (and men), who are oppressed and powerless, are,
understandably, hardly ever treated ethically or legally—or kindly—
by others.

Frigidity

> A hoarder of secret sexual grievances, a wife.
>
> Joan Didion[19]

A great deal of information has recently been circulated regarding the political basis of female frigidity; women are sexually
repressed by patriarchal institutions which enforce fear, dislike,
and confusion about female sexual and reproductive anatomy in
both men and women. Phallus-worship is well represented in myth,
painting, sculpture, and modern bedroom practices: clitoris-wor-
ship and/or non-reproductive vagina-worship is not. I do not wish
to repeat or even review this information here, except as briefly as
possible.

Clinical case histories, psychological and sociological surveys
and studies[20]—and our own lives—have documented the extent
to which most twentieth-century women have not been having
orgasms; or not having the "right" kind of orgasms**; or not hav-

** One psychoanalyst, Marie Robinson, has characterized the proper
female orgasm as one in which the woman may be rendered unconscious for
up to three minutes.

ing *any* kind of orgasms very frequently or very easily; or having orgasms only under conditions of romantic monogamy, legal prostitution, or self-degradation; or only after much purposeful "learning." Women have been seen as sexually "insatiable" by witchhunters and modern scientists[21]; they have also been seen as not really "needing" orgasms as much as they need love, maternity, and fine silverware. Nevertheless, the psychoanalytic tradition (combined with a growing addiction to instant materialism and pleasure) has viewed "neurosis" and even "psychosis" as stemming from sexual repression. Consequently, most clinicians have tried hard to help their female patients "achieve" heterosexual orgasms— usually by counseling a joyous and/or philosophical acceptance of the female role as envisioned and enforced by men: as Madonnahousewife and mother, or as Magdalene Earth Goddess. Even sexual liberationist pioneers, such as Wilhelm Reich, have posited the primacy of vaginal eroticism, and viewed bisexuality and lesbianism as "regressive" or "infantile." Most clinicians have not thought deeply about the sociopolitical—*or* the psychological—conditions that are necessary for female sexual self-definition. Women can never be sexually actualized as long as men control the means of production and reproduction. Women have had to barter their sexuality (or their capacity for sexual pleasure) for economic survival and maternity. Female frigidity *as we know it* will cease only when such bartering ceases. Most women cannot be "sexual" as long as prostitution, rape, and patriarchal marriage exist, with such attendant concepts and practices as "illegitimate" pregnancies, enforced maternity, "non-maternal" paternity, and the sexual deprivation of "aging" women. From a psychological point of view, female frigidity will cease when female children are surrounded by and can observe non-frigid female adults.

Suicide Attempts

> I have done it again.
> One year in every ten
> I manage it——
> . . . .
> Dying
> Is an art, like everything else.
> I do it exceptionally well.
>
> I do it so it feels like hell.
> I do it so it feels real.
> I guess you could say I've a call.
>
> Its easy enough to do it in a cell.
> Its easy enough to do it and stay put
> Its the theatrical
>
> Comeback in broad day
>
> Sylvia Plath[22]

Men commit actions; women commit gestures. Both sexes are imprisoned by separate vocabularies. "Manfully," men kill themselves, or others—*physically*. Women *attempt* to kill themselves physically far more often than men do, and fail at it more often. Suicide is not an apolitical occurrence: the politics of caste (sex and race) shape American patterns of suicide. One study found that 69 per cent of attempted suicides in America are female and, conversely, that seventy per cent of completed suicides are male.[23] They also found that housewives comprised the "largest single category of both "attempted and completed suicides" and, further, that about five times as many widows *commit* suicide as attempt suicide (20 per cent vs. 4 per cent). Twice as many widowers commit suicide as attempt suicide (6 per cent vs. 3 per cent). A recent government pamphlet entitled *Suicide Among Youth*[24] documented that attempted suicide is far more frequent among student-age females than males but that student-age males complete more suicides. Non-white males between fifteen and twenty-five have the highest suicide commitment rate.

Physical action—even the exquisitely private and *self*-destructive act of taking one's own life—is very difficult for women. Conditioned female behavior is more comfortable with, is defined by, psychic and emotional self-destruction. Women are conditioned to experience *physicality*—be it violent, destructive, or pleasurable— more in the presence of another, or at male hands, than alone or at (their own) female hands. Female suicide attempts are not so much realistic "calls for help" or hostile inconveniencing of others as they are the assigned baring of the powerless throat, signals of ritual readiness for self-sacrifice. Like female tears, female suicide attempts constitute an essential act of resignation and helplessness —which alone can command temporary relief or secondary rewards.†† Suicide *attempts* are the grand rites of "femininity"— i.e., ideally, women are supposed to "lose" in order to "win." Women who *succeed* at suicide are, tragically, outwitting or rejecting their "feminine" role, and at the only price possible: their death.

SCHIZOPHRENIA IN THREE STUDIES

It is important to realize that schizophrenia, or madness, is crucially different from female symptoms such as depression or anxiety. Schizophrenia, in both women and men, always involves opposite as well as same-sex behavior. For instance, female schizo-

†† As we have noted, however, women who try to kill themselves are not necessarily treated very kindly.

phrenics are more openly hostile or violent, or more overtly concerned with sexual and bisexual pleasure, than are female "de-
pressives." Both groups of women still share many "feminine"
traits such as mistrusting their own perceptions, feeling inferior,
helpless, and dependent. Just as schizophrenia is no entrée into
power for women, neither are "female" diseases such as depression, paranoia, frigidity, and suicide attempts. Such "disorders,"
whether hospitalized or not, constitute female role rituals, enacted by most women. As we shall see, whether and what kind
of "treatment" is afforded these rituals is a function of age, class,
and race.

During the last decade three psychologists have discussed
"schizophrenia" in terms of sex-role alienation or sex-role rejection. In 1961, Dr. Shirley Angrist[25] compared female ex-mental
patients who were returned to asylums with those who weren't.
She found that the rehospitalized women had refused to function
"domestically" in terms of cleaning, cooking, child care, and
shopping. The rehospitalized women were no different from the
ex-mental patients in terms of their willingness to participate in
"leisure" activities, such as traveling, socializing, or enjoying themselves. The rehospitalized women were, in Angrist's terms, slightly
more "middle class and more frequently married than their non-
returned counterparts." Further, the husbands who readmitted their
wives expressed significantly lower expectations for their total human functioning. They seemed more willing to tolerate extremely
childlike and dependent behavior in their wives—such as incessant
complaining and incoherence—as long as the dishes were washed.
These husbands also expressed great alarm and disapproval about
their wives' "swearing," "cursing," and potentially violent "temper
tantrums."

In 1968, Dr. Angrist published a book, entitled *Women After
Treatment*,[26] in which she compared both early and late "re-

turnees" with "normal" or housewife female controls.‡‡ She found that the original differences between returned and non-returned women in the domestic performance area had completely disappeared. *All* "returned" women and *all* female ex-mental patients performed more poorly domestically than did "normal" housewives. In a further refinement of her data, in which she controlled for educational level, age, race, and social and marital status, these differences in domestic performance were eliminated. The differences between ex-mental patients and "normal" housewives were now in the "psychological" area—at least according to Angrist's informant-observers. Ex-patients, whether they were rehospitalized or not, swore more often, attempted aggressive acts more frequently, got drunk, did not want to "see" people, and "misbehaved sexually"—behaviors considered more "masculine" than "feminine." However, the ex-patients also exhibited many "feminine" behaviors, such as fatigue, insomnia, pill-taking, and general "inactivity."

It is interesting to note that both ex-patients and housewives equally displayed certain behaviors—behaviors which are negatively viewed. Angrist notes:

> [It was surprising] that so many of the controls [the normal housewives] were reported to have evidenced similar behavior as the ex-mental patients. 46% were described as restless; 59% as worn out; 60% as tense and nervous; 57% as "grouchy."

The husbands and mothers of both groups of women described them as

> making no sense when talking; walking, sitting, or standing awkwardly; moving around restlessly; saying she hears voices; trying to hurt or kill herself; needing help in dressing; being bad tem-

‡‡ A double standard of mental health accounts for such methodological and ideological practices as defining the "normal" woman as the "unemployed" housewife.

pered; not knowing what is going on around her; saying she sees people who aren't there.

In 1964, Dr. Frances Cheek published a study entitled "A Serendipitous Finding: Sex Role and Schizophrenia."[27] She compared male and female "schizophrenics" between the ages of fifteen and twenty-six with their "normal" counterparts, expecting to find a classic profile of schizophrenic passivity, withdrawal, and emotionally constrained behavior.* Instead she found that female schizophrenics were more dominant and aggressive with their parents than were female—or male†—normals or male schizophrenics. The male schizophrenics presented a more "feminine" (or schizophrenic) pattern of passivity, more so than schizophrenic females and normal males.

It is important to note that the male schizophrenics were still very similar to normal males in the expression of negative social-emotional behavior, such as expression of hostility and disagreement.‡ The female schizophrenics were less "negative" emotionally than were female or male normals or male schizophrenics. Nevertheless, female schizophrenics were perceived by both their parents as the "least conforming" of all the groups. Their parents remembered them as unusually "active" (for girls?) during childhood. This reference to "activeness" may not refer as much to physical or aggressive behavior as to perceptual, intellectual, or verbal behavior. Perhaps it was this rather specific rejection of one aspect of the female role that caused family conflict, and ultimately led to psychiatric labeling and incarceration.

Dr. Cheek refers to an earlier study done by Letailleur,[28] in

* Dr. Cheek observed and rated a mainly verbal patient-parent interaction. The task behavior that Dr. Cheek rated as "dominant" or "aggressive" involved opinion-giving or clarification of the subject being discussed.
† This information was obtained in a private communication.
‡ For example, the male ex-mental patients involved in various Mental Patients Liberation Projects are aware—and troubled by their excessive hostility and indifference to women.

which he suggests that "the overactive dominating female and the underactive passive male are cultural anomalies and are therefore hospitalized."** Letailleur thinks that the "role reversal" is a function of the disease process. I think that what Cheek calls the role "reversal" or "rejection" *is* what is labeled "crazy," or is, partly, what the disease is about. However, I do not think "role rejection" is the appropriate term. The male schizophrenics were similar in many ways to normal males; the female schizophrenics were similar to—or even more "female" than—the "normal" females. Sex-role alienation is probably a better term—and is the exact phrase used by Drs. David McClelland and Norman Watt in a 1968 study.[29]

McClelland and Watt compared twenty male and twenty female *hospitalized* schizophrenics between the ages of twenty and fifty with a number of "normal" control groups: "employed" males and females and "unemployed" housewives. The study measured conscious attitudes and preferences, attitudes to one's own body, fantasy and storytelling patterns, and preferences for abstract geometric figures. (Most of these measures had previously been standardized among "normal" populations, and clear sex differences had emerged.) The researchers found a general pattern of more "masculine" test behavior among female schizophrenics and more "feminine" test behavior among male schizophrenics.†† For example, female schizophrenics significantly favored the "intruding" and "penetrating" abstract geometric figures, usually preferred by normal males; female schizophrenics were significantly less "nurturant" and "affiliative" than normal female controls—but, in this regard, were no different from either normal or schizophrenic males; female schizophrenics chose "male" roles in imaginary plays: they preferred being "devils" to "witches" "police-

---

** The "passive" female schizophrenic is probably not hospitalized at so early an age, any more than is the "active" male schizophrenic.

†† There are many methodological criticisms to be made of this study. However, I think that the study's findings are essentially correct.

men" to "secretaries," "bulls" to "cows."‡‡ When shown a picture of a bull in a bullring, female schizophrenics evidenced "normal" male reaction—i.e., they said they would kill the bull. Male schizophrenics reacted as "normal" women and said they would flee the bullring.

Perhaps this study's most significant finding concerned satisfaction or dissatisfaction with various body parts, such as lips, face, elbows, body hair, hands, etc. Female schizophrenics were significantly less sensitive to their "feminine" appearance than were either normal female or male schizophrenics.* In fact, female schizophenics were more satisfied with their male or "strength" body parts than even normal males were.† Again, it is important to note that male schizophrenics were as "satisfied" with their male body parts as were male normals: they were simply more "satisfied" with their feminine or appearance body parts than normal males were. Female schizophrenics were relating to their bodies—at least verbally, in fantasy, or during a test—in a more recognizably "male" fashion. McClelland and Watt feel that concern with the body is a "primary and unconscious mode of expressing identity" and predates more secondary sex-role reversal behaviors, such as female wage-labor 'employment' or 'intellectual assertiveness.' "

The researchers are confused by the greater schizophrenic female than male "indifference" to all parts of their bodies.

‡‡ Unfortunately, McClelland doesn't make much of the fact that, to a great extent, the housewife control group preferred to play opposite-sex roles in this imaginary play.

* As we shall see in Chapter Three, this lack of concern has dire consequences for female mental patients in terms of releasing them from asylums.

† Sixty-nine per cent of the female schizophrenics compared with fifty per cent of the male normals were "satisfied" with their male or "strength" body parts. This should be compared with Cheek's finding that female schizophrenics were more "dominant" (verbally) than male normals. McClelland and Watt do not always compare female schizophrenic performance to male normal performance. It is therefore difficult to evaluate how much female schizophrenics are "threatening" because they have not only deserted certain posts of the "feminine" role but have adopted certain "masculine" posts even more boldly than normal men.

By itself such indifference might be attributable to long hospital-ization but this explanation would not account for the differen-tial results for the schizophrenic males. It seems plausible to con-clude that some parts of the schizophrenic woman's unconscious self-image is insensitive and more masculine, whereas some part of the schizophrenic man's self-image is sensitive and more feminine. Whether this difference predates their entry to mental hospitals is a question for further research.

Most women, while morbidly concerned with their "appear-ance," are actually quite removed from their bodies in terms of either "satisfaction," "confidence," or "activity." It is not surprising to find a continuation of this among female schizophrenics—who are, after all, "females." More important, however, is the fact that the essentially female nature of psychiatric confinement is, in a certain sense, more enraging to women—who have already been through it and been driven "mad" by it—than to men. If asylums are where you go for being alienated from your sex role, then you might as well act out that alienation as much as possible; there is nowhere else to do so. It is not surprising, therefore, that female psychiatric wards have been characterized as generally "noisier" than male wards[30]; as more "excitable" than the "apathetic" male wards[31]; as dominated by more mood swings, more belligerent, bossy, and interpersonally disruptive behavior[32]; and as more po-tentially "violent" than male wards.[33] What we must remember, however, is that such "masculine protests" are both ineffective and effectively punished, and are ultimately self-destructive. Patients on female wards have also been characterized as generally unable to make effective decisions, or to reason abstractly, and have been characterized by a marked lack of "ego strength."[34] Such traits often characterize long-term psychiatric patients and may, indeed, also be a function of hospitalization.

A THEORETICAL PROPOSAL

Neither genuinely mad women, nor women who are hospitalized for conditioned female behavior, are powerful revolutionaries. Their insights and behavior are as debilitating (for social reasons) as they are profound. Such women act alone, according to rules that make no "sense" and are contrary to those of our culture. Their behavior is "mad" because it represents a socially powerless individual's attempt to unite body and feeling. For example, Valerie Solanas‡ is both "crazy" and a "criminal" for *acting on* what many people are content simply to "name" and verbally criticize: the existence of misogyny and asexuality in patriarchal culture.

What we consider "madness," whether it appears in women or in men, is either the acting out of the devalued female role or the total or partial rejection of one's sex-role stereotype. Women who fully act out the conditioned female role are clinically viewed as "neurotic" or "psychotic." When and if they are hospitalized, it is for predominantly female behaviors such as "depression," "suicide attempts," "anxiety neuroses," "paranoia," or "promiscuity." Women who reject or are ambivalent about the female role frighten both themselves and society so much so that their ostracism and self-destructiveness probably begin very early. Such women are also assured of a psychiatric label and, if they are hospitalized, it is for less "female" behaviors, such as "schizophrenia," "lesbianism," or "promiscuity."**

Men who act out the female role and who, for example, are "dependent," "passive," sexually and physically "fearful" or "inactive," or who, like women, choose men as sexual partners, are seen as "neurotic" or "psychotic." If they are hospitalized they are

‡ The author of *The Scum Manifesto* and the woman who shot Andy Warhol, the film maker.
** "Promiscuity," like "frigidity," is both a "female" and a "non-female" trait: either can mean a flight into or a flight from "femininity."

usually labeled as "schizophrenic" or homosexual. It is important to note, however, that men in general are still able to reject more of their sex-role stereotype without viewing themselves as "sick," and without being psychiatrically hospitalized, than are women. Women are so conditioned to need and/or to service a man that they are more willing to take care of a man who is "passive," "dependent," or "unemployed"—than men are willing to relate to, no less take care of, a "dominant," "independent," or "employed" woman. What this means is that clinically "depressed" or "suicidal" females who do not serve men (or husbands) are as often rejected by them, and thereby subjected to relative poverty, or illegal prostitution, as are clinically "schizophrenic" or "hostile" females. Married men seek psychiatric help less frequently[35] and remain in asylums for shorter time periods than do married women or single men. Homosexuals, although psychiatrically "labeled" and legally persecuted, seek help less frequently than lesbians do[36] and, like male schizophrenics, still exhibit fewer (devalued) female traits than do lesbians or female schizophrenics.

Men who act out the male role—but who are too young, too poor, or too black—are usually incarcerated as "criminals" or as "sociopaths," rather than as "schizophrenics" or "neurotics." In order to be "men," less powerful men in our society have to "steal" what more powerful men can "buy." (And they are punished for doing so.) The kinds of behaviors that are considered "criminal" and "mentally ill" are sex-typed,†† and each sex is conditioned accordingly. Psychiatric categories themselves are sex-typed. Many more women than men manifest, seek help, and are hospitalized for what we categorize as a "psychiatric disease." It is important to know what type of clinical treatment these psychiatric patients receive; how many clinicians there are, the theories on which the clinicians draw, and how these psychiatrists and psychologists view their patients.

†† They are also typed by race and class.

Chapter Three

THE CLINICIANS

I met Wilhelm Reich in October 1939 shortly after his arrival in the States. I became his wife, secretary, laboratory assistant, bookkeeper, housekeeper, and general factotum, soon thereafter, the mother of his son in 1944. . . . I had to continue my work, which at that time and place consisted mainly of typing Reich's manuscripts. I also had to take care of the baby. I remember well typing away at a manuscript while pushing the carriage back and forth with one foot to keep the baby quiet because Daddy could not bear to hear him cry. Or Reich, very graciously telling me in the late afternoon to take off for a while and go fishing out on the lake while he would look after the baby, then after half an hour, his waving to me frantically because the baby needed to be changed, an ordeal which he could not face.

Ilse Ollendorf Reich[1]

At home [Freud's] family revolved around him and his work. . . . "I am afraid I do have a tendency toward tyranny" he admitted more than once. . . . Unlike his success with adopted [intellectual] daughters, Freud had trouble with all his "sons" in psychoanalysis. Especially for men, working for such a genius could be very frustrating: it was bound to offend a man's sense of autonomy. . . . [Helene Deutsch's] career seems to contradict the Freudian theories of femininity which she expounds in her book. Far from being clinging and dependent, as a psychiatrist she was both active and independent, yet toward Freud and his concepts, which she did so much to make popular, Helene remained passive and receptive. . . . [Freud psychoanalyzed Deutsch's] "Oedipal situation" [and told her to continue her "identification" with her father—and with himself].

Paul Roazan[2]

Freud was merely a diagnostician for what Feminism purports to cure . . . a thorough restatement of Freud in Feminist terms would make a valuable book.

Shulamith Firestone[3]

The Women's Liberation Movement cannot afford to indulge the bad poetry about women, when we have a science we can use, explore, criticize, amend. For psychoanalysis, like all sciences, is open, not closed.

Juliet Mitchell[4]

> By an irony nearly tragic, the discoveries of a great pioneer [Freud], whose theories of the unconscious and of infant sexuality were major contributions to human understanding, were in time invoked to sponsor a point of view essentially conservative . . . the effect of Freud's work, that of his followers, and still more that of his popularizers was to rationalize the invidious relationship between the sexes, to ratify traditional roles, and to validate temperamental differences. . . . Although the most unfortunate effects of vulgar Freudianism far exceeded the intentions of Freud himself, its anti-feminism was not without foundation in Freud's own work.
>
> Kate Millett[5]

Psychiatrists and psychologists are no more sexocidal than politicians, soldiers, poets, physicists, or bartenders are. However, they are no less so—despite their rather special concern with and power over individual women. We owe our familiarity with feminine "hysteria," as well as our ambivalence about whether such behavior is universal and "normal," or universal and "abnormal," to such scientific fathers. I do not think that any one social or professional group is "responsible" for or can change the entire fabric of social reality, although at a given moment, each group or individual threads its way rather unalterably through it. I do believe that individual exceptions exist, and are valuable, as well as limited to those individuals involved. Individual exceptions are also irrelevant to any understanding of the rules or forces to which they take exception. Harping on or clinging to the doctrine of "individual exceptions" is usually a privilege of cowardice, ignorance, or vested interest.

In this chapter, I would like to present some general facts about clinicians:

(1) The extent to which the professions of psychiatry and psychology in America are numerically dominated by men.

(2) The extent to which most *contemporary* female and male clinicians, whether they are disciples of a particular psychoanalytic or psychological theory or not, currently share and act upon traditional myths about "abnormality," sex-role stereotypes and female inferiority.

(3) The extent to which most traditional psychoanalytic and therapeutic theories and practices perpetrate certain misogynistic views of women and of sex-role stereotypes as "scientific" or "curative."

(4) The extent to which both modern and traditional ideologies are played out within the *institution* of private therapy, which is, like that of the mental asylum, a mirror of the female experience in patriarchal culture.

HOW MANY CLINICIANS ARE THERE IN AMERICA?

Clinicians, like ghetto schoolteachers, do not study themselves or publicize their own motives, personalities, and values as easily or frequently as they do those of their neurotic patients or "culturally deprived" pupils. Most clinicians are too busy, too unwilling, or too "important" to fill out questionnaires or be experimental subjects. Over the last decade, the response of psychiatrists and psychologists to questionnaire inquiries is generally rather low; they are not willing subjects.[6] Nevertheless, the major professional organizations do publish membership lists; government research bureaus do publish estimates of psychiatric hospital staffing patterns; psychologists and psychiatrists have published studies about their profession's attitudes, behaviors, and "personal" life styles; psychoanalytic theorists and clinicians have published their case histories and theories; their disciples have often published their biographies.

In 1960 the membership of the American Psychiatric Association totaled 11,083, of whom 10,100 were men and 983 were women. In 1970 their membership increased to 17,298, of whom 14,267 were men and 1691 were women.* Thus 90 per cent of all psychiatrists during the last decade were men. It is important to remember that psychiatry is the most powerful of the mental illness professions, in terms of prestige, money, and *ultimate* control over psychiatric policies, both in private practice and in mental hospitals. Psychiatrists, both medically and legally, decide *who* is insane and *why; what* should be done to or for such people; and *when* and *if* they should be released from treatment. (As we shall see, both their medical training and their legal responsibility predispose most psychiatrists to diagnose "pathology" everywhere—even, or especially, where non-experts are blind to it.)

I italicized the word "ultimate," above, because, powerful as psychiatrists are, there are far too few of them to carry out their opinions in all psychiatric wards at every moment. For example, in 1970 the National Institute of Mental Health conducted a survey of staffing patterns in transitional mental health facilities.[7] Based on a January 1970 sample, they documented that psychiatrists comprise no more than 5 per cent of the staff—and that the majority of them are employed on a part-time basis. Sixty-eight per cent of the full-time and 37 per cent of the part-time staff in these facilities are "non-professionals." Social workers constitute 10 per cent of the full- and part-time staff; psychologists comprise about 2 per cent of the staff. In community mental health facilities, psychiatrists were seen as constituting 14 per cent of the staff involved in consultation and education.[8]

Within mental asylums, most psychiatrists function as well-paid administrators whose minimal and prima donna presence lends a paternal air of scientific and legal efficiency. Nevertheless,

* The sex of 1340 names on the 1970 membership list is unclear.

their will be done—even in their absence. The non-professional staff is influenced by their "expert" views which, after all, are not very different from the supposedly less enlightened views and practices of social workers, nurses, dieticians, and orderlies. (Also, since the less prestigious hospital professionals are mainly women, there is a conditioned and much reinforced tendency to serve, please, and second-guess the male psychiatrist before he even makes his judgment known.)

In 1960 the American Psychological Association totaled 18,215 members. This increased to 30,839 members in 1970. This Association does not publish an accurate sex-ratio count of their members but, in a personal communication,† estimated that twenty-five per cent are women. This would mean that approximately 4580 women in 1960 and 7500 women in 1970 were psychologist-members at all levels of "expertise." We must remember that not all psychologists are clinicians. Many teach and/or do research—exclusively. (Most psychiatrists combine their research or teaching with clinical responsibilities in both hospital and private settings.) In any event, however many *clinical* psychologists there are, they occupy positions subordinate to psychiatrists, especially within the hospital hierarchy. I would estimate that women have comprised 15 per cent of all clinical psychologists and that they, together with female psychiatrists, comprise no more than 12 per cent of America's two most powerful clinical professions.‡ Predictably

---

† Personal communication from Ms. Jane Hildreth, American Psychological Association Membership Office, May 1971.

‡ Of course, there are more clinicians in America, both male and female, than are listed as members of the American Psychiatric and Psychological Associations. The number of lower-"ranking" clinicians has increased tremendously during the last decade, and include degreed and non-degreed social workers, lay analysts, behavior therapists, traditional and anti-traditional and/or encounter group specialists, marriage and family counselors, school and vocational counselors, and "trained" and "untrained" paraprofessionals involved in community mental health and drug addiction projects. All such clinicians are subordinate to and take their cues from psychiatrists and psychologists. The male-female ratio is probably more equal in some of these professions—and to less avail.

enough, these women are disproportionately involved in "women's work" within the profession: they see preadolescent children and women. "Troubled" male adolescents are usually referred to male therapists for fatherly role-modeling; and adult males—as well as females—prefer male therapists.[9]

Dr. William Schofield[10] sent basic information questionnaires to randomly selected practitioner members of the American Psychiatric and Psychological Associations, and to the National Association of Social Workers.** He found that clinical psychologists were predominantly male, in a ratio of two to one; that ninety per cent of the psychiatrists were male; and that social workers (the least prestigious and well-paying of the three professional groups) were predominantly female, in a ratio of two to one. He also found that the psychiatrists and psychologists were about the same age (an average of forty-four), and were married. (Two per cent of the psychiatrists and 10 per cent of the psychologists were divorced.) Both the psychiatrists and psychologists had backgrounds that Schofield characterized as containing "pressure toward upward social mobility." Also, of those psychiatrists and psychologists who expressed a preferred sex in their "ideal" patient, the majority "preferred" a young, attractive female patient—with no more than a B.A. degree. Perhaps this preference makes good sense. A male therapist†† may receive a real psychological "service" from his female patient: namely, the experience of controlling and feeling superior to a female being upon whom he has projected many of his own forbidden longings for dependency, emotionality, and subjectivity, and from whom, as a superior expert, as a doctor, he is protected as he cannot be from his mother, wife, or

** Complete returns were obtained from 140 psychiatrists, 149 psychiatric social workers, and 88 clinical psychologists.

†† Whose "masculinity" is already somewhat compromised by his involvement in a "soft" and "helping" profession.

girl friend. There are other reasons for this preference which I will discuss later.

It is obvious that a predominantly female psychiatric population in America (see Chapters Two and Four) has been diagnosed, psychoanalyzed, researched, and hospitalized by a predominantly male professional population. Despite individual differences among clinicians, most have been steeped, professionally and culturally, in both contemporary and traditional patriarchal ideologies—ideologies which they put into some sort of practice within a patriarchal *institution*, such as private therapy or the mental asylum.

Before reviewing some traditional psychological or psycho-analytic theories and practices regarding sex roles and women, I'd like to review some studies about what contemporary clinicians believe and practice—regardless of what kind of traditional ideologies they may have been taught.

CONTEMPORARY CLINICAL IDEOLOGY

Most contemporary professionals (like most non-professionals) unthinkingly consider what happens to men as somehow more important than what happens to women. *Male* psychiatric illness or "impairment" is viewed as more "disabling" than female illness. The ghost of female expendability and "outsidedness" haunts almost every page of psychiatric and psychological journals—even when the subject of the article is female illness. Fewer (male) "virtues" are expected of women: it is not catastrophic or even surprising when they don't manifest any—even though their absence is both socially devalued and psychiatrically diagnosed as neurosis or psychosis.

Women as subjects have remained quite literally "outside" of many psychological experiments, particularly in learning or achievement-motivation: female performance proves too variable or too "minimal" to yield up the manly and publishable phenomena being sought.[11] Women—even the college sophomore subject—constitute a troublesome "error" or "noise" factor which must be excluded. Unfortunately, the results of just such experiments have been accepted as the standards for normal learning or "performance," standards which, by definition, women cannot achieve.

The clinical research literature documents, challenges, and is guilty of certain biases shared by most practicing clinicians. I would like to discuss five major biases—all of which I have been "taught" either directly or indirectly, in my training as a psychologist.

(1) Everyone is "sick"

In general, most clinician-theorists are trained to find "pathology" everywhere: in women, in children, in men, in nations, in entire historical epochs.‡‡ This bias has been more easily attacked than avoided, and I will not dwell on it at length. Dr. Maurice K. Temerlin in 1968[12] described an experiment that took place in Oklahoma, which demonstrated the extent to which psychiatrists and psychologists are predisposed to diagnose "pathology"—wherever they look—significantly more so than non-professionals; and the extent to which the prestige of authority accounts for the kind of diagnoses made in hospital settings. Temerlin asked a group of psychiatrists, clinical psychologists, and graduate students in clinical psychology to watch a taped, televised interview, on the basis of which they would make diagnoses of "psychotic," "neurotic," or "healthy." (The interviewee was a male actor who had memorized a script that was prepared in accordance with consensus judgments of what is "normal" and "healthy.") Before watching him each of the three professional groups were told by a "high-prestige"

‡‡ This is dangerous because, in doing this, we banish the concepts of good and evil from the arena of human responsibility.

person within their own field that the man was "very interesting because he looked neurotic but actually was quite psychotic." Sixty per cent of the psychiatrists, 28 per cent of the clinical psychologists, and 11 per cent of the graduate students diagnosed "psychosis." Control (or comparison) groups, composed of professionals who did not hear any prestige suggestion, never diagnosed psychosis. Most important, perhaps, is the fact that a control group composed of non-professional people, who were randomly selected from a jury wheel and asked to watch the tape at a county courthouse, unanimously considered the man "sane." (They were told that the court was experimenting with new sanity-hearing procedures.) Temerlin interprets these findings in terms of the medical training that predisposes judgments of "illness"—especially when in doubt —combined with the tendency toward diagnostic conformity which prestige figures enforce and reward. After one of the subject-psychiatrists was "debriefed," he still defended his diagnosis as follows: "Of course he looked healthy, but hell, most people are a little neurotic, and who can accept appearances at face value anyway?"

(2) Only men can be mentally healthy

Thus, many clinicians think their patients are "crazy" but they think their female patients are "crazier" yet. Many double standards of mental health and treatment exist: one for blacks, another for whites, one for the poor, another for the wealthy, and, of course, one for women and another for men. A recent study by Dr. Inge K. Broverman et al.[18] demonstrates the extent to which contemporary clinicians still view their female patients as Freud viewed his—and still hold to a double standard of mental health. Seventy-nine clinicians (forty-six male and thirty-three female psychiatrists, psychologists, and social workers) completed a sex-role stereotype questionnaire. The questionnaire consisted of 122 bipolar items, each of which described a particular behavior or trait. For example:

> very subjective_____very objective
> not at all aggressive_____very aggressive

The clinicians were instructed to check off those traits that represent healthy male, healthy female, or healthy adult (sex unspecified) behavior. The results were as follows:

1. There was high agreement among clinicians as to the attributes characterizing healthy adult men, healthy adult women, and healthy adults, sex unspecified.
2. There were no differences among men and women clinicians.
3. Clinicians had different standards of health for men and women. Their concepts of healthy mature men did not differ significantly from their concepts of healthy mature adults, but their concepts of healthy mature women did differ significantly from those for men and for adults. Clinicians were likely to suggest that women differ from healthy men by being more submissive, less independent, less adventurous, more easily influenced, less aggressive, less competitive, more excitable in minor crises, more easily hurt, more emotional, more conceited about their appearances, less objective, and less interested in math and science.

Finally, what was judged healthy for adults, sex unspecified, and for adult males, was in general highly correlated with previous studies of social desirability as perceived by non-professional subjects.

It is clear that for a woman to be healthy she must "adjust" to and accept the behavioral norms for her sex even though these kinds of behavior are generally regarded as less socially desirable. As the authors themselves remark, "This constellation seems a most unusual way of describing any mature, healthy individual." The ethic of mental health is masculine in our culture. This double standard of sexual mental health, which exists side by side with a single and masculine standard of *human* mental health, is enforced by both society and clinicians. Although the limited "ego resources," and unlimited "dependence," and fearfulness of most women is pitied, disliked, and "diagnosed," by society and its agent-clinicians, any other kind of behavior is unacceptable in women! The disquieting "submissiveness," "shyness," and "pettiness" of female children is never treated as a problem: it is viewed as evidence that girls "grow up" (into their eternal childhoods) more quickly than boys do.* Female adolescents and adults run serious risks when they persist in "male" activities.† Their parents and husbands will ostracize and psychiatrically commit them for this— and the psychiatrists will keep them in hospitals until they assert their "femininity." Less educated[14] and more "attractive" women are probably released sooner and more easily from state hospitals and from private treatment; they are probably also sexually propositioned more often within the hospital (a blessing or a curse, depending on your viewpoint). Certainly, "feminine" domestic tasks— as opposed to "man's work"—is the slave labor of choice for women in state asylums.

In a 1971 study by Dr. Nathan Rickel,[15] entitled "The Angry Woman Syndrome," husbands who "put up" with their middle-aged wives' "angry" and malelike behavior are described

---

* The only reason that the "aggressive" behaviors of male children are treated as a problem is because patriarchy wants male youth to wait until it grows older, whiter, and richer before being given its license to practice "masculinity." Female adolescents as well as adults are more censured for "aggressive" rather than "sexually" delinquent behavior than are male adolescents and adults.

† The reverse is often true too, of course.

as suffering from a "Job complex." The author notes that while the reverse is often seen, namely, "where men are the angry protagonists and women the passive recipients . . . our society is so geared that it more readily accepts this as only an exaggeration of the expected masculine-feminine roles." Rickel's "angry" women are all highly successful professionally and are "neurotic" because they exhibit "male" behaviors such as

> an inability to brook criticism or competition; bursts of uncontrollable temper; the use of foul language; possessiveness or jealousy; the use of alcohol or drugs; and consorting with spouses who accept such behaviour.‡

If such "male" behavior is "neurotic" or "self-destructive," then it should be seen as such for both sexes. (Of course, when women do the very same things as men, it always has a completely different meaning and set of consequences: even here, it is the *wives* who are seeking treatment—the husbands, for all their "female"-like suffering, are not.)

Whenever sex-role stereotype lines are crossed, clinicians enforce the double standard of mental health. For example, a 1963 report tells how a male psychiatrist, Dr. Herbert Modlin, "managed" a group of "paranoid" women back to "feminine" health[16]: he helped them re-establish their relationships with their husbands. The author's therapeutic technique is as reprehensible as his goal. He decided that his "paranoid"** patients needed "strong" male control, both within their marriages and within the hospital. He notes that many of these women's husbands were too "passive

‡ Like Angrist's and McClelland's female schizophrenics (Chapter Two), they also exhibit much female behavior such as suicide threats and attempts and a "very good memory for minor slights."
** I wonder whether he would have treated white middle-class men this way. Certainly, many psychiatrists in city hospitals serving the poor treat drug addicts and blacks, Latins, and/or female patients similarly: their professional competence or *machismo* is measured by their contempt for and distance from their "sneakily" "manipulative" patients.

and compliant." He therefore "demonstrated to the man his wife's need of him [and helped] him assume a stronger position for her sake." Within the hospital, the psychiatrists were instructed to be firm and authoritarian, to disbelieve and be wary of the women's "inclinations to interpret, react to, and manipulate [their] environment on the basis of their distorted perceptions."†† Of course, their perceptions are not "distorted" at all: they represent an appropriately panicked reaction to reality. For example, Modlin notes that the "precipitating factor" in all the "paranoid" cases was "an actual alteration in the husband-wife relationship" which often led to a decrease or cessation of sexual intercourse. Many of the husbands were involved in work that was "more" important to them than their marriages, and were not only happily absent from home for long periods but sexually ungiving when present. These women were not only sexually deprived—they were nearly out of jobs. Their "paranoia" was both a way of fulfilling and avoiding the consequences they feared and saw approaching: psychic and financial unemployment.

Dr. Modlin may have listened to his patients but he did not hear what they were saying. He neatly glides over the meaning of such "delusions" as "conversations with the Devil," reported by one of his "paranoid," sexually deprived, and probably monogamous patients. The "Devil" is persuading her to become a "prostitute" —i.e., the only image of a sexually *involved* woman in our culture is that of a prostitute, and she (the patient) wished to be sexually involved. Accusations of "infidelity" are also considered as "delusionary" as is one of Dr. Modlin's female patient's complaints that twenty-one "previous shock treatments" had "ruined her brain." Rickel also somewhat underestimates (but does not overlook) the

†† In another 1963 study by Dr. Franklin Klaf, the majority of female paranoid patients reported that *men* were "persecuting" them.

fact that one of his patients, like Freud's patient Dora, was in treatment as a "captive." He says:

> . . . she constantly expressed the fear with some basis, that her mother and older brother would like to see her put away. In fact, the brother called me with that thought in mind.

Another psychologist,[17] in a study of female psychology, glosses over the perceptiveness of those female college students who explained their "frigidity" in terms of what the author calls "unconscious prostitution fears." There is nothing very unconscious—or distorted—about such fears. For two thousand years the male "brotherhood" and, more recently, psychiatric and psychological journals have testified to what extent men are socialized to separate love and sex and to fear the former and condemn the latter—in women.

Traditional patriarchal themes, like bad dreams, have reappeared in several recently published accounts of female psychology and sexuality.‡‡ For example, Dr. Judith Bardwick has written the first academic book about female psychology since the second feminist movement occurred in America.[19] Bardwick presents a reasonable, thoughtful, and comprehensive review of various studies, accompanied by deceptive protestations of objectivity and political neutrality. Despite her clear understanding that American females never develop "selves" or "independence," she is still a Dutiful Daughter, in the best Helene Deutsch-Esther Harding tradition. She apparently accepts a double standard of mental health, lauding the "female virtues" for women but not for men. Although she criticizes Freud's views of women, she joins him in the comfort of an "anatomy is destiny" bias. Like Horney, her version of it is "my vagina is bigger than your penis."

‡‡ I am thinking of Mary Jane Sherfey's conclusions at the end of her long and excellent monograph on female sexuality, i.e., that "civilization" at its best would be undermined by female sexual liberation.[18]

Many of her "professional" opinions sound remarkably similar to conventional opinions. She proclaims that female children develop sexuality later than male children; that, because the clitoris is so anatomically small, female children do not masturbate or "suffer" sexual frustration, nor do they experience prepubertal vaginal sensations; that male children suffer a harsher socialization than female children; that sex for women is much more tied up with love than it is for men; that the most basic pleasure for women is that of maternity; that the vaginal orgasm exists "psychologically" and "involves fusion with a loved man"*; that women are more dependent on men than on women because of the "indifferent (or hostile) relationships they've had with their mothers and girlfriends."† These are all familiar and "unprovable" views which, however, are more rewarded than an opposite and equally "unprovable" set of views would be.

(3) Maternity and maternality are exclusive female properties

Clinician-theorists share the idea that women need to be mothers and that children need intensive and exclusive female mothering in order for both to be mentally "healthy." The absoluteness of this conviction is only equaled by the conviction that mothers are generally "unhappy" and inefficient, and are also the cause of neurosis, psychosis, and criminality in their children. Child-development textbooks are filled with these views; as is the research literature on the "schizophrenogenic" mother;

---

* I do not question that women report and/or experience different intensities of orgasm. What I do question is whether this female "greater" sexual sensitivity is indeed biologically predetermined or whether it is culturally and economically predetermined; and further, whether there is—or should be—only one kind of orgasm for men.

† She does not interpret this in feminist terms at all.

the mother who produces "promiscuous" daughters, "homosexual" sons, and "criminal" or "neurotic" children.

Joseph Rheingold, in his *The Mother, Anxiety and Death*,[20] claims that he has "been struck by the number of women who almost indifferently admit the desire to abuse, rape, mutilate, or kill a child, any child. I have never known a man with this cold-blooded animosity for children."

(4) Lesbianism and homosexuality are diseases

Most clinicians view lesbianism and homosexuality as "pathological" or, at best, as "second best." Heterosexuality, rather than bisexuality, is the norm. Few clinicians differentiate between (male) homosexuals and (female) lesbians.

(5) Certain pregnancies are illegitimate; certain women are promiscuous

Clinician-theorists accept patriarchal notions of "illegitimate" pregnancies; female "promiscuity"; female "seductiveness"; and, paradoxically, female "sexlessness."[21] They act on such views in rather powerful ways: by convincing women that they are true, or by psychiatrically incarcerating women, especially adolescents and wives, for "promiscuity."‡ Female children whose fathers rape them are seen as "seductive"—or the mothers are blamed for not preventing the rape-incest, or for secretly "wanting" it.[22] In any

‡ In a personal communication, dated 1971, a practicing psychiatrist told me about a middle-aged American woman who was psychiatrically committed by her husband and psychiatrist twenty years ago for having taken a lover; she died ten years later in the asylum. A lawyer told me the following story: a woman in her thirties was privately hospitalized by her husband. In 1969 she began a sexual-emotional relationship in the asylum with a man younger than herself. Both seemed much happier. The asylum authorities forcibly separated them; both suffered "relapses" and, to her (the lawyer's) knowledge, both are still hospitalized.

event, the tone is one of "no great harm has been done anyway." The few cases of maternal seduction and incest reported are all seen as the cause of the male child's ultimate "schizophrenia."[23] Professional prostitution is clinically viewed as female "revenge" and "aggression"—and not as female victimization.[24]

These five major clinical viewpoints or biases may or may not be derived from having read the works of traditional theorists and/or from having been professionally trained. In any event, these and other similar biases certainly reflect many themes in the traditional clinical literature.

TRADITIONAL CLINICAL IDEOLOGY

Although the ethic and referent of mental health in our society is a masculine one, most psychoanalytic theoreticians have written primarily about women. Whether this choice simply reflects the greater abundance or cooperativeness of female patients, as well as the male desire to "save" and mold them, is unclear. I think something deeper has tempted and excited male psychiatrists for the last century to write about the Eternal Feminine gone "mad." I think it was both safe and "therapeutic" for them to do this. In women, they could study madness without dread. They would not be turned into stone or pigs (Valerie Solanas is no Medusa; Zelda Fitzgerald is no Circe.)** Also, while many "mad" women are hostile and unpredictable, they are still women, and not as physically dangerous as their male counterparts.†† More important, men of science (and art) cannot, except momentarily and romantically, and therefore safely, identify strongly with their female subjects. Their own sanity can remain firmly moored between their legs.

** What I'm saying is that mad women have no power. I am not saying that Medusa or Circe was mad. On the contrary, precisely because such women had power, they have become images that are despised and feared.
†† Although certainly some are—and are feared as such.

The subject of women has traditionally elicited the most sentimental yet authoritative pronouncements in the psychoanalytic literature, all of which imply, accept and desire a double standard of mental health or normality.

Sigmund Freud:

[Women] refuse to accept the fact of being castrated and have the hope of someday obtaining a penis in spite of everything. . . . I cannot escape the notion (though I hesitate to give it expression) that for woman the level of what is ethically normal is different from what it is in man. We must not allow ourselves to be deflected from such conclusions by the denials of the feminists who are anxious to force us to regard the two sexes as completely equal in position and worth.[25]

We say also of women that their social interests are weaker than those of men and that their capacity for the sublimation of their interests is less . . . the difficult development which leads to femininity [seems to] exhaust all the possibilities of the individual.[26]

Erik Erikson:

For the student of development and practitioner of psychoanalysis, the stage of life crucial for the understanding of womanhood is the step from youth to maturity, the state when the young woman relinquishes the care received from the parental family and the extended care of institutions of education, in order to commit herself to the love of a stranger and to the care to be given to his or her offspring . . . young women often ask, whether they can "have an identity" before they know whom they will marry and for whom they will make a home. Granted that something in the young woman's identity must keep itself open for the peculiarities of the man to be joined and of the children to be brought up, I think that much of a young woman's identity is already defined in her kind of attractiveness and in the selectivity of her search for the man (or men) by whom she wishes to be sought.[27]

Bruno Bettelheim:

. . . as much as women want to be good scientists and engineers, they want, first and foremost, to be womanly companions of men and to be mothers.[28]

Joseph Rheingold:

. . . woman is nurturance . . . anatomy decrees the life of a woman. . . . When women grow up without dread of their biological functions and without subversion by feminist doctrines and therefore enter upon motherhood with a sense of fulfillment and altruistic sentiment we shall attain the goal of a good life and a secure world in which to live.[29]‡‡

Carl G. Jung:

"But no one can evade the fact, that in taking up a masculine calling, studying, and working in a man's way, woman is doing something not wholly in agreement with, if not directly injurious to, her feminine nature." . . . [Female] psychology is founded on the principle of Eros, the great binder and deliverer; while age-old wisdom has ascribed Logos to man as his ruling principle.[30]

M. Esther Harding:

A personal motive will carry a woman through an almost unlimited amount of monotonous work, without risk of losing her soul. For instance, she can make an infinite number of stitches if the embroidery is for a special place in her house; or she can

‡‡ Anatomy, like the bubonic plague, is history, not destiny. Of course, there are bio-anatomical differences between the sexes. The question now is whether these differences—or the cultural conclusions drawn from them—are either necessary or desirable.

knit sweaters and socks indefinitely for her husband and boys.
. . . [Woman's real goal is the] creation of the possibility of
psychic, or psychological, relation to man. . . . It is a significant
turning point in [the successful woman's] relation to a man,
when she finds that she can no longer look him frankly in the
eyes, for it means that her real feeling which may not be shown
openly has begun to stir . . . one of the factors accounting for
an older woman's interest in a man much younger than herself,
lies in her own emotional immaturity. Such a woman has put
all her energies and attention into developing her individual
and professional qualities but little into developing her feminine
values . . . so long as her own emotional nature is immature,
she will continue to seek her fulfillment by making someone
else dependent on her, her own inner childishness being projected, or reflected, in the man to whom she is attracted.[81]

These are all familiar, prescribed, and therefore extremely
seductive views of women. Their affirmation by experts has indirectly strengthened such views among men and more directly
tyrannized women: events such as childbirth and marriage which,
in others centuries, was unavoidable, common, and unromanticized,
are here being touted by experts as spiritual luxuries, which women
must *strive for*. The unchosen necessities of the past (perhaps no
different from poverty, disease, or early death) were revived as
salvation myths for twentieth-century women by the major psychoanalytic theorists. American middle-class women were also "seduced
and abandoned" by the institution of psychotherapy and the
tyranny of published "expert" opinion which stressed the mother's
importance (and deadly responsibility) for healthy child development. Most child development research, like most birth control
research, has centered around women, not men: for this is "woman's
work," for which she is totally responsible, which is "never done,"
and for which, in a wage-labor economy, she is never directly

paid. She does it for love and is amply rewarded—in the writings of Freud et al.

Freud's views and self-professed confusion about women have been embraced, often romantically and devotedly, by female theoreticians, such as Freud's analysand and disciple Helene Deutsch, and by Marie Bonaparte, Marie Robinson, and Marynia Farnham, and by male theoreticians such as Frederick Lundberg, Erik Erikson, Bruno Bettelheim, and Joseph Rheingold. Freud's views have been more subtly supported by C. G. Jung and his disciple, Esther Harding, whose approach to human psychology is more "spiritual" and anthropological than Freud's.*

The "Freudian" vision beholds women as essentially "breeders and bearers," as potentially warmhearted creatures, but more often as cranky children with uteruses, forever mourning the loss of male organs and male identity. The headaches, fatigue, chronic depression, frigidity, paranoia, and overwhelming sense of inferiority that Freud recorded so accurately about his many female patients was never *interpreted* in any remotely accurate terms. Female "symptoms" were certainly not viewed by Freud as the indirect communications characteristic of slave psychologies. Instead, such symptoms were viewed as "hysterical" and neurotic productions, as underhanded domestic tyrannies manufactured by spiteful, self-pitying, and generally unpleasant women whose *inability to be happy as women* stems from unresolved penis envy, unresolved Electra (or female Oedipal) complexes, or from general, intractable, and mysterious female stubbornness.

In rereading some of Freud's early case histories of female

* However, their female ideal is essentially a chivalrous one. Women are biologically and therefore psychologically different from men and *vive la différence!* Woman's real problems stem from a resistance to her very unique and glorious capacity for a life of love, feeling, and maternity. Of course, modern society devalues such a life, but then, more's the pity. Women, preferably well-educated and wealthy women, like Jung's female disciples, should, as individuals, transcend such devaluing.

"hysterics," particularly his "Case of Dora,"[82] what is remarkable is not his brilliance or his relative sympathy for the female "hysterics"; rather, it is his tone: cold, intellectual, detective-like, controlling, sexually Victorian. He really does not like his "intelligent" eighteen-year-old patient. For example, he says:

> For several days on end she identified herself with her mother by means of slight symptoms and peculiarities of manner, which gave her an opportunity for some really remarkable achievements in the direction of intolerable behaviour.

The mother has been diagnosed, unseen, by Freud, as having "housewife's psychosis."

Dr. Leonard Simon reviews the plight of Dora, whose father brought her for therapeutic treatment for a variety of Victorian "symptoms."[33] He notes that Freud's case study

> could still stand as an exemplary effort were it not for a single, but major, problem having to do with the realities of Dora's life. For throughout his therapeutic examination of Dora's unconscious Freud also knew that she was the bait in a monstrous sexual bargain her father had concocted. This man, who during an earlier period in his life had contracted syphilis and apparently infected his wife . . . was now involved in an affair with the wife of Mr. K. There is clear evidence that her father was using Dora to appease Mr. K., and that Freud was fully aware of this. . . . At one point Freud states: "Her father was himself partly responsible for her present danger for he had handed her over to this strange man in the interests of his own love-affair." But despite this reality, despite his full knowledge of her father's predilections, Freud insisted on examining Dora's difficulties from a strictly intrapsychic point of view, ignoring the manner in which her father was using her, and denying that her accurate perception of the situation was germane. . . . Freud

appears to accept fully the willingness of these men to sexually exploit the women around them.

Although Freud eventually conceded (but not to Dora) that her insights into her family situation were correct, he still concluded that these insights would not make her "happy." Freud's own insights—based on self-reproach, rather than on Dora's reproaching of those around her—would hopefully help her to adjust to, or at least to accept, her only alternative in life: housewife's psychosis. If Dora had not left treatment (which Freud views as an act of revenge), her cure presumably would have involved her regaining (through desperation and self-hypnosis) a grateful respect for her patriarch-father; loving and perhaps serving him for years to come; or getting married and performing these functions for a husband or surrogate patriarch.

Freud was not the only one who disliked Dora. Twenty-four years later, as a forty-two-year-old married woman, Dora was referred to another psychiatrist, Felix Deutsch, for "hysterical" symptoms. Let me quote his description of her[34]:

> The patient then started a tirade about her husband's indifference toward her offerings and how unfortunate her marital life had been . . . this led her to talk about her own frustrated love life and her frigidity . . . resentfully she expressed her conviction that her husband had been unfaithful to her . . . tearfully she denounced men in general as selfish, demanding, and ungiving. . . . [She recalled that] her father had been unfaithful to her mother, [spoke] of her unhappy childhood because of her mother's exaggerated cleanliness . . . and her lack of affection for her . . . she finally spoke with pride about her *brother's* career, but she had little hope that her son would follow in his footsteps . . . more than 30 years have elapsed since my visit at Dora's sickbed . . . from [an] informant I learned the additional pertinent facts about the fate of Dora .

she clung to [her son] with the same reproachful demands she made on her husband, who had died of a disease—"slighted and tortured by her almost paranoid behaviour, strangely enough, he had preferred to die . . . rather than divorce her." Without question, only a man of this type could have been chosen by Dora for a husband. At the time of her analytic treatment she had stated unequivocally "men are all so detestable that I would rather not marry. This is my revenge!" Thus her marriage had served only to cover up her distaste of men. . . . [Dora's] death from cancer of the colon, which was diagnosed too late for a successful operation, seemed a blessing to those who were close to her. She had been, as my informant phrased it, "one of the most repulsive hysterics" he had ever met.

Thomas Szasz comments on the "hysterical" symptoms of another of Freud's female patients, Anna O., who fell "ill" while nursing her father.[35]

Anna O. thus started to play the hysterical game from a position of distasteful submission: she functioned as an oppressed, unpaid, sick-nurse . . . young middle-class women in Freud's day considered it their duty to take care of their sick fathers. . . . Notice how similar this is to the dilemma in which many contemporary women find themselves, not, however, in relation to their fathers, but rather in relation to their young children. Today, married women are generally expected to take care of their children; they are not supposed to delegate this task to others.

To Freud, however, it was to Anna's "great sorrow" that she was no longer "allowed to continue nursing the patient."

All or some of Freud's views about women have been extensively reviewed, criticized, and rejected by many female theoreticians: by Karen Horney, Clara Thompson, Margaret Mead, and

more recently Simone de Beauvoir, Betty Friedan, Kate Millett,
Shulamith Firestone, Eva Figes, and Germaine Greer. Male theoreticians such as Bronislav Malinowski, Alfred Adler, Harry S. Sullivan, Wilhelm Reich, Ronald Laing, David Cooper, and Thomas
Szasz have refuted him also but not necessarily or primarily because of his views of women.

In her 1926 essay entitled "The Flight from Womanhood"[36]
Karen Horney says:

> The present analytical picture of feminine development (whether
> that picture be correct or not) differs in no case by a hair's
> breadth from the typical ideas that the boy has of the girl.
>
> We are familiar with the ideas that the boy entertains. I
> will therefore only sketch them in a few succinct phrases, and for
> the sake of comparison will place in a parallel column our ideas
> of the development of women.

THE BOY'S IDEAS	OUR PSYCHOANALYTIC IDEA OF FEMININE DEVELOPMENT
Naive assumption that girls as well as boys possess a penis	For both sexes it is only the male genital which plays any part
Realization of the absence of the penis	Sad discovery of the absence of the penis
Idea that the girl is a castrated, mutilated boy	Belief of the girl that she once possessed a penis and lost it by castration
Belief that the girl has suffered punishment that also threatens him	Castration is conceived of as the infliction of punishment
The girl is regarded as inferior	The girl regards herself as inferior. Penis envy

The boy is unable to imagine how the girl can ever get over this loss or envy	The girl never gets over the sense of deficiency and inferiority and has constantly to master afresh her desire to be a man
The boy dreads her envy	The girl desires throughout life to avenge herself on the man for possessing something which she lacks

Freud's indirect rejoinder, made in his 1931 essay entitled "Female Sexuality,"[87] is as follows:

It is to be anticipated that male analysts with feminist sympathies, and our women analysts also, will hardly fail to object that such notions have their origin in the man's "masculinity complex," and are meant to justify theoretically his innate propensity to disparage and suppress women. But this sort of psychoanalytic argument reminds us here, as it so often does, of Dostoevsky's famous "knife that cuts both ways." The opponents of those who reason thus will for their part think it quite comprehensible that members of the female sex should refuse to accept a notion that appears to gainsay their eagerly coveted equality with men. The use of analysis as a weapon of controversy leads to no decision.

At this point I would like to discuss the views of four of Freud's critics who are regarded as "revolutionary" theorists, or as profoundly innovative clinicians.†

† Earlier theoreticians such as Karen Horney and Clara Thompson certainly criticized Freud specificially in terms of his views of women. However, they are not popularly considered as "radical" theoreticians or clinicians—and in a certain broad sense they are not. They were not political or social visionaries, nor did they develop single standards of mental health for both women and men. I suppose that a closer reading of these theoreticians—and of others such as Melanie Klein, Anna Freud, Edith Jacobson, etc., might surprise even me with the extent of their "radicalness." I am not yet familiar enough with their work to competently review them here.

I am concerned with whether these theoreticians' frame of reference for what is "human" is female. I feel that any clinical theory or practice which does not have, or is opposed to, this concern, is philosophically limited and socially oppressive to both women and men. The theorists are all male psychiatrists: Wilhelm Reich, Ronald Laing, David Cooper, and Thomas Szasz.‡

All four theorists are concerned with normality as well as abnormality, and with society as well as personality. All are "important": Reich for his vision of sexual and political freedom; Laing for his descriptions of schizophrenia and for his clinical call to emotional arms; Cooper for his attempt to exorcise the demons of the family and for his feminist sympathies; Szasz for charting the psychology of power relationships, and for his moral and legal sensitivity. I will not weigh, sum up, or compare them on the basis of *all* their work. I will share my thoughts with you about each theorist in terms of only *some* of their writing.

Wilhelm Reich

> Of course I knew about his jealousy, but I found at that time a moralistic attitude in him such as he usually attacked in others. The double standard of sexual behavior was quite apparent in his attack. I was not allowed to question his faithfulness to me during that period, but I was quite certain that he did not apply to himself the same standards that he expected of me. In fact I knew that he had had an affair although he didn't tell me so.
>
> In Oslo, I talked at length to Grethe, the woman who shared Reich's life during this period. Many of the agonies that I had experienced during my last three years with Reich were repeated in her experiences. Accusations of infidelity during

‡ Frantz Fanon will be discussed in Chapter Eight, "Third World Women."

the last month of their life together when the relationship had deteriorated—interestingly enough with some of the same men that had figured in his accusation of me—demands of confessions, often heavy drinking, and frightening moments. . . .

Dr. Havrevold . . . once tried to refer a very worthy professional man to Reich for training, but when Reich heard that the person was a homosexual he not only refused to accept him, but said, *"Ich will mit solchen Schweinereben nichts zu tun haben* [I don't want to deal with such filth.]

Ilse Ollendorf Reich[38]

As a theoretician, Wilhelm Reich was a feminist.[39] He consistently condemned the patriarchal family as the primary institution of sexual and political repression in general, and of female enslavement in particular. He was fiercely opposed to prostitution, "compulsive marriage," and alienated labor. He sought a single (pan-sexual) standard of mental health for women and men. And, although he attaches a clinician's sense of importance to his own patient's individual "breakthrough" into sexual-mental health, he nevertheless remained convinced that mental health could never exist without the elimination of poverty and the oppression of women. Ideal mental health, like freedom, exists for one person only if it exists for all people. He stressed the importance of "preventive social measures" in order to rid people of the "psychic plague." He conducted free sex education clinics and stressed the importance of therapy for the poor at a time when his colleagues were trying to become respectable in order to attract a middle-class clientele. He rarely romanticized the psychology of oppression:

The well-to-do citizen carries his neurosis with dignity or he lives it out in one way or another; in working class people, it shows itself as the grotesque tragedy it really is.

He was as sensitive to the often early, traumatic, and brutal introduction of poor women to sex as he was to the middle-class woman's lifelong non-introduction to it.

Reich's ideas about the nature and importance of "orgastic potency" (or "healthy" orgasms) can easily be, and have been, misinterpreted as "proof" that "good sex will make you free." Reich's repetitive expositions about orgasm, and about what constitutes a "healthy" one, does assume the proportion of a staunch and hysterical religious doctrine, an idée fixe,** that often bizarrely and shrilly invades his analyses of fascism, poverty, the family, and madness.

His definition of "orgastic potency" is

the capacity for surrender to the flow of biological energy without any inhibition, a complete discharge of all dammed up sexual excitation through involuntary pleasurable contractions of the body.

Reich certainly understood why feminists, "bluestockings," the majority of women, and male "moralists" were—and are—intolerant of male-originated notions of "free sex" or sexual liberation. He describes (with a little too much naïveté) how, in his clinical practice, he discovered that sex is experienced by the average man as a debased and degraded activity, in which power and mastery (his) must be expressed. Reich describes the universality of his male patient's pornographic and sadistic masturbation and other sexual fantasies, and his female patient's masochistic and passive fantasies. Male fantasies, then as now, involved the penis as a "murderous weapon"; as a means of "proving" potency; as a compulsively Don Juan-like "ejaculation followed by a reaction of

** But no more so than are Freud's ideas about infantile sexuality, repression, and death, or Skinner's about conditioned learning. Perhaps all *authoritative* statements (in a world where authority is corrupt) concerning certain facts, such as sexuality or death, are especially threatening to the modern male-designed ego. Perhaps therefore it is a matter of scientific integrity to call these assertions to our attention again and again.

disgust." Reich considered such sexuality as "perverse"—no matter how many orgasms are achieved.

> This sexuality is a pathological caricature of natural love. The usual evaluation of sexuality refers to its caricatures and its condemnation is justified. Thus, any controversy in the sense of fighting for or against sexuality is senseless and leads nowhere. In such a controversy the moralists would and should win. The caricature of sexuality should not be tolerated. The sexuality exercised in brothels is disgusting.

Reich claimed that once his male patients became "orgastically potent" they were

> no longer able to go to prostitutes . . . wives, once they were orgastically potent, could no longer submit to husbands they didn't love or submit when they were unaroused.

Unlike Freud, he does not suggest that we "sublimate" our sexuality for the sake of "civilization": quite the contrary. Reich claims that, once healthy genitality was asserted in his patients, they tried to find more meaningful relationships in work and in love. He claims (with no less and no more proof than Freud's) to have found a "decent nature" in every patient—if he (Reich) was able to penetrate deeply enough. "Sex-economy regulation" always led to a natural morality that was superior to a compulsive morality.

Reich, like all those who wish to understand and "champion" the insane, is caught in a dilemma: on the one hand, he says that "the profundity of some mental patients makes them more valuable from the human point of view than the Babbitts with their nationalistic ideals"; yet he also sees the insane as people who "act out," often grotesquely and suicidally, and with a great deal of suffering, both what is "wrong" and what is "repressed" in all of us. The insane are both heroines and victims, courageous and doomed.†† For Reich, the schizophrenic *is* schizophrenic because she is overwhelmed by anxiety (as she has been conditioned to be), when pleasurable genital and body sensations "break through"—sensations which she has *not* been conditioned to feel, and which, therefore, break through rather mysteriously. Reich is absolutely correct in stressing the importance of the body in madness. I think, in fact, that a person is considered mad, both by herself and by others, when she *acts out* her thoughts and feelings with her body. When a person does this *alone,* without any group support or consensus, she is considered "mad." As I noted elsewhere, Valerie Solanas is "crazy" (as well as "criminal") because she *acted on* what many people are content to just think about or criticize in print: namely, the extent of Andy Warhol's misogyny and asexuality.‡‡

Like Freud, Reich found sexual repression at the heart of every neurosis and psychosis. Its purpose was the ultimate and total submission of the individual to the family, to the state, and to work. It is sexual repression, beginning with the repression of infantile sexuality, that leads to the "fixation" on the family, i.e., to the necessity of re-creating family-like relationships for the rest of one's life.* The prohibition against adolescent sexuality makes the now twice-repressed child "submissive" and capable of "compulsive marriage."

Reich sees sexual energy at work in the whole body, not just

†† Doomed, certainly, in no small part, because of the way they are treated by their "betters."

‡‡ Traditionally, misogyny, or woman-hating, has been so widespread that it is almost invisible; and, when highly visible, has been deemed understandable and acceptable.

* It is never quite clear whether Reich is seriously recommending that we break the incest taboo and, if so, in what manner; i.e., women in a patriarchal society are already, and to their detriment, encouraged to break the incest taboo. Further, he is unclear about the types and stages of infantile sexuality and in what way it is repressed in the infant.

in the genitals. He is careful to distinguish between perverted and healthy sexuality, and between sexuality and reproduction. He views, without contempt or superficiality, the results of total and lifelong sexual unhappiness in women. He is seriously concerned with the role of the body, and with our difficulty in uniting body and mind. He views an element of "involuntary surrender" as essential for both men and women in "healthy" heterosexual intercourse.

However, in a patriarchal culture it is destructively romantic to talk too much about female "surrender" in heterosexual inter-course and, for that matter, to talk too much about the im-portance of female sexual happiness, without talking about the importance of female *power*. The use of sex, like drugs, can become a compulsive pacification-opiate, especially to those with-out the power to define themselves.

In his zeal to create a pan-sexual, normal psychology (and in his sympathy for men), Reich fails to emphasize the *enormous* male-female differences that exist in the quality and quantity of "submissiveness" and "sexual monogamy" in women and men. The family *does* repress both male and female children—but female children more so. We may also have to consider the possibility that what Reich calls a "caricature" of sexuality is actually *male* sexuality. As such, men may not be as sexually unsatisfied as women—or as open to making certain changes in the interest of sexual happiness. (Men may not really be that interested in a female-dictated definition of sexual happiness.)

Reich proclaims the existence of a primary vaginal eroticism in female children, which he feels is "socialized" out of them. This, together with the fact that he is far too silent on the importance of the clitoris in female sexuality, is disturbing; but for a pioneer of sexual liberation to *also* proclaim that all bi-and homosexuality is "unhealthy" and "regressed" is positively alarming.† Does Reich mean to deny the paternal-male body as a source of physical and sexual gratification to male or female infants? Is mother-daughter physicality to be banned from the Garden of Sexual Liberation also?

Reich is dangerous or certainly limited when he or his devotees romanticize human sexuality to the exclusion of other human activities—or when they assume, rather naively, that ego, self, peace and love will, like children, simply and "naturally" follow the Pied Piper of orgasm. The right to "sexual happiness" may exist in the most advanced technological-fascist state.

Ronald D. Laing

> What we call "normal" is a product of repression, denial, splitting, projection, introjection and other forms of destructive action on experience . . . it is radically estranged from the structure of being . . . if our experience is destroyed, our behavior will be destructive.
>
> Jack may act upon Jill in many ways. He may make her feel guilty for keeping on "bringing it up." He may invalidate her experience. This can be done more or less radically. He can indicate merely that it is unimportant or trivial, whereas it is important and significant to her. Going further, he can shift the modality of her experience from memory to imagination: "It's all in your imagination." Further still, he can invalidate the content: "It never happened that way." Finally, he can invalidate not only the significance, modality and content, but her very capacity to remember at all, and make her feel guilty for doing so into the bargain.
>
> This is not unusual. People are doing such things to each other all the time. In order for such transpersonal invalidation

† Of course, he doesn't clearly differentiate homosexuality from lesbianism.

to work, however, it is advisable to overlay it with a thick patina of mystification. For instance, by denying that this is what one is doing, and further invalidating any perception that it is being done by ascriptions such as "How can you think such a thing?" "You must be paranoid." And so on.

There are sudden, apparently inexplicable suicides that must be understood as the dawn of a hope so horrible and harrowing that it is unendurable.

In our "normal" alienation from being, the person who has a perilous awareness of the non-being of what we take to be being (the pseudo-wants, pseudo-values, pseudo-realities of the endemic delusions of what are taken to be life and death and so on) gives us in our present epoch the acts of creation that we despise and crave.

From the moment of birth, when the Stone Age baby confronts the twentieth-century mother, the baby is subjected to these forces of violence, called love, as its mother and father, and their parents and their parents before them, have been. These forces are mainly concerned with destroying most of its potentialities, and on the whole this enterprise is successful.

We are effectively destroying ourselves by violence masquerading as love.

Ronald D. Laing

In the book entitled *Sanity, Madness and the Family*,[40] Laing, like Freud before him, chose women as his subjects. Like Freud, he is "sympathetic" to his English female "schizophrenic" subjects.‡ His clinical and journalistic method of interviewing is highly successful. Like Freud, however, Laing is describing the phenomena correctly, but without understanding their significance. Throughout the book, he remains unaware of the universal and objective op-

‡ The New York *Times* (February 6, 1971) reported that there are thirty-five women to every one man in English mental asylums. This ratio is reversed in prisons.

pression of women and of its particular relation to madness in women.

Most of the "schizophrenogenic" families that Laing describes are not atypical in their treatment of their daughters. All the families are involved in: (1) the sexual and intellectual repression of their daughters; (2) covert and overt patterns of paternal tyranny and incest; (3) the deep division between mother and daughter, which is characterized, on the mother's part, by an obsessive "policing" coupled with a lack of physical affection for her daughter, and on both mother's and daughter's parts, by a preference for the father-husband, and a sacrificing of each other for family stability or for temporary feelings of well-being.

(1) This repression occurs in all eleven families that Laing depth-interviewed. One of the women, Ruby Eden, became pregnant when she was seventeen. Her mother and aunts call her "slut," blame her for the "mess"** and "disgrace" she got herself into, and subject her to all the well-known home ordeals to induce an abortion. Another of the women, Lucie Blair, is *sterilized* after giving birth to a baby girl. Both her family and the psychiatrists have viewed her as "sexually wanton." Her father says he wanted her to be a pure, virginal, "spinster gentlewoman"—(when she "grew up," I suppose). Maya Abbott's family is obsessed with "cleanliness and neatness" for her; Hazel King's mother is completely—and typically—sexually uninformed. According to Laing, Mrs. King

> doesn't know whether she has an orgasm, whether she has intercourse "properly" with her husband or not, whether or not he uses a contraceptive, or whether he ejaculates inside or outside of her.

** So much for the reification of maternity in male-dominated society. We should really be asking, How do women cope with such brutal rejection of their bodies?

This same Mrs. King has "hardly ever been outside the house un-
accompanied by her own mother and father"—*since her marriage.*††

The intellectual and artistic repression of daughters (and
wives) is fairly total in these eleven families. Only one of the daughters interviewed (Ruth Gold) even *wants* to be an artist—and, unlike her brother, she is discouraged and punished for it. The fact
that she even attempts such a task is what makes her family think
she is "mentally ill." Most of these families act as if their daughters
won't even have to work at *menial* employment in the outside
world—let alone at higher forms of self-development. Lucie Blair
says:

> "My father doesn't believe in the emancipation of women. He
> doesn't believe women should support themselves."

She further tells the interviewer that she "gets no support in anything she wants." Ruth Gold, the would-be artist, answers Laing's
question, "Do you feel you have to agree with what most of the
people around you believe?" with "Well, if I don't, I usually land
up in a hospital." Women are often psychiatrically incarcerated
for rejecting their "femininity" as defined by those close to them—
and are released or are considered as "improved" when they re-
gain it.

(2) Lucie Blair's father is typically maniacal in his (sexual)
possessiveness of his daughter. He constantly told her that she
would be "raped or murdered" if she went out alone. Lucie's
"illegitimate" child (illegitimate because her father had not conceived it) could never be mentioned in the house. Another of the
daughters, Agnes Lawson, sat on her father's (not her mother's)
lap every evening while he read stories to her until she was fourteen.

†† Either the King family are Moslems in disguise—or Mrs. King was
just not allowed to go by herself to the asylum, and sent her daughter in her
place.

(3) All of Laing's subjects had mothers of the extreme "feminine" variety: psychologically insecure, sexually repressed, poorly educated, and economically dependent—prisoners and guards of The Home, in an era when The Home is devalued. From whom could their daughters learn to be both female and human? Mrs. Blair, according to Laing, "sees herself as the subject of a forty-year-long persecution by her husband." She says she hasn't left him

> "because the world outside is just as persecutory, if not more so . . . the only solution is to accept one's helplessness in the persecuted position; there is nothing to be done."

While the presence of so deformed a spirit as Mrs. Blair's tempts us (and Laing) to consider *her* as "mentally ill" also, let us pause for a moment: Mrs. Blair's analysis of things is essentially correct. She has chosen the evil of persecution within the family, rather than the evil of persecution in a mental asylum, or in the "outside" world. Finally, despite paternal tyranny, most of the daughters typically preferred their fathers—at least at some time—to their mothers. The only act of near violence reported, in fact, took place when one of the daughters, Maya Abbott, took a knife to her mother.

If most of Laing's subject-families are typical in their treatment of women, the question still remains: Why are *these* eleven daughters hospitalized and/or "schizophrenic"? It may be argued that what exists in most families exists in an *extreme* form in the schizophrenogenic one. Perhaps madness is just "more of the same." It may also be argued that perhaps the mothers are as "hospitalized" within their marriages as their daughters are within the asylums. It may also be argued that sooner or later most women become, are perceived as, or think they are mad. If Laing had used "normal" (non-hospitalized) control groups he would find the same patterns. If he *followed* his "normal" control groups over time, he might even have found the "normal" control "daughters" eventually embarking on careers as psychiatric patients.

In general, Laing is correct in placing the schizophrenic process within its social setting; correct in "making sense" out of what our society has stubbornly insisted is the essence of senselessness. Ideally, this is what *all* psychiatrists are supposed to do. However, his standards of "mental health" are as obscure or absent as were Freud's; his occasional and increasing equation of madness with mass political revolution or art forms is just that—a confusion.‡‡

Laing is his own best critic. In his most recent introduction to *Sanity, Madness and the Family*, he says that the concept of "family pathology" is a "confused" one.

> It extends the unintelligibility of individual behaviour to the unintelligibility of the group. It is the biological analogy applied now, not just to one person, but to a multiplicity of persons . .
> [it is a form of] "pan-clinicism"* . . . in which all of society is seen in need of psychological "curing."

The danger of such pan-clinicism is its fearful optimism. While society may indeed be in need of "curing," the traditional psychoanalytic method, with or without insight, and based on the illusion of individual freedom, cannot do such "curing"; especially if the major social institutions remain "uncured"; and if the "patient" has had to suffer their socializations for many, many years.

‡‡ While madness and art may both be protests against and escapes from forms of oppression, and while both experiences involve pain *and* being discriminated against, I suppose I still "discriminate" between the totally *personal* and *invisible* modes of madness and the potentially *public* and *tangible* modes of art. (Perhaps this is indeed a form of discrimination. . . .)
* Thomas Szasz calls this "psychiatric imperialism."

David Cooper

> [paranoia is a] poetic protest against the invasion by one's family and by others . . . the poetry is unappreciated by society and gets treated by psychiatry if spoken too loud . . . (paranoia) is not a resolvable fantasy . . . we must use and not resolve our persecution anxieties.
>
> David Cooper

David Cooper, in his recent book, *The Death of the Family*,[41] presents a poetic summary of much of Reich's and Laing's condemnation of the nuclear family, sexual repression, and society's misunderstanding and brutalization of madness. He makes some good statements about female socialization such as

> A little girl, before she can be her own baby is plied with object-babies [the more "perfect" dolls being the most expensive], so that she can learn to forget her experiences of birth and childhood and become not her own child but childlike; so that if later in life, she wants to return to this area, she can become childish, [regressed, hysterical, etc.] . . . she was educated to be a mother like her mother, like all other mothers who are educated not to be themselves but to be "like mothers."†

Cooper often writes as if he were the Abbie Hoffman of psychiatry: he is a sleight-of-phrase clown, a self-proclaimed Holy Idiot, a prophet for the sexual and cultural indulgences of (white)

---

† However, with even this much of a feminist consciousness, Cooper still systematically refers to his idealized "non-leader" leaders and therapist-prophets as "he" rather than "she." He begins using the pronoun "she" as often as "he" only when he refers to patients or children. He is still more linguistically and therefore psychologically advanced than other theoreticians, to be sure. Also, while he doesn't *blame* mothers for the evils of family-influences, he talks more about the mother-child relationship than the father-child relationship—which, to me, connotes his acceptance or romanticization of the female as the *exculsive* maternal agent in civilization.

men.‡ Telling men to withdraw from deep or monogamous commitments is not very revolutionary: few men are committed to the ethic of love or sexual monogamy. The majority of women cannot "withdraw" from these ethics and practices as long as prostitution remains their only mode of psychological and economic survival, and as long as they do not control the means of reproduction. Telling white men to "ready" themselves *culturally* for the *structural* revolution that the brown, black, and yellow people of the world will accomplish *for* them (with their blood and bodies) is hardly "revolutionary." Cooper also contradicts himself here: he admires Mao and Castro as "embodiments" of the "leadership principle"— and these are two men who put their bodies where their principles were and, unlike mad people and Holy Idiots, "won" their battles—in their lifetime and in the flesh.

The problem is that Cooper is unable to come to terms with biology, with the body.** For example, he (incorrectly) analogizes the spiritual hunger of the "first world" with the physical hunger of the "third world": he emphasizes the desirability of same-sex relationships but, like Reich, rather nervously and glibly insists that it is "immaterial" whether or not we make love—sexually—with members of our own sex. He displays his most dangerous misunderstanding of the body's role, especially in relation to female oppression—and just where he is trying to be most sympathetic. Let me give two examples.

First: Cooper has a typically male voracious longing for the incorporation of experience in general,†† and for colonizing or, in his case, "embodying" the "female principle" in particular. He

‡ I hope my comments are not too influenced by the "fashionableness" to which Cooper has been subjected and for which he is not to blame.
** He certainly is not alone in this failing.
†† Women are conditioned to shun "experience" or adventure as destructive to their non-self selves; men are conditioned to accumulate it in order to develop their non-self selves.

is, from a liberal point of view, *commendably* interested in "being" (which is "female") as well as in "doing" (which is "male"). He proclaims that men must live out the reality of the "woman," the "child," and the "wise old woman-man." However, men simply *cannot* live out the reality of women—who, by definition, cannot *choose* to live the female reality but are condemned to do so.‡‡ It is no accident that Cooper shies away from male homosexuality. Despite the fact that in one sense it is an extreme expression of misogyny, it is also the closest that some men come to experiencing the "female reality" in our culture, i.e., other men despise and brutalize them. Cooper is interested in what he conceives to be the "spiritual" aspects of being female—more than in its reality. How different is what he is implying from what the countless myths of male maternity* have implied, namely, the devaluation or distortion of that very same activity in women?

Men can only *be* when women can *do:* perhaps both sexes can both *be* and *do* only after the *biological* differences between them are completely eliminated. Further, the cultural revolution's dictum that *being* is better than *doing* places women in a rather familiar (and disadvantaged) position: now, they are barefoot, pregnant, psychologically dependent, and abandoned on communes rather than in suburbs. As for the "wise old woman-man" principle: only when female biological aging is as valued and rewarded (by sexual and political power) as is *some* or (ideal) male aging, then, and only then, will what Cooper suggests here be meaningful.

When Cooper suggests that "we must learn to play with pain" and that "irony is the most revolutionary sentiment of all," I am

‡‡ In order to live out the female principle, Cooper would have to give up the privileges and psychology of the male principle—which is impossible. Perhaps Cooper is *able* to desire or experiment with "femaleness" only because he already has "maleness" under his belt (literally).

* Zeus, as Athena's mother, Adam as Eve's mother, the Church as the mother of us all.

reminded of Chekov's Dr. Ragin, in the story "Ward Six." Dr. Ragin philosophizes about the "pain" involved in being a mental patient—until be becomes one himself. Then, behind bars, he is seized with terror, despair, rising anger, and complete impotence. After being beaten, he goes "mad" with very unphilosophical anger, and is dead by the next day.

Another example of how crucially Cooper misunderstands the role of the body in female oppression is his comparison of the traditional therapist (whom "one pays by the hour" to be "all things for anyone") with the female prostitute. There is a very obvious and important difference between female (non-legal) prostitutes and male therapists. Prostitutes are degraded and punished by society; it is their *humiliation* through their *bodies*—as much as their *bodies*—which is being purchased.† Psychotherapists are (at least in some circles) the priests of our society. Their patients do not pay for their humiliation. And even when therapists do have sexual relations with their female patients, the psychological dynamics never involve a reversal of sex-roles.

Cooper espouses many of Reich's and what are now the "counterculture's" myths or, more realistically, hopes: (1) that, contrary to Freud's pessimistic and, therefore, bourgeois concepts, we have unlimited energy at our disposal; (2) that we can "love" many people; (3) that spontaneous "groupings" of people are sufficiently better and different from the nuclear monogamous family, and that unlike every other social institution, they would not mirror it, or would not impose a family or state-like tyranny over individual liberty‡; (4) that charismatic anti-leader leaders are *not* leaders, or conversely, that "leadership" is intrinsically evil; (5) that

† Of course, in a wage-labor and advanced capitalist society, people are encouraged or forced to "sell" most things, their time, skills, physical labor, etc. Female prostitution may exist in a somewhat separate category from these other "sales" of self.
‡ This is like saying we can truly escape our history.

"madness" is somehow "revolutionary"—when in fact, in our culture, it is a cry of powerlessness which is mercilessly punished.

Thomas Szasz: Witches and Madness

The fundamental conflicts in human life are not between competing ideas—one of which is true and the other false, but rather, between those that hold power and use it to oppress others, and those who are oppressed by power and seek to free themselves of it.

Witches and mentally ill patients are actually created through the social interaction of oppressors and oppressed. If the observer sympathizes with the oppressor, then the witches are "mad." If the observer sympathizes with the victim, then the oppressor is "mad." Both explanations bypass, conceal, excuse and explain away the terrifyingly simple but all important fact of man's inhumanity to man [and I add: to woman] . . . the image of the knight in armor, the symbol of mobility, and of the black witch as a symbol of depravity embodies the sexocidal hatred of women . . . [for the] knight is always male [and the] witch is always female in all the fairy tales and mythologies of (medieval and modern) times.

There can be no abuses in institutional psychiatry because institutional psychiatry, by definition, is an abuse.

Social oppression in any form, and its manifestations are varied, among them being . . . poverty . . . racial, religious, or sexual discrimination . . . must therefore be regarded as prime determinants of direct communication of all kinds (e.g. hysteria).

Thomas Szasz

Thomas Szasz has been concerned with the extent to which "politics" produces medical and ethical consequences which are psychiatrically "incurable." In *The Myth of Mental Illness* he analyzes the psychology of (female) "hysteria" as a "slave state," and criticizes Freud's patriarchal and authoritarian theories and practices. In *Law, Liberty and Psychiatry* he condemns the violation of the legal and constitutional rights of the "mentally ill"; the cruel irony of the humanely intended insanity defense; and the pervasive correlation between poverty and psychiatric incarceration. In *The Manufacture of Madness*[42] he develops Elizabeth Packard's analogy between institutional psychiatry and the Inquisition: he labels the persecution of witches as "sexocidal," and compares their treatment to that of mental patients.

Our knowledge of witches is at best conjectural. Their case histories were kept by their more socially powerful male persecutors—just as hospital records are kept by psychiatrists and psychologists, and not by the mental patients themselves. Were witches really cultural and political revolutionaries, matriarchs, and Amazons come back to do battle with the Church? Were they wealthy and powerful women whose property was coveted? Were they beautiful women whose sexuality was both feared and desired? Perhaps all of these things—perhaps none. Jules Michelet in *Satanism and Witchcraft: A Study in Medieval Superstition*,[43] suggests that many witches were midwives and doctors, whose knowledge of painkillers, abortion, and herbal or "faith healing" threatened the Church's anti-scientific, anti-sexual, and anti-female doctrines.** Szasz suggests that, "by aiding the weak, the white witch†† tended to undermine the established hierarchy of

---

** I am suspicious of women romantically identifying with witches, who, after all, were tortured and martyred. Whoever they "really" were, witches were defeated; whatever their psychological and religious truths, they attained too little material power. Further, they (supposedly) still worshiped a *male* Devil and had ritual intercourse with phallus substitutes.

†† The designation of witches as (good) "white" or (bad) "black" witches once more denotes Christian cultures' deep racism—predating both slavery in America and industrialization.

dominance—of priest over penitent, lord over peasant, man over woman—and herein lay the principal threat of the witch and [is] why the Church set out to crush her." Una Stannard, in an article entitled "The Male Maternal Instinct,"[44] describes the Church's successful attempt to both usurp the female power of childbirth (the Church, through baptism, really gives "birth" to children) and devalue this same function in women (Christ's was a Virgin birth). Male "spirits" can enter "receptacle" women to plant their holy or devilish seeds. Thus women could, indeed, be "possessed" —or, worse still, through contraception, could control whether and by whom they would be "possessed."‡‡ On either count, they were dangerous to and therefore persecuted by the male Church.

Michelet also suggests that the combination of feudal poverty and Catholicism so brutalized women that some turned "strange": they lived alone, or with each other, and were not subject to husbands. He suggests, further, that witches were persecuted for their presumed (or actual) ritualization of sexuality, including incest, lesbianism, homosexuality, and group sex. In celebrating what the Church prohibited—and which occurred anyway—the witch cults constituted a strong opposition, or complementary religion.

Szasz notes that

> . . . the witch, like the involuntary mental patient, is cast into a degraded and deviant role against her will; is subjected to certain diagnostic procedures to establish whether or not she is a witch; finally is deprived of liberty and often of life, ostensibly for her own benefit.

Of course, many witches—and most female mental patients—are all too willing that this should happen: they wish to commit suicide, but at somebody else's hands. Szasz quotes an English

‡‡ The Malleus, a kind of religious doctrine of male superiority, claimed that "among women midwives (who often could perform abortions), surpass others in wickedness . . . all witchery comes from carnal lust [which in women] is insatiable."

witch, who, when led to the stake, tells the crowd not to blame her judges:

> "I want to die. My family shunned me. My husband repudiated me. If I live I could only be a disgrace to my friends. I longed for death and I lied to gain my end."

The role of the witch—or the mental patient—is often, like suicide, the only resolution (the "cure") for having been born female. Psychiatrists and inquisitors share certain views of women-witches: because they aren't men, they are mysterious and therefore dangerous; they are really inferior beings—but with hidden powers*; they are responsible for male sexual aggression because of their "sinfully" seductive natures. Witch-hunters often considered masturbation as proof of "witchcraft"; nineteenth-century psychiatrists thought it caused "insanity" and sometimes cured it by performing clitoridectomies.

Szasz describes the inquistors' insatiable and psychiatric-like curiosity about their victims' sexual fantasies and activities. Isolation, social ostracism, hydrotherapy, physical beatings, shock therapy—all psychiatric techniques—were first practiced by witch-hunters. Although the strait jacket, solitary confinement, brain surgery, and systematic physical violence were traditionally psychiatric "treatments," they are now being replaced by tranquilizers, antidepressants, and shock therapy. The Inquisition's more *obviously* violent methods are no longer needed to attain a female's submission and belief in her inferiority and sinfulness.† Twentieth-century mental patients are not burned at the stake or subjected

---

* Today, the world of the spirits is located in our own backyards, or in our own childhoods. Women have "power" not because they are Satan's agents but because the psychiatrist's mother was a woman—and she had (and still has) "power" over him.

† However, we shouldn't write off as non-violent the often serious negative effects involved in the long-term administration of standard psychiatric drugs.

to the "water ordeal"—in which a witch's "innocence" was established if she *drowned*. Many mental patients *are* sexually and physically assaulted; their earning capacity (as wives or in other capacities) is even more seriously damaged than a criminal inmate's; their property and money are handed over to their husbands or children when they are declared "insane and incompetent"; like witches, they are publicly and constantly humiliated, and made to "confess" their sexual and other wrongdoings. While all of their body hair is not shaved off in a search for the "Devil's mark," many (male) mental patients are close-shaved and both male and female patients are kept short-haired and "anonymous"-looking, in regulation hospital-prison clothing.

Szasz notes the similarity of zeal with which inquisitors and psychiatrists hunt and classify (or diagnose) witches and mental patients. (I have rarely heard of a psychologist diagnosing "normality" or "health" on the basis of projective test results; even more rarely have I heard of a psychiatrist presenting a "healthy" case history at a hospital staff meeting.) Armed with a fearful knowledge of illness and sinfulness, both the Holy Father (the inquisitor) and the Scientific Father (the psychiatrist) are interested in saving female souls. Their methods: confession, recantation, and punishment. Of course, modern psychiatrists would not think that "helping" an "unhappy" woman accept her feminine role is at all similar to "helping" a witch return to Christ.

Szasz is a provocative and political thinker, with a strong commitment to civil liberty, and a highly developed moral sensibility. I do not agree with him that private therapy is either very "private" or that it is necessarily freed from a variety of social abuses. Nor do I believe that "madness"—as I defined it in Chapter One—does not exist. I agree that "madness" can be understood in terms of "oppression" and "conditioning," but I am not sure *our understanding* alone will be enough to change what oppression has wrought—in our lifetime. Szasz is certainly right when he concludes that our treatment of "madness" is itself unethical and oppressive. However, I think he underestimates the deeply conditioned nature of woman's *compliance* with her literal and psychological self-sacrifice. Many female mental patients view themselves as "sick" or "bad" and commit themselves, quite voluntarily, to asylums or to private psychiatrists. The fear of economic, physical, and sexual deprivation or punishment teaches women to value their own sacrifice so highly that they quite "naturally" perform it. And if their anger about this natural self-sacrifice drives them "mad," asylum practices will exact their sacrifice anyway.

The "revolutionary," contemporary, and traditional ideologies and practices I've discussed thus far all ascribe to a double standard of mental health and/or to many patriarchal myths about "femininity"—e.g. female inferiority or female evil. As I've mentioned earlier, not every American clinician necessarily believes or acts upon *all* of these beliefs. However, he or she probably believes a good many. Further, all clinicians are involved in the *institution* of private practice—an institution which, like a mental asylum, is structurally modeled upon that of marriage and the family.

THE INSTITUTIONAL NATURE OF PRIVATE THERAPY

A great deal has been written about the covertly or overtly patriarchal, autocratic, and coercive values and techniques of psychotherapy. Freud believed that the psychoanalyst-patient relationship must be that of "a superior and a subordinate."[45] The psychotherapist has been seen, by his critics as well as by his patients, as a surrogate parent (father or mother), savior, lover, expert, and teacher—all roles that foster "submission, dependency, and infantilism" in the patient: roles that imply the therapist's omniscient and benevolent superiority and the patient's inferiority. (Thomas Szasz has remarked on the dubious value of such a role for the patient and the "undeniable" value of such a role for the "helper."[46]) Practicing psychotherapists have been criticized for treating unhappiness as a disease (whenever it is accompanied by an appropriately high verbal and financial output); for behaving as if the psychotherapeutic philosophy or method can cure ethical and political problems; for teaching people that their unhappiness (or neurosis) can be alleviated through individual rather than collective efforts (or can't be alleviated since the human condition is "tragic"); for encouraging and legitimizing the urban middle-class tendency toward moral irresponsibility and passivity; and for discouraging emotionally deprived persons from seeking "acceptance, dependence, and security in the more normal and accessible channels of friendship."[47] The *institution* of psychotherapy can also be viewed as a form of social and political control that offers those who can pay for it temporary relief, the illusion of freedom, and a self-indulgent form of self-knowledge; and as an institution that punishes those who cannot pay for such illusions by being forced to label *their* unhappiness as psychotic or dangerous, thereby helping society consign them to asylums.

The institution of private therapy is a patriarchal one—regardless of whether the individual clinician is female or male. As such, most clinicians are no more divinely inspired or in touch with their own emotions than anyone else is in our culture. Our culture's criteria for an "expert" are the same for engineers and soul-healers: objectivity, rationality, impersonality. Clinicians, with rare and feared exceptions, are not oracles, priestesses, prophets, or tribal shamans. They do not make *personal* intercessions for their patients with the unknown or with the unconscious. As scientists they probably do not believe in the "unknown," or, if they do, wish to conquer it. Clinicians are more respected and trusted by their teachers, colleagues, and patients if they remain unavailable and impersonal.‡

Traditionally, any analysis or comparison of private therapy with mental asylums would be a class-based one. Poor people are hospitalized; middle and upper class people are not; or are hospitalized privately for a shorter time; or have access to private treatment. Nevertheless, with the increase in psychiatric outpatient clinics, community mental health centers, and "therapeutically" oriented case work in social agencies and schools, poor and black people, especially women, are experiencing more contact with some of private therapy's practices and ideas. Many more women than men are involved in private therapy, both as private and as clinic outpatients.

For most women (the middle-class-oriented) psychotherapeutic encounter is just one more instance of an unequal relationship, just one more opportunity to be rewarded for expressing distress and to be "helped" by being (expertly) dominated. Both psychotherapy and white or middle-class marriage isolate women from each other; both emphasize individual rather than collective solutions to woman's unhappiness; both are based on a woman's helplessness and dependence on a stronger male authority figure; both may, in fact, be viewed as re-enactments of a little girl's relation to her father in a patriarchal society; both control and oppress women similarly—yet, at the same time, are the two safest (most approved and familiar) havens for middle-class women in a society that offers them few—if any—alternatives.

Both psychotherapy and marriage enable women to express and defuse their anger by experiencing it as a form of emotional illness, by translating it into hysterical symptoms: frigidity, chronic

‡ Unfortunately, many male clinicians who agree with this sort of criticism, have gotten involved in self-revelatory and "touching" or sexual behaviors with their patients. But given our culture, such behaviors are especially abusive to their female patients.

depression, phobias, and the like. Each woman, as patient, thinks these symptoms are unique and are her own fault: she is "neurotic." She wants from a psychotherapist what she wants—and often cannot get—from a husband: attention, understanding, merciful relief, a *personal solution*—in the arms of the right husband, on the couch of the right therapist. The institutions of therapy and marriage not only mirror each other, they support each other. This is probably not a coincidence but is rather an expression of the American economic system's need for geographic and psychological mobility, i.e., for young, upwardly mobile "couples" to "survive," and to remain more or less intact in a succession of alien and anonymous urban locations, while they carry out the function of socializing children and making money. Most therapists have a vested interest, financially and psychologically, in the supremacy of the nuclear family. Most husbands want their wives to "shape up" or at least not to interfere with male burdens, male pleasures, or male conscience.

The institution of psychotherapy may be used by many women as a way of keeping a bad marriage together or as a way of terminating it in order to form a good marriage. Some women, especially young and single women, may use psychotherapy as a way of learning how to catch a husband by practicing with a male therapist. Women probably spend more time during a therapy session talking about their husbands or boy friends—or lack of them—than they do talking about their lack of an independent identity or their relations to other women.

The institutions of middle-class psychotherapy and marriage both encourage women to talk—often endlessly—rather than to act (except in their socially prearranged roles as passive women or patients). In marriage, the talking is usually of an indirect and rather inarticulate nature. Open expressions of rage are too dangerous and too ineffective for the isolated and economically dependent women.

Most often, such "kitchen" declarations end in tears, self-blame, and in the husband graciously agreeing with his wife that she was "not herself." Even control of a simple—but serious—conversation is usually impossible for most wives when several men, including their husbands, are present. The wife-women talk to each other, or they listen silently, while the men talk. Very rarely, if ever, do men listen silently to a group of women talking; even if there are a number of women talking and only one man present, the man will question the women, perhaps patiently, perhaps not, but always in order to ultimately control the conversation from a superior position.

In psychotherapy the patient-woman is encouraged—in fact directed—to talk, by a therapist who is at least expected to be, or is perceived as, superior or objective. The traditional therapist may be viewed as ultimately controlling what the patient says through a subtle system of rewards (attention, interpretations, and so forth) or rewards withheld—but, ultimately, controlling, in the sense that he is attempting to bring his patient to terms with the female role, i.e., he wants her to admit, accept, and "solve" her need for love. However, such acceptance of the human need for other people, or for "love," means something very different when women are already our culture's "acceptors" and men our culture's "rejectors." Such acceptance is further confused by the economic nature of the female need for "love."

Traditionally, the psychotherapist has ignored the objective facts of female oppression. Thus, in every sense, the female patient is still not having a "real" conversation—either with her husband or with her therapist. But how is it possible to have a "real" conversation with those who directly profit from her oppression? She would be laughed at, viewed as silly or crazy and, if she persisted, removed from her job—as secretary or wife, perhaps even as private patient.

Psychotherapeutic talking is indirect in the sense that it does not immediately or even ultimately involve the woman in any reality-based confrontations with the self. It is also indirect in that words—any words—are permitted, so long as certain actions of consequence are totally avoided—such as not paying one's bills.

Private psychoanalysis or psychotherapy is still a commodity available to those women who can buy it, that is, to women whose fathers, husbands, or boy friends can help them pay for it. Like the Calvinist elect, those women who can *afford* treatment are already "saved." Even if they are never happy, never free, they will be slow to rebel against their psychological and economic dependence on men. One look at their less privileged (poor, black, older and/or unmarried) sisters' position is enough to keep them silent and more or less gratefully in line. The less privileged women have no real or psychological silks to smooth down over, to disguise their unhappiness; they have no class to be "better than." As they sit facing the walls, in factories, offices, whorehouses, ghetto apartments, and mental asylums, at least one thing they must conclude is that "happiness" is on sale in America—but not at a price they can afford. They are poor.

Given the traditional and contemporary psychological ideologies about women and/or the patriarchal nature of the *institution* in which they are practiced, in what way should women relate to either the ideologies or the institutions? In what ways can therapy "help" women? Can female therapists "help" female patients more differently than male therapists? Can feminist or "radical" therapists "help" female patients in some special or rapid way? Can a technique based on transference, or on the resolution of an Oedipal conflict—i.e., on a romanticization of a rape-incest-procreative model of sexuality—wean women away from this very sexual model? What new "curative" techniques can emerge from a feminist analysis of human psychology?

There are a number of contemporary clinicians, who as "radicals" or feminists, wish to "help" women.** Many still share the profession's and our culture's bias against or genuine ambivalence and confusion about feminisim. Many such clinicians are trying to develop new views that will lead to new techniques. Many clinicians are trying to return to the originally revolutionary implications of Freudian psychoanalysis. And many women, dedicated feminists and anti-feminists alike, are still seeking "help" of some sort. I would like to share several thoughts with both the patients and the clinicians.

First, contrary to what their hysterical detractors may think, "radical" clinicians are not hot headed nihilistic extremists. As a group, they are predominantly young, white, male and middle-class and have been steeped in "social reformism" and the importance of the individual. (None of which is bad.) As a group, they have little power, and consequently are often too unreflectively or impractically idealistic. They often tend to be as ideologically inflexible as "establishment" groups. "Radical" projects such as therapy communes and "freak-out" centers may be short-lived, and at best palliative, if larger social forces (over which clinicians have little control) don't change.††

The role that insight plays in effecting behavioral and emotional change is, like the effect of ideas on history, a matter resolved more by faith and experience than by scientific proof. To achieve "political" insight about one's own oppression is no more a sure road to paradise on earth than is the achievement of "personal" insight a guarantor of individual happiness. Group defined and achieved insights or "alternative" working and living arrangements may not prove any more invulnerable to the pull of early condition-

** Contemporary clinicians' views regarding feminism is discussed in Chapter Nine.
†† Another paradox or danger in radical as well as in any other mass psychiatric project involves viewing basic human needs for security and communication as "therapy," rather than as normal human needs—and rights.

ing or surrounding social forces than do individual solutions. Unfortunately, reality is not so easily captured, no less proclaimed away, by either tragic ideologies, for example by Freudian, Christian or liberal myths, or by optimistic ideologies, for example by Reichian, pagan, or "radical" myths. People and social structures change slowly if at all. More people inherit than experience revolutionary change. Very few people are transformed by myths before those myths have become the justificatory images of a New Order. Most people simply obey new myths, as inevitably as they did old myths.

The ideas and alternative structures of a "radical" or feminist psychotherapy both excite and disturb me. I don't know how much "professionalization" of either ideology might come to parallel hippie capitalism or limited social reformism or authoritarianism with a new party line. Part of the difficulty that a "service" or freedom-loving profession faces in being "revolutionary" is that people won't voluntarily patronize what isn't already palatable to them—and shouldn't be forced to do so. Also, the difficulty of translating one's ideology into action remains a problem for clinicians and people, whether traditional, radical, or feminist. For example, what happens to us as children in families may be very difficult to "will" away psychologically, even in the best of peer-group structures, even by the most scrupulous "contracts" between a therapist and her patient, or between a group and an individual.

Chapter Four
THE FEMALE CAREER AS A PSYCHIATRIC PATIENT

The insistence that femininity evolves from necessarily frustrated masculinity makes femininity a sort of "normal pathology."

Judith Bardwick[1]

We must always wonder, comparing absolute totals from two separate populations, whether apparent differences are due to inadvertent differences of method that have crept in. If the two populations have contrasting cultures or economic levels this kind of doubting is increased. Does population x, for instance, appear to have more cases than population y because culture x produces more cases or is it because culture x affects the criteria and methods employed so as to make it seem as if there were more cases? Put another way, when two populations differ markedly in their sociocultural condition, these differences may, in effect, make any attempt to count cases amount to using a different indicator in each culture.

Dorothy C. Leighton[2]

Since clinicians and researchers, as well as their patients and subjects, adhere to a masculine standard of mental health, women, by definition, are viewed as psychiatrically impaired—whether they accept or reject the female role—simply because they are women. Given this fact, it is not surprising that most studies of non-hospitalized populations report greater female than male "neurosis" or "psychosis," often regardless of marital status, age, race, social class,* or nationality.† From 1950 to 1970, women in America, England, Canada, and Sweden have been seen and consider themselves as more "disturbed" than their male counterparts. A study published in 1970 by the U. S. Department of Health, Education, and Welfare[3] indicated that, in both the black and white populations, in America more women than men *reported* having suffered nervous breakdowns, having felt impending nervous breakdowns, psychological inertia, and dizziness. Both black and white women

* Psychologists and sociologists have always considered women as part of the social class their husbands and fathers belong to. This is not a valid classification, from either a psychological or an economic point of view.
† Within the Western world.

also reported higher rates than men for the following symptoms: nervousness, insomnia, trembling hands, nightmares, fainting, and headaches (see Table 2).

White women who were never married reported fewer symptoms than white married or separated women. These findings are essentially in agreement with an earlier study published in 1960, by the Joint Commission on Mental Health and Illness.[4] The Commission reported the following information for non-hospitalized American adults:

(1) Greater distress and "symptoms" are reported by women than by men in all adjustment areas. Women report more disturbances in general adjustment, in their self-perception, and in their marital and parental functioning. This sex difference is most marked at the younger age intervals.

(2) A feeling of impending breakdown is reported more frequently by divorced and separated females than by any other group of either sex.

(3) The unmarried (whether single, separated, divorced, or widowed) have a greater potential for psychological distress than do the married.‡

(4) While the sexes did not differ in the frequency with which they reported "unhappiness," the women reported more worry, fear of breakdown, and need for help.

‡ This is a very controversial issue. For instance, in a study of the psychiatric "health" of the Manhattan community conducted by Srole et al. in 1962,[5] higher psychiatric "impairment" was found among single men when compared with married men than among single women when compared with married women. Among married people the sexes did not differ in the proportions rated psychiatrically "impaired." The 1970 HEW report also documents the fact that single white women in the general population report less "psychological distress" than married or separated white women. Hagnell, in his study of a Swedish population, found a higher probability of mental disorder in married than single women. Perhaps women who are single and employed behave, in some ways, more like men than married women do: as such they are seen as "healthy"—but only up to a point.

TABLE 2: SYMPTOM RATES BY SEX, SEX AND AGE, AND SEX AND RACE: A NATIONAL INSTITUTE OF MENTAL HEALTH STUDY

Symptom and sex	Total, 18-79 years	Age								Race	
		18-24 years	25-34 years	35-44 years	45-54 years	55-64 years	65-74 years	75-79 years		White	Negro
Nervous breakdown											
Male	3.2	1.3	1.8	3.5	3.0	5.4	5.4	1.5		3.2	2.8
Female	6.4	1.0	3.6	5.0	7.3	12.7	10.7	13.1		6.0	10.4
Felt impending nervous breakdown											
Male	7.7	6.9	7.4	8.6	11.7	6.4	3.1	2.2		7.7	8.2
Female	17.5	14.6	21.6	19.3	18.8	14.5	13.8	10.2		17.8	16.1
Nervousness											
Male	45.1	43.5	47.5	51.9	48.1	37.7	36.6	30.2		47.2	31.2
Female	70.6	61.4	74.4	75.0	72.5	72.6	62.9	65.6		73.2	55.2
Inertia											
Male	16.8	17.2	16.1	17.6	16.3	16.9	18.2	12.1		16.9	17.1
Female	32.5	31.0	34.0	35.2	31.1	29.7	31.9	35.6		33.1	29.5
Insomnia											
Male	23.5	20.4	16.7	20.8	26.8	27.0	35.9	26.5		24.1	20.4
Female	40.4	28.0	33.5	33.7	42.8	53.8	59.0	51.0		40.9	38.9
Trembling hands											
Male	7.0	7.6	6.5	5.4	5.7	8.8	10.0	8.5		6.9	7.1
Female	10.9	10.4	12.2	12.1	10.6	9.3	9.2	13.0		10.6	12.3
Nightmares											
Male	7.6	5.7	9.4	7.7	7.7	8.2	5.8	6.5		6.9	13.0
Female	12.4	12.8	15.8	14.7	9.9	7.5	11.6	11.8		12.3	14.3
Perspiring hands											
Male	17.0	23.2	24.9	17.7	14.7	11.0	7.9	3.0		17.0	16.8
Female	21.4	28.6	27.7	24.2	19.6	15.0	9.2	5.9		22.2	16.0
Fainting											
Male	16.9	17.6	15.7	15.7	18.1	17.3	17.8	17.2		17.5	13.8
Female	29.1	28.5	33.2	29.9	27.0	26.2	29.7	24.8		30.4	20.5
Headaches											
Male	13.7	13.0	12.8	13.8	15.2	15.6	11.3	10.0		13.8	11.9
Female	27.8	24.0	31.6	29.6	29.5	25.9	24.2	19.3		27.5	30.9
Dizziness											
Male	7.1	6.3	3.0	5.0	7.6	10.7	12.8	14.3		6.9	9.2
Female	10.9	8.4	9.5	8.5	10.1	14.3	16.9	16.6		10.3	15.7
Heart palpitations											
Male	3.7	3.3	2.0	2.1	3.9	7.2	6.4	1.5		3.6	4.8
Female	5.8	1.7	3.1	4.7	6.2	9.7	10.4	14.8		5.7	6.4
SCALE MEAN VALUE[1]											
Male											
White	1.70	1.72	1.70	1.72	1.78	1.69	1.66	1.19		1.70	—
Negro	1.55	1.25	1.03	1.37	1.79	1.87	2.23	2.99		—	1.55
Female											
White	2.88	2.61	3.07	2.93	2.89	2.86	2.82	2.80		2.88	—
Negro	2.65	1.91	2.61	2.60	2.52	3.27	3.79	2.62		—	2.65

[1]Scale is from 0 to 11.

Table Description: This survey was conducted in 1960–62 on a probability sample of 7,710 persons selected to represent the 111 million adults in the U.S. civilian non-institutionalized population aged 18–79 years. The symptom rates shown are projected percentages for the total population.
SOURCE: Harold J. Dupuy, Arnold Engel, Briand K. Devine, James Scanlon and Linda Querec. "Selected Symptons of Psychological Distress." Vital and Health Statistics. U. S. Department of Health, Education and Welfare. Public Health Service. Health Services and Mental Health Administration. August 1970.

Dr. Dorothy Leighton *et al.*,[6] in a 1963 study of English- and French-speaking Canadians, found that between 1951 and 1958 women had a higher risk of "psychiatric disorder" than did men, at all ages (twenty to seventy), and that "symptomatology" increased with age. Dr. Olle Hagnell found a greater incidence of "mental disorder" among Swedish women than men in 1947 and again in 1957.[7]

A double standard of mental health** affects women far more seriously than by presenting relatively unflattering academic studies of them. Only some of the studies mentioned above are concerned with how many of these "psychologically distressed" women are also in various kinds of psychiatric and psychological treatment.

Many factors have already been discussed that would suggest or predict a large female involvement with psychiatric facilities. For example, the real oppression of women—which leads to real distress and unhappiness; the conditioned female role of help-seeking and distress-reporting—which naturally leads to patient "careers" as well as overt or subtle punishment for such devalued behavior; the double or masculine standard of mental health used by most clinicians—which leads to perceiving the distressed (or any) female as "sick," whether she accepts or rejects crucial aspects of the female role††; the comparatively limited social tolerance for "unacceptable" behavior among women—which leads to comparatively great social and psychiatric pressure to adjust—or be judged as neurotic or psychotic; the female need for some sort of vacation from the female role, yet one that would satisfy her needs for dependence and nurturance; and finally, the female nature of

---

** Combined, of course, with misogyny and the female help-seeking and distress-reporting role.

†† Men are not usually seen as "sick" if they act out the male role fully—unless, of course, they are relatively powerless contenders for "masculinity." Women are seen as "sick" when they act out the female role (are depressed, incompetent, frigid, and anxious) and when they reject the female role (are hostile, successful, sexually active, and especially with other women).

the psychotherapeutic and hospital institutions—which leads to their being accepted more easily by women than by men. Additional facts would also predict a large and increasing female psychiatric population. For example, female longevity, coupled with the relative shortening of the child-rearing years (and the emphasis on female youth), leaves many women "unemployed" at an early age; just as public employment discrimination against women and lack of job training and opportunities leave most women "unemployed" at every age—and with few alternatives to home life.

The data shown in Tables 4 through 9 and presented more fully in the Appendix document a consistently large female involvement with psychiatry in America, an involvement that has been increasing rather dramatically since 1964. The total number of women in psychiatric facilities (including the predominantly all-male Veterans Administration psychiatric facilities) increased from 479,167 in 1964 to 615,112 in 1968. In 1964 there were 1079 more women than men in psychiatric facilities. By 1968, 50,363 more women than men were psychiatrically hospitalized and publicly treated.‡‡[8] (See Tables 4 and 5.) During the 1960s, adult women, far more than adult men, constituted the majority of private psychotherapy patients, as well as the majority of patients in general psychiatric wards, private hospitals, public outpatient clinics and community mental health centers.[9] In 1968, for example, adult women comprised 60 per cent of the patients in general psychiatric wards, 61 per cent of the population in private hospitals, and 62 per cent of the population in outpatient clinics. In 1968,

---

‡‡ From 1964 to 1968 female psychiatric "involvement" often exceeded, in many ways, what we would expect from a greater female than male existence in the population at large. In any event, if there *are* more women than men in the U.S. population at large, many are being stigmatized as "mentally ill" and incarcerated without much justification and without much effective "rehabilitation."

women of all ages comprised 50 per cent of the population in state and county hospitals. From 1964 through 1968, 125,351 more women than men were patients in all psychiatric institutions. Between 1950 and 1968, 223,268 more women than men (many of them "old" women), were confined in state and county hospitals (see Tables 4, 5, and 7).

A pattern of frequent and recurring hospital commitments, as well as lengthy stays, seems to characterize the female "career" as a psychiatric patient.[10] There is some evidence that women are detained longer and die sooner than men with the same psychiatric diagnosis, and that the personality characteristics of long-term hospital "stayers" are "feminine" in nature.[11] In 1971, although more men than women were admitted to state and county hospitals, women were detained for much longer periods—especially women over thirty-five.

The female "career" as a psychiatric patient in America seems to follow a certain pattern as a function of age, marital status, social class, race, and most certainly "attractiveness" (of course, this last is hard to document).* In 1968, general psychiatric wards and outpatient clinics serviced the most people. State and county hospitals serviced somewhat fewer people,† and private hospitals serviced the smallest patient population (see Table 5). Looking at these four facilities from 1966 to 1968, we see that, in

* These other factors—race, social class, marital status, etc.—are discussed more fully in the Appendix. It is also important to remember here that many more people are hospitalized for "mental illness" than for "mental retardation" —a basically genetic and biological phenomenon which, as a biological event, shows a relatively stable prevalence rate over time. "Mental illness," a primarily cultural event, increases and decreases over time. Also, more people are incarcerated in America for "mental illness" than for criminal offenses (See Appendix).

† The decrease in state patient populations is due to drug therapy and to the growth of Community Mental Health Centers—facilities which NIMH has not yet adequately reported on. An NIMH report regarding the CMHC population in 1969 documents a consistently female outnumbering of males in all adult age groups.[12]

terms of age, women are most concentrated in outpatient facilities between the ages of twenty and thirty-four. Kadushin has noted that among all the private therapy patients he surveyed, "young housewives [had] the most complaints."[18] In terms of age, twenty to thirty-four are women's "prettiest" and childbearing years. Even if they are "unhappy" or functioning at low levels, their child-rearing responsibilities and/or sexually youthful appearance keep them within the "outside" patriarchal institutions such as marriage and private psychotherapy. The largest number of women in both general and private hospitals (institutions where women have pre-dominated as psychiatric patients) are between the ages of thirty-five and forty-four.‡ White and/or wealthy women in private hos-pitals, black and/or poor women in general psychiatric wards are reacting to being both overworked and, paradoxically, to the begin-ning signals of their sexual and maternal "expendability." Hospitals provide them with warning therapy (via pills, shock treatments, and humiliation) to make as little protest about this state of affairs as possible. If they persist in being "depressed" about this state of affairs, or reacting with "hostility," repeated or longer con-finements in private and public hospitals await them. State and county asylums function as a final dumping-ground for "old" women. Thirty-two per cent of the total female population in-carcerated in state and county hospitals in 1968 were over sixty-five (see Table 7).

The female "career" as a psychiatric patient requires a closer and more thoughtful analysis than statistics or small-sample studies can yield. Therefore, I wanted to talk to women about their pa-tient experiences. I was curious to see to what extent the kind of psychiatric patient "career" suggested by national statistics also

‡ This is also true for men, i.e., men between the ages of thirty-five and forty-four are the largest group of men in general hospitals: but there are *still* significantly fewer men than women in this age bracket who are psychiatrically hospitalized.

exists at a grass-roots level. I also wanted to see how much my theoretical approach to "madness" would describe the circumstances surrounding female psychiatric hospitalization or treatment. I wanted to see how many of the clinical biases I outlined in Chapter Three would be spontaneously reported by "naïve" women.

THE INTERVIEWS

As women, most of our lives with men are dramatic and theatrical affairs. We "play" at being women; we dress up like Mommy—for Daddy's sake; we're always on stage, working at being some other woman—a "beautiful" woman, a "happy" woman, a well-paid-for woman.

Our lives with women are generally less dramatic. The "play," for better or worse, ended long ago. We talk more to women. Men don't have the time, the interest, or the capacity to engage in "woman's talk"—which never seems to "go" anywhere and often makes no "sense." Thus, dialogue, words, interviews between women, reveal more about the female condition than do test scores or statistics.

From November 1970 to June 1971, I spoke with sixty women, whose ages ranged from seventeen to seventy, about their experiences in private therapy and mental asylums. Collectively, their experiences spanned a quarter century (from 1945 to 1971) and a continent (from Rhode Island to California).** The majority of these experiences took place in large cities in New York, New Jersey, Illinois, and California.

The interviews were very informal and were held in either of our homes, over long cups of coffee, and often more than once.

** Two women were also in private therapy and mental asylums in England.

They were tape-recorded—as long as and whenever it didn't interfere with spontaneity or rapport. I encouraged and answered any questions about myself and about why I was, in effect, "interviewing" them. I did have a standard questionnaire form, which usually wasn't properly filled out (by either the women or myself). We tended to "talk out" the details. I participated very actively in the conversations and, after no more than an hour's grace, expressed my views, sometimes beyond the point of mild disagreement.

I met some kindred spirits—and some not; I made and received many midnight phone calls, some of which were exhausting and depressing. Hope often united with humor: for example, when someone would exclaim, with great surprise, that she was "telling me things she would never even tell her therapist!" I was as exhilarated as an amateur detective when different women told me about the *same* therapist or hospital. Unknowingly, they duplicated and corroborated one another's experiences, and helped me re-create several years in the life of a particular therapist or hospital. I was more exhilarated when several of the women, who at first were even reluctant to talk to me privately, attended professional conferences of psychiatry and psychology some four months later in New York City where they were very vocal, angry and thoughtful about their experiences.

More often, sorrow, anger, helplessness, and guilt marked my interviewing days. I remember arguing with someone about whether or not she was "crazy": after six years of therapy and two hospital commitments, she thought she was, I thought she wasn't. Slowly, some remembered fear silenced her. Slowly, and quite emphatically, she began agreeing with me—with *Dr*. Chesler, of course.††
I helped a lonely and unmarried woman avoid an unwanted psy-

†† There is a possibility that that type of "experimenter effect" happened *throughout* the interviews—without my awareness. My report of the interviews, like any scientific or artistic report, will be as "truthful" as my sensitivity, integrity, and basic premises allow.

chiatric commitment. Afterward, quite understandably, she wanted to live with me "for a while." I offered her money and other temporary shelters, both of which she refused. I never saw her again. I was constantly asked to find lawyers, physicians, employers, landlords, therapists, and baby sitters. I failed these requests more often than not. I am not by temperament and therefore, by ideological conviction, a "social worker." My failings and strengths are those of an intellectual and an artist rather than those of a "crisis-intervener" or a revolutionary organizer. However, these requests for help were from women who were less in need of "social work" than of a station on a feminist underground railroad.

At no time did I wish to classify these already "overclassified" women. I *did*, however, originally seek them out in terms of one of five categories of experience‡‡: women who (1) had sexual relations with their therapists (SWT women); (2) had been hospitalized in mental asylums (MA women); (3) were lesbians*; (4) were Third World women (TW women); and (5) were feminists in therapy. This categorization wasn't simple. For example, in talking to a particular lesbian about her experiences in private therapy, it sometimes became apparent that she had also been psychiatrically hospitalized and had since become a feminist. Some Third World women, feminists, and SWT women had *also* been psychiatrically hospitalized. Naturally, since they were all women, their "psychiatric careers" often turned out to be rather extensive.

Table 3 presents a comparison of these five groups in relation to some aspects of their psychiatric patient careers. Fifty-four

‡‡ These women comprise a non-random sample, in that they were sought because they *had* certain kinds of experiences.

* The word "lesbian" is problematic: it identifies a woman as strictly in terms of her *sexual* activities as the word "woman" does. It also, unfortunately, has a historically negative valuation. However, many lesbians think it a very "respectable" word—and those who don't, think it should be used more often and positively in order to make it so.

women are presented.† As is indicated, the averages for a particular variable within each experience-category are based on a *different* number of women. Not all the SWT women were psychiatrically hospitalized (only four were, as compared to eleven MA women); not all the women in any of the five categories ever saw a female therapist, etc. Thus, there are usually unequal and often small numbers of women being compared on a particular category average. I decided not to run any statistical tests for this reason— and for a more important reason. Those trends that are important are as visible to my eye as to your own. Trends which echo those found in the national statistics (and there are many) will be better understood by an intelligent discussion of the individual interviews than by a clean bill of statistical "health." Also, each of these fifty-four women has a universe of experience to relate—a universe that cannot be inhabited by any other woman. And what happened to this group as a whole happened absolutely. However, their experiences seem to parallel and make human sense out of the studies and statistics cited earlier and in the Appendix.

Since racism is as deep, as complicated, and as absolutely evil a factor in American society as is sexism, I decided to view the Third World women shown in Table 3 as a separate group— regardless of any differences in their class origins, educational backgrounds, political beliefs, sexual preferences, and types of psychiatric experience. For a similar reason, I viewed all the (white) lesbians shown in Table 3 separately, regardless of any differences in class origins, political beliefs, types of psychiatric experience, etc. These two decisions, which I made beforehand, and for strictly ideological reasons, were fruitful ones.

Looking at Table 3, it is evident that these fifty-four women

---

† Of the original sixty interviewed, five women were sexually propositioned by their therapists and refused him. They are not here included. One black woman who was also a lesbian but who had no private therapy experience, is not included either.

were experts about the "mental illness" profession.‡ They had seen a total of 136 therapists and "averaged" (by category) between three and four therapists apiece. By category, they had remained in private therapy from about two years to more than four years.

They were also experts about mental asylums: twenty-four of the women had been psychiatrically committed at least once, ten for suicide attempts and five for depression. They had been hospitalized from a minimum of about four months to a maximum of about sixteen months. The average duration in hospitals for all of the twenty-four hospitalized women was about a year. However, individual variation was very great. Some women had been hospitalized only once for a relatively brief period (for two- or three-month "stretches"); still others had been hospitalized only a few times for very long periods (five years or more.) By category, the women had been in private hospitals (white middle- and upper-class enclaves) from a minimum of about two months to a maximum of about eight months; in both general psychiatric wards and state hospitals from a minimum of about two and a half months to a maximum of about ten months; and in state hospitals alone from a minimum of three months to a maximum of nearly two years.

In terms of private therapy, all of the women had seen about as many female as male therapists. However, with only one important exception,** they had remained in treatment at least twice or three times as long with male as with female therapists. Among white women, the lesbians saw female therapists for the longest average

‡ Nearly half of the women (N=26) are or were legally married at least once. Nearly a fifth of them (N=12) have children. Twelve of the forty women in the non-feminist categories expressed some feminist awareness or defined themselves as feminists (one of the SWT women; seven of the lesbians; two of the MA women; and two of the TW women.)
** The important exception here are the Third World women, who stayed in therapy longer with female than with male therapists, and whose total duration in therapy was shorter than that of any other group.

TABLE 3:
FIFTY-FOUR WOMEN: SOME COMPARATIVE IMFORMATION
REGARDING THEIR PSYCHIATRIC HOSPITALIZATION AND
PRIVATE PSYCHOTHERAPEUTIC EXPERIENCES: 1945–1971*

	SEX WITH THERAPIST N – 11	LESBIANS N – 9	MENTAL ASYLUM N – 11	THIRD WORLD N – 9	FEMINIST N – 14
Average Age at First Hospital Commitment	N – 4 AV. – 25	N – 6 AV. – 21	N – 11 AV. – 29	N – 3 AV. – 26	N – 0 AV. – 0
Total Average Duration in Hospital *(in days)*	N – 4 AV. – 103	N – 6 AV. – 320	N – 11 AV. – 476	N – 3 AV. – 428	
Private Hospitals *(in days)*	N – 2 AV. – 131	N – 4 AV. – 245	N – 6 AV. – 60	N – 0	
General and State Hospitals *(in days)*	N – 2 AV. – 75	N – 4 AV. – 190	N – 9 AV. – 550	N – 3 AV. – 428	
State Hospitals *(in days)*	N – 1 90	N. – 1 730	N – 6 AV. – 722	N – 2 AV. – 575	
Number of Therapists Seen	N – 11 TOT. – 35 MODE – 3.0	N – 8 TOT. – 21 MODE – 3.0	N – 8 TOT. – 29 MODE – 4.0	N – 7 TOT. – 18 MODE – 3.0	N – 14 TOT. – 33 MODE – 2.0
Number of Male Therapists Seen	N – 11 TOT. – 23 MODE – 2.0	N – 5 TOT. – 9 MODE – 2.0	N – 5 TOT. – 21 MODE – 3.0	N – 6 TOT. – 10 MODE – 2.0	N – 10 TOT. – 15 MODE – 2.0
Number of Female Therapists Seen	N – 8 TOT. – 12 MODE – 2.0	N – 7 TOT. – 12 MODE – 2.0	N – 8 TOT – 29 MODE – 4.0	N – 3 TOT. – 8 MODE – 2.0	N – 10 TOT. – 15 MODE – 2.0
Total Duration in Therapy *(in months)*	N – 11 AV. – 51	N – 9 AV. – 44	N – 8 AV. – 40	N – 7 AV. – 25	N – 14 AV. – 39
Total Duration with Male Therapists *(in months)*	N – 11 AV. – 40	N – 5 AV. – 39	N – 8 AV. – 35	N – 6 AV. – 17	N – 10 AV. – 30
Total Duration with Female Therapists *(in months)*	N – 8 AV. – 14	N – 7 AV. – 21	N – 5 AV. – 8	N – 3 AV. – 24	N 10 AV. – 19

*TABLE CODE
N=No. women   Mode=Number most frequently given
Av.=Average   Tot.=Total number of therapists

time period (twenty-one months). The feminists remained with female therapists for an average of 19 months. However, both the
lesbians and the feminists still saw male therapists for twice as long
a period as they saw female therapists.

Table 3 may be viewed in terms of my concept of a female
career as a psychiatric patient—a career whose shape is influenced by the extent to which the "feminine" role is accepted or
rejected, as well as by the woman's age (or "expendability"), race,
class, and marital status. For example, let's look at the age at which
the women were *first* committed to asylums. Lesbians were committed at the youngest age (when they were twenty-one) of any
group. What is perceived (and experienced) as an extreme rejection of one's "feminine" role is the most stressful and dramatically
punished of all female offenses in our society. Let's compare the
"psychiatric patient careers" of the least "feminine" of the women
—the Lesbians—with those of the most "feminine"—the SWT
women. (I am defining "femininity" mainly in terms of dependence
on a man.)

The SWT women had committed a dramatic version
of father-daughter incest—a sine qua non of "femininity" in patriarchal society. Nine of the eleven SWT women were legally married at least once *before* therapy while only one of the nine lesbians
had ever been heterosexually married. The psychiatric careers of
the SWT women reflect their "femininity" in several ways:

(1) they remained in therapy (a marriage-like institution)
longer than any other group (for an average of fifty-one months,
seven months longer than the lesbians did). For SWT women,
going to therapy both reflected the problems they were having
with their "feminine" role and provided another way of acting
out that role. The fact that lesbians remained in treatment for
the second longest period of time (for an average of forty-four
months) underlines the extent to which therapy is a culture for

both female accepters and female rejectors of the "feminine" role
—and how similarly socialized both types of women are.

(2) *Fewer* of the SWT women were ever psychiatrically committed at all; four of the eleven SWT women (less than a third)
were hospitalized, as compared with six or two thirds of the nine
lesbians.†† Here we may remember in what ways clinical as well as
societal bias rewards "femininity" in both psychiatric and social
settings—up to a certain point—as long as the woman is young
and/or attractive. The totally attractive "feminine" woman is not
usually hospitalized. (She may still be "depressed" or "anxious"
without being incarcerated for it.)

(3) Not only were the lesbians psychiatrically committed at
an earlier age, but they remained in asylums for a total average of
more than three times as long as the SWT women (for an average
of ten months compared with an average of three and one-half
months).

Perhaps one can argue that the SWT women were simply
"caught" here (in Table 3) at an earlier stage of their patient
"careers." When they grow older their patient careers may resemble
those of the MA women and may involve even greater hospitalization periods than those of the lesbians. The SWT-type woman
may get so "depressed" or "anxious," that she will have to be
treated for these extreme expressions of "femininity." However, I
don't think this is true. For example, the ages of the SWT women
at the time I interviewed them ranged from twenty-five to fifty;
the MA women ranged in age from nineteen to seventy. I think
we're dealing with two different kinds of women. The SWT
women may be "unhappy" but they remain committed to a
"feminine" ideal throughout their lives. As such, they are not as
stressed or punished by the fact and meaning of psychiatric hos-

†† It is important to note that two of the four SWT women were committed right after, and one during, their "affairs" with their therapists.

pitalization—as the lesbians are. The lesbians, in turn, for a number of reasons, are not as trapped into a *hospitalized* psychiatric career as are the MA women.‡‡

The mental asylum (MA) women in Table 3 were *first* committed at the oldest average age of any of the groups (when they were twenty-nine years old). These eleven women probably reflect the scores of women on the national level who begin filling the psychiatric wards in general, state, and private hospitals when they reach their thirties. They have already had patient careers in private or outpatient clinic treatment during their twenties. Now, no longer "young," they are both more desperate and more "expendable." By this age they are stressed either by marriage and children—or by being unmarried and childless.* Psychiatric hospitalization is perceived by them as an escape from and as deserved punishment for their desperation, unhappiness, etc.

Third World women remained in private therapy for the shortest time period of any group, for an average of twenty-five months. They were also the only group who remained in treatment longer with female than with male therapists. The simplest explanation for both these facts is that of poverty. Third World women couldn't easily afford the white middle-class luxury of "feminine" father-worship. This is not to say they didn't *want* to see male therapists or didn't *want* to remain in therapy for longer periods. Six of the nine TW women interviewed saw (and *wanted* to see) male therapists; only one saw only female therapists; two saw both

‡‡ Here we may remember the various studies that found greater "mental health" among single than married women. Of course, what is usually measured as "mental health" is male characteristics—some of which economically independent women (or women independent of men) would exhibit more than economically dependent women would.

* Four of the eleven MA women were legally married, and two had children. Of the two women who were hospitalized for the longest time period, one was a single white woman and the other a very much married Puerto Rican mother.

male and female therapists. The three women who saw female therapists saw agency or hospital social workers or predoctoral psychologists. It was at a price they could afford: it was free. Explanations other than "poverty" to account for the comparatively short therapy duration among TW women would include: the fact that, for better or worse, TW women are not as well "trained" for careers as psychiatric patients as are white women (although they are better "trained" than TW men); the fact that they mistrust, fear, and usually have no easy access to a professional world that is usually threatening, unsympathetic, and unable to "cure" them; the fact that some of their family and friendship needs are satisfied within the ghetto culture—as long as they are willing to remain within it, on its terms.

Only three of the TW women I interviewed were hospitalized—too small a number to reveal anything conclusive about the comparative effect of race and sex on the frequency or duration of hospitalization. It is possible that female psychiatric patient careers are primarily white and/or middle-class phenomena. Third World women are hospitalized, controlled, and commit suicide in many other ways: in jails, in medical experimentation and mistreatment; in abortion or childbirth; in doomed attempts to be treated as "white."†

Table 3 seems to suggest that feminists are never psychiatrically hospitalized or, as Shulamith Firestone has suggested in *The Dialectics of Sex,* that feminism is the cure for all the female disorders described by Freud. Actually, six of the twenty-four feminists were hospitalized: five were lesbians who became feminists after their hospital experiences. They are not shown as feminists in Table 3. The fourteen non-hospitalized (white) feminists ranged in age from twenty to forty-five and were certainly involved in the culture of private therapy. They saw therapists for a total average of

† I will discuss this more fully in Chapter Eight.

more than three years. Among white women, feminists remained in therapy with female therapists for the second longest time period—for an average of nineteen months.

There are many other inferences to be drawn from the information in Table 3. I will not draw any. Instead, I would like to discuss each of the interviews in greater depth, beginning with the most unambivalently "feminine" of the women—those who had sexual relations with their therapists.

WOMEN

To the Daddy's Girls we were—and are no longer—I dedicate this poem and chapter.

SOMETHING BORROWED, SOMETHING BLUE

More and more lately,
there's a man
on my couch
talking about his
girl friend or his wife.

I've always loved
to borrow things
from women:
library books, perfume, cigarettes and shawls
                          delicious
this dressing up for Daddy,
and as safe
as playing a part
in a play
that must end
before bedtime.

So I listen,
a gravely curious
little girl,
with eyes so clear
a woman can
drown in them
silently.

Phyllis Chesler
1970

Chapter Five

SEX BETWEEN PATIENT AND THERAPIST

"I am a doctor of the soul" [the Guru] said quietly. "I am certainly not interested in that silly little body of yours. . . . [Under my guidance you will learn] control of your senses, whereby you may come at will—instantaneous orgasm at my command. . . . [Regard my erection] impersonally, not as an object of love, but as a demonstration of spiritual advancement." [The Guru teaches Candy various yoga exercises, some of which] . . . in any other context would suggest the sexual and perhaps even the obscene. Candy crossly blamed herself for making the association and attributed it to her own insecure and underdeveloped spirit. [When Candy's period is overdue, the Guru] gives her a plane ticket to Tibet [where Candy meets a holy man in a Buddhist temple]. Candy began her meditation at once, concentrating all her attention on a single spot, the tip of Buddha's nose. It was wonderful for her—all her life *she* had been needed by someone else—mostly boys—and now at last she had found someone that she herself needed . . . Buddha!

[The temple is struck by lightning and, with the dung-crusted holy man seated beside her, they watch as] the huge Buddha . . . toppled forward, pitching headlong to the temple floor in a veritable explosion. Although it seemed to fall right on top of them, Candy and the holy man were miraculously unscathed, and were left bunched together. . . . In fact, she felt the holy man's taut member ease an inch or two into her tight little lamb-pit. [And pressing against her] was a section of her beloved Buddha's face—the nose! And a truly incredible thing was happening—it was slipping into Candy's marvelous derriere . . . it was then she realized . . . that wonder of wonders, the Buddha, too, needed her! She gave herself up fully to her idol, stroking his cheek, as she gradually began the esoteric Exercise Number Four—and only realizing after a minute that this movement was having a definite effect on the situation in her honey-cloister as well, forcing the holy man's member deeply in and out as it did, and she turned to him at once, wanting to tell him that it wasn't meant the way it seemed certainly, but she was stricken dumb by what she saw—for the warm summer rain had worked its wonders there as well, washing the crust of dung and ash away as the eyes glittered terrifically while the hopeless ecstasy of his huge pent-up spasm began, and sweet Candy's melodious voice rang out through the temple in truly mixed feelings: "GOOD GRIEF—IT'S DADDY!"

Terry Southern and Mason Hoffenberg,
Candy

If only 25% of these specific reports [made by women about having had sexual relations with their therapists] are correct, there is still an overwhelming issue confronting professionals in this field.

William Masters and Virginia Johnson

Dramatic or extreme forms of exploitation always signify the pervasiveness of less dramatic forms. Atrocities and scandals are everyday events—writ large. Physical brutality in American state mental asylums and prisons signifies the dailiness of brutality in when they reach their thirties. They have already had patient the "outside" society. Prostitution,[1] rape,[2] and sexual molestation of female children by adult males[3] are so common they are usually invisible—except when sensationalistic accounts focus them, distortedly, into view.*

"Sex" between private female patients and their male psychotherapists is probably no more common—or uncommon—an occurrence than is "sex" between a female secretary or housekeeper and her male employer.†[4] Both instances generally involve an older male figure and a young female figure.[5] The male transmits "unconscious" signals of power, "love," wisdom, and protection, signals to which the female has been conditioned to respond automatically. Such a transaction between patient and therapist, euphemistically termed "seduction" or "part of the treatment process," is legally a form of rape[6] and psychologically a form of incest. The *sine qua non* of "feminine" identity in patriachal society is the violation of the incest taboo, i.e., the initial and continued "preference" for Daddy, followed by the approved falling in love with and/or marrying of powerful father figures.‡ There is

* Female prostitution and harems have existed among all races, in nearly every recorded culture, on every continent, and in all centuries: it predates Catholicism and industrial capitalism. It *always* signifies the *relatively* powerless position of women and their widespread sexual repression. It *usually* also signifies their exclusion from or subordination within the economic, political, religious, and military systems.

† From a financial point of view, the therapist and not his patient is the employee. Psychologically, however, the female is as much—if not more—a dependent supplicant here as she is elsewhere.

‡ Men may marry mother figures but only if they are safely powerless. Wives are generally younger, less mobile, and physically smaller than their husbands—and than their husbands' *childhood* mother. Men do not violate the incest taboo; they do not re-create certain crucial conditions of their childhood in marriage.

no real questioning of such feminine identity in psychotherapy. More often, an adjustment to it is preached—through verbal or sexual methods.

. Although there are many individual therapists and several therapist "families" in New York and California who have systematically preached and practiced "sex" with their female patients for over a decade,** such intercourse is by no means a recent innovation. Many analysts in Freud's time had "love affairs" or married their female patients—when the comparatively short (three- to six-month) treatment process was completed. Paul Roazen reports that Reich's first wife, Bernfeld's last wife, Rado's third wife, and one of Fenichel's wives were former patients; that Freud's disciple Tausk had a love affair with a former female patient, sixteen years his junior; and that Freud himself encouraged a prominent American analyst to marry a former patient.[7] Judd Marmor writes about the "tragic end of the career" of W. Bern Wolfe, a gifted psychiatrist who was forced to flee the United States in the 1930s for "impairing the morals of a girl whom he had under treatment[8], the late James L. McCartney, who encouraged "sex" between male therapists and their female patients (when "necessary"), claims that a number of well-known psychiatrists (Hadley, Sullivan, Alexander, and Reich) "told him, despite their writings to the contrary, that they allowed their patients physically to act out."[9] Freud is quoted by Marmor[10] as chiding Ferenczi on his habit of kissing his patients:

> If you start with a kiss [you risk an ultimately very] lively scene . . . Ferenczi, gazing at the lively scene he has created, will perhaps say to himself, maybe I should have halted my technique of motherly affection.

** There are even therapists who "specialize" in treating *other* therapists' "guilt" or "conflict" about having sexual relations with their patients.

I do not seek a simple alliance with those Puritans who censure sexual and other forms of doctor-patient contact. I am not in favor of great and grave professional distances between people, especially between therapists and patients. (Many "schizophrenics" need and should have access to specifically physical contact.) However, Puritanism usually implies an acceptance of the myth of "feminine evil" and the practice of other evils.†† Also, there are many kinds of "distance," other than sexual, to be tenderly and/or experimentally bridged between therapist and patient. "Sexual" contact does not necessarily insure any other kind of "communication—be it a "traditionally" or "radically" desired one: it often impedes it. Most important is the fact that most such "sexual" contacts take place between middle-aged male therapists and younger female patients.[12] It does not usually occur between female therapists and male (or female) patients of any age[13]; or between male therapists and male patients, unless the therapist is homosexual.‡‡

The fact of the matter is that sexually seductive (or assault-ive) therapists are quite ordinary in their ethical failure. Despite their occasional pretenses of being radicals whom society crucifies, they are not very "radical," i.e., they do not perceive or challenge basic assumptions and social behavior.* For example, they are

†† For example, Leon J. Saul,[11] in an article condemning patient-thera-pist sexual contact, is more sensitive to the *analyst's* than to the patient's vul-nerability. He says: "Let the analyst beware. In the face of sexual love needs, let him recall the Lorelei and Delilah and the many other beauties who have revealed that appearance need not be reality . . . if the analyst is tempted to follow Ferenczi in experimenting with Eros let him be certain . . . [that] no matter how obvious Eros may be, hostility is the inevitable middle link."

‡‡ Dahlberg[14] reports one case of an attempted seduction by a male homosexual therapist. The male patient, who was also homosexual, refused his advances. Perhaps men are more conditioned than women to refuse sexual en-counters that they do not initiate, cannot control, or in which they see neither pleasure nor profit.

* The issue of sexuality, childhood, and family life is a crucial and "radical" one. The fact that we do not experience sexual pleasure with our childhood relatives, but with strangers, no doubt limits our sexuality as well as our level of civilization. Nevertheless, I don't think that remedial psychotherapy

generally extremely anti-homosexual and anti-lesbian. McCartney,[15] who was ousted from the American Psychiatric Association for publicly favoring "overt transference," limits it to overt heterosexual transference. He recommends "transferring" his sexually aroused male patients to a female therapist—or sends them home to "practice" on their wives and girl friends.† McCartney also seems to measure "success" in terms of the female patients' subsequent marriage and maternity. Further, McCartney treats his female patients who are in need of "overt transference" (sex) as children: he asks for their parents' or husbands' permission before sexual contact occurs. Most important, he recommends that the therapist remain as emotionally uninvolved, as removed from risk-taking, as "performance"-oriented, as a Playboy stereotype. He emphasizes the distinction between "transference love" and "romantic love," and describes the therapist's role as passive, unemotional, and "responsive" to the patient's initiative.‡

for adults is the place, time or way to solve this particular moral mystery. Further, while McCartney is correct in condemning the originally harmful distance between parent and child, and the harmful effects of sexual repression, he is shortsighted in his understanding of the differences in treatment of male and female childhood sexuality. Female children have already been (over) exposed to heterosexual sexuality with their fathers; male children, while well nurtured maternally, are forced to severely repress their heterosexual sexuality in relation to their mothers. Few men achieve "mature" heterosexuality—and I don't think sexual intercourse with a female therapist is the solution to this problem. Also, both male and female children are deprived of sexuality with their same-sex parent or with other nurturant same-sex adults. I doubt whether such bisexual deprivation could be remedied for adults through "acting out" in psychotherapy.

† McCartney notes that "it is not so easy for a female [as for a male] analysand to find a [sexual] surrogate, so the analyst may have to remain objective and yet react appropriately, in order to lead the immature person into full [heterosexual] maturity."

‡ Perhaps male therapists, like male artists in our society, are seen, or fear themselves, as more "feminine" than business executives, soldiers, or politicians. Thus, it is important to them to be able to "have" as many women as their presumably more "masculine" counterparts do. Male poets and novelists are as notorious (as they are "forgiven") for their frantic and sexually selfish and abusive treatment of women. Some psychotherapists, although less inspired, may behave similarly.

Dr. Charles Dahlberg[16] presents the seductive therapist as a man who chose to practice psychotherapy between 1930 and 1945, and who was probably

> withdrawn and introspective, studious, passive, shy . . . [more] intellectually [than] physically adventurous . . . among other things, this adds up to being unpopular with the opposite sex. None of this stops a person from having fantasies of sexual conquest. It may well encourage sexual fantasies.

Such typically "deprived" men now find themselves in a professional position where many young women may be expressing fantasies of sexual desire for them. The therapists *can't help* being "flattered" by the situation; and they *refuse* to help exploiting the situation for their own ends.

Dahlberg, in his presentation of nine cases of patient-therapist "sexual" contact, draws a composite portrait of the "seductive" therapist as "always over 40; from 10 to 25 years older than the patient; always a man; and with the [one] exception of the homosexual, the patient is always a young female." Most of Dahlberg's nine therapists are married; many experience premature ejaculation with their patients; some "seduce" the wives of their male patients; some terminate therapy—or payment for therapy—once sexual contact begins; others continue both therapy and payment.

Many of these therapists are what Dahlberg terms "grandiose." He cites the example of one therapist who offered to "cure" his married female patient's "frigidity" on a two-week holiday.** Another therapist hypnotized his female patient and then suggested to her that sexual contact might increase her "transferential" in-

----

** This patient panicked, told her husband, and together they sought legal action. The suit wasn't pursued because of the patient's "paranoid" tendencies: the lawyers feared that the woman would not be believed and would lose the case.

volvement with him. When she finally refused to pay for such treatment and began seeing another therapist, the first therapist told her he would continue seeing her for "sex," and would not "charge" her for it—but neither would he listen to her "problems" any longer. Dahlberg's paper presents only two cases where sexual contact occurred during therapy; four such contacts took place almost immediately after therapy was terminated, and three were propositions for sexual contact which never took place.

I was interested in talking with women whose sexual contact with their therapists took place during treatment.†† Ten of the eleven women I interviewed had "sex" with their therapists during the treatment process. Five of these sexual contacts were initiated and continued in the therapist's office. For seven of the women, therapy continued after such contact. Seven women continued paying for therapy for an average of four months. The duration of these contacts ranged from one night to eighteen months.

At the time of sexual contact, the women's ages ranged from twenty-two to forty-five. Their average age was thirty-one. Four women were married, four were separated or divorced, and three were single. The husbands of the four married women were in treatment with the same therapist at the time of sexual contact. The ten therapists‡‡ were, on an average, fifteen years older than their patients. Their average age was forty-seven. Seven of the therapists were married, two were separated or divorced, and one was single. Seven were psychiatrists and three were psychologists.

Nine of the ten therapists assumed a "missionary" position during sexual intercourse for the first time and in general throughout the sexual "treatment." Seven of the women did not experience

†† I also spoke to five women who refused their therapists' sexual propositions.

‡‡ Two of the women saw the same therapist—and did not know about each other, or about his many other female patients similarly "contacted."

orgasm at this time; four women never did throughout the "treatment"; seven of the women eventually experienced orgasm, from within one to nine months. Four of the therapists had difficulty maintaining an erection throughout the sexual contact period.*

As a group, these women were the most reluctant to talk with me.† They were indecisive about meeting times, broke appointments, set time limits, and forgot about time once we started talking. Their lives were filled with the clamor and escape of people and crises. They received many phone calls: their children needed them, their lovers were waiting, their *lovers'* children needed them. And yet—a very quiet and despairing eye looked out at me from the center of this storm.

Those women who were over thirty-five when the sexual encounter occurred seemed more "worldly": sophistication was their body armor, compassion their shield. They were the most vocal advocates of "pity" and "understanding" for the therapists—and for all men.

MELISSA: I have tremendous sympathy, compassion for men. I think from my experience that they need much more assurance and love and affection and sympathy. . . .

PHYLLIS: Even when they aren't capable of giving it to you?

MELISSA: Right. In fact, people are seldom capable of giving it, they're so wrapped up in pain . . . he [the therapist] had trouble maintaining an erection. It had to do with his being sixty, I think. He fumbled around a lot, which was a little bit surprising. I began to feel a little anxious too. I began to fall into old patterns of reassuring him as I had been reassuring men all my life, that it didn't matter [that I didn't have an orgasm], that I was so happy with him . . . but he wasn't very skillful. . . .

PHYLLIS: Did you tell him?

---

* At the risk of superficiality, one might simply conclude from this information that "seductive" therapists are lousy lovers.

† I did, however, manage to speak to every woman I contacted.

MELISSA: No, because it didn't really matter. Now it would matter . . . but he said that I was so lovely, that I was a beautiful thing, and he was an old man . . . that I was not a doll or a child but a charming, fully mature woman, intelligent and delightful.‡

Three of the over-thirty-five "sophisticated" women refused to reveal their therapists' names (even before I asked), for fear of "harming his reputation." They insisted that *they* were to blame; *they* were the real seducers.

MELISSA: I think that he just finally couldn't resist me any more. I think I just put too much pressure on him. . . . I was making moves from the very beginning. . . .

DONNA: I had a fantastic tan . . . and I was high, and I'm very attractive when I'm high. I'm irresistible. . . . I wanted to look nice for my therapy sessions. I always took off my glasses and combed my hair before I went.

ROSLYN: Actually, in a certain way, I was seducing him all along . . . unconsciously. I wasn't aware of it until one time he came to a party at my house. . . . I always had to seduce every man.

MARTHA: He was really attracted to me . . . and I was attracted to him beforehand . . . the night he gave me flowers I was hoping he'd make love to me. But I wasn't as conscious about those things then.

And yet these women described as many fantasies of love and marriage about their therapists, and felt as little-girl betrayed, as the younger, less "sophisticated" women did.

ELLEN: I wanted him to marry me but he wouldn't. His wife and children, his reputation, and his failing health made it hard for him. . . . I haven't been able to shake the relationship and it's been eight months . . . he won't see me at all now.**

‡ This somewhat sad and very "human" aging male therapist was married—and had also been treating Melissa's husband for several years, for marital and sexual problems.
** She had been in therapy for six years before the sexual affair began.

MARTHA: I had just left my husband after twenty years and was I depressed! I was living alone for the first time in my life and needed everything: emotional support, solace, approval, friends, a better job—everything. . . . I guess I really wanted another husband. . . . I was still looking to romantic love for security. . . . Do you know, I found out much later that he was involved with at least one other woman at the same time as me.

ROSLYN: I thought, I fantasied, that he would leave his wife and marry me . . . that he was going to give up his other life and start a new life with me. . . . I was so happy that my therapist loved me. Who cared about anything else? . . . Look how worthy I am. . . . I said to him, "You don't have to leave your wife. You don't have to do anything like that. Just see me." But he couldn't do that either . . . he didn't want to get involved.

STEPHANIE: I finally asked him if he would marry me and he just laughed and said no. . . . I thought, he's going to be really old soon and needs someone to take care of him. I *thought* I loved him, that he had it within his power to make me happy, that he could do it if he only will . . . but he was more interested in my typing for him than in talking about this.

DONNA: I was enamored. I guess I would have been in love had I let myself think that at thirty an intelligent woman could fall in love with a man so fast. . . . I left my husband. . . . [The therapist] was a doorway to finding things out about myself. . . . We haven't slept apart since I moved in with him.

JOYCE: I know I needed him very, very badly. It was like he was God. . . . He was mistreating me, and I didn't want to admit that, because I needed him badly. I loved him. . . . Then he offered me a job as his typist but he wouldn't sleep with me any more. I was so depressed and upset and I wanted some help and called up, hysterical, "Please talk to me on the phone," and he said, "I can't talk to you now, I'll call you back." And he never called back. I felt deserted and all alone and usually when I talk about this with my shrink [now] I'm just in tears.

Although many of the women described being humiliated and frustrated by their therapists' emotional and sexual coldness or ineptitude, it was the therapist, more often than the patient, who ended the "affair." And in every case the woman was further hurt by the abandonment.†† After the therapist's withdrawal, one woman tried to kill herself; two others lapsed into a severe depression; a fourth woman's *husband,* who was also in treatment with the same therapist, killed himself shortly *after* if not *because* he found out about the affair. This particular therapist's rather sadistic and grandiose attempt to cure this woman's "frigidity" one night resulted in her developing a "headache" that wouldn't subside for a year.‡‡ His behavior was depressingly typical.

SHEILA: I got stoned on grass because I was so scared. And he never even took his clothes off. He just dropped his pants. . . . I was up for having an affair, but this didn't feel like an affair. . . . He told me I was blocked, that there were things I had to work out with my father and that maybe we could solve it on a non-verbal level if I would just trust him . . . and that I was going to have to trust him. So maybe he's bizarre and unattractive —I didn't feel too straight myself. . . . Oh, God. Then he got up, dropped his pants, said, "Take your pants down," or something really insensitive, unsensual, and he just got on top of me. He came, I didn't

CINDY: He'd interpret everything I said as "transference love" or sexual desire for him . . . but there was very little affection between us. . . . We started having a drink after the session was over . . . then one night he said he wanted to see what my place looked like. He got undressed all at the same time and we went to bed together—and it was a very strange thing, there was almost no tenderness or prelove play . . . and I remember thinking afterwards when I said, "That was great," or "That was very good"— some insane comment that I made, thinking that it wasn't really . . . then all of a sudden, "Excuse me, I have to make a train," because his wife

†† Women *are* conditioned to "suffer"—as long as it keeps them in a relationship to a man. The "suffering" matters less than the "relationship."
‡‡ This therapist systematically had "sex" with as many of his female patients as he could. He also "employed" them as baby sitters, secretaries, cooks, errand-runners, chauffeurs, etc.

come. And then I said, "I'd like to get on top of you." And then he told me that that was my problem, that I wanted to be in control. . . .

STEPHANIE: It took ten minutes. He jumped up, washed in the bathroom, and was back at his typewriter. I thought we'd talk till four in the morning . . . if anyone should know what he's doing a therapist does. If I don't have an orgasm here, then it's really my fault.

was sitting out in the Bronx with this kid. I'd never slept with a married man before. . . . It was probably the coldest affair I've had in my life.

JOYCE: He was always on top of me. And he said things to me, too. He'd say: "Cock. I want to put my cock in your cunt." And he wanted me to say that back to him. I couldn't handle it. . . . It was extremely stimulating. . . . I was being very whorey. . . . I was depraved and he was a beast, he grunted and groaned louder than any animal I had ever heard. . . . He asked, "Does the thought of having another couple watch stimulate you? Should I smack you on the behind?" He said he wouldn't hurt me, not in the face, but on the behind. I was beginning to get terrified. . . .

Victims make us uncomfortable. We grow uneasy, guilty, finally annoyed by the sight of them. Our pity turns to anger. Their suffering, their mutilation, which we fear so much ourselves, must somehow be their own doing. That beggar in rags is to blame for his misfortune: pass him by without a backward glance. "Naïve" women who are "taken advantage of"—how positively *Victorian* it all is: are there still shopgirls and serving-maids stupid enough to be seduced? Well, if they can't learn to protect themselves,* they, like Candy-Candide, deserve whatever they get. . . . But "shopgirls" still exist. With the exception of one woman, the earning capacity and educational level of these women was never more

* As "men" do? Or as women *try* to do by getting "married"?

than a fraction of that of their therapists.† Yes, these women like most women, *are* tremendously "naïve": their naïveté proclaims their "helplessness," which alone may earn them a Benefactor, a Savior, a Father.

As I noted in Chapter Four, these eleven women were the most overtly or superficially unambivalent about being "feminine." They were all conventionally and frantically "attractive"; they were all economically limited and intellectually insecure; they were both sexually fearful and sexually compulsive; they were paralyzed by real and feared loneliness and self-contempt; they all blamed themselves for any "mistreatment" by men; they all confused economic and selfhood needs with romantic "love"; and they were slow to express any anger. (Anger is a painful and dangerous display for those who feel and are relatively powerless.)

For example, at the beginning of one conversation with one of the "sophisticated" women, she described her therapist as a "really nice guy," and her experience with him as "her fault" and as "not really important." After about an hour (during which I was relatively silent), she described this period in her life as one in which she "went through the most severe pain." Surprised by this memory, she suddenly grew angry:

MARTHA: I was really very vulnerable and dependent upon him. . . . How could he so miscalculate the situation . . . and behave so selfishly? He was reinforcing my dependency needs without questioning them—or even satisfying them.

Very quickly though, she moved on to another topic: her intense dislike for her next therapist—who was a woman.

I was able to speak to two women who had "sex" with the

---

† At the time of sexual contact two of the women were students, two were secretaries, two were housewives, one was a waitress, one a recreational counselor, one a saleswoman, one a private secretary, and one a sociologist.

same therapist, and to a number of women who were all sexually propositioned by another therapist—all but one of whom refused him. I also spoke with several other of this same therapist's non-propositioned female and male patients. On the basis of these interviews, a certain composite portrait emerged.‡

Both men were involved in creating a primal patriarchal family-empire, consisting of one male guru (themselves) and many "wives" (female patients, legal wives, mistresses).** Both men used their female patients as secretaries, typists, baby sitters, sexual partners, errand-runners, plant-dusters, therapy "assistants," and all-round cheering squad. Both men kept very odd office hours, and even odder treatment hours. "Sessions" lasted from ten minutes to four hours, and no questioning of this arbitrary "spontaneity" was brooked—even from other patients who had to wait long beyond their scheduled appointment times. Both men were married. Both described their wives as "crazy," "hopeless," "dependent," and "too old." Both men were cold and/or inadequate sexual partners and lovers; both apparently had "sex" with as many of their female patients—simultaneously—as they could, often presenting it as either necessary for the "cure" or as a unique instance of "love."

Both of these therapists prescribed drugs for everyone for anything. Both were very authoritarian in directing and ordering their patients' lives: they *told* their patients whom to sleep with and when; what jobs to leave and what jobs to take; where to live

‡ One of these psychiatrists had an office on Central Park West, the other on the Upper East Side in New York City. The New York psychiatrists and psychologists discussed in this chapter are all highly "reputable" professionals in terms of legitimate medical or doctoral training, some sort of psychoanalytic or clinical training, well-established practices and office locations in expensive buildings on the Upper East side, the Upper West Side and Greenwich Village.
** We may note that while Freud certainly never had "sex" with his patients—and, reportedly, not too frequently with his legal wife, he was nevertheless polygamous: according to Roazen,[17] his wife and his wife's sister both lived with him and took care of his domestic and emotional needs; and his many female disciples served him as Dutiful Daughters.

and with whom. Both thundered at sexually reluctant female patients about how "unhealthy" their sexual "repression" was and how they'd "better start fucking a lot" if they wanted to get rid of their "hangups." Both therapists insisted that only they could "help" or "save" their patients—and warned their unhappy or rebellious female patients to leave only at their own risk. Both therapists were quite cruel to protestors or deserters. For example, one woman refused to sleep with one of these therapists—and told her husband, who was also in treatment with him, about the proposition. She also decided against continuing "treatment."

SANDRA: I decided, though, that I owe it to Mark [her husband] to go up with him and confront the group we're all in together. So I go up and there's Dr. X and his two assistants sitting there and I figure, well, the cards are stacked against me. . . . Dr. X says, "Well, well, tell us what happened." So I tell the story again and then he proceeds to tell the group how I was provocative to him, how I wore a miniskirt—which I always wear. . . . He made it look as if I were coming up there to seduce him, not to have a session. . . . Then he says I'm using this lie of a proposition to cop out of therapy. He reminded me that I didn't quit a job I once had just because my boss made a pass at me. . . . Then all of a sudden we're sitting there and he's starting to say things like: "Sandra, you know how dishonest you are, how dishonest you are with Mark, there are things you haven't told him" [he was referring to a brief affair she'd had], and I started crying, "I'm getting out of here," I mean it was like a kangaroo court . . . and when we left, Mark said to me, "What haven't you told me, what did you do?" He forgot all about what Dr. X did. . . . Everything got twisted.††

†† Another woman who refused her therapist's sexual advances told her group therapy mates about it. The therapist denied everything and told the group she was "crazy." This woman—and her boy friend—were also both involved in "consciousness-raising" groups. The woman's group sympathized with her outrage: the male group went together to confront the therapist and "beat him up." The woman told me this anecdote proudly, and couldn't understand my crestfallen expression (the men were still engaged in protecting "their" female territory; the women were still incapable of defending themselves). When she understood, we laughed and moaned in unison.

Both of these therapists exhibited another trait, one often found among certain "seductive" men over sixty,‡‡ and traditionally attributed to "schizophrenogenic" mothers: they said something —and denied they'd said it; they made sexual advances, and then, half teasingly, half testingly, but totally seriously, denied having made them.

JOYCE: And then I had a dream about going to bed with him. And he said, "Ah, transference at last"—in his accent. The week before he'd made me put my head on his lap just like I used·to do with my father when I had a bad headache, and he'd stroked my hair. It was very warm; I was a little girl and he was my father. Then his hand slipped. . . . The next session he helped me on with my coat, turned me around to him, and kissed me quite passionately. And I was quite shocked . . . and then I burst into tears. I'm melodramatic anyway, but I was really upset. Because I didn't know what to make of it. And I said, "Why did you do that?" It was a stupid question to ask, really, and he said, "What? Do what? What are you talking about?" And I said, "Kiss me." "I don't know what you mean," he said . . . he was really playing into my hangup. Because my parents would do that to me. Whenever my mother did something or said something and I said: "Why did you do that?" she'd go "What? I didn't do anything."

Clearly, none of these women were "helped" by their seductive therapists. They were neither helped into self-definition, self-esteem or independence, nor were they tenderly indulged or protected for their conditioned helplessness. I cannot *measure* how "hurt" they were by having sexual contact with their "soul-doctors." What I can do is introduce two of the women. Both are thirty-two and are self-supporting. Joyce has a twelve-year-old daughter but receives no child support. Stephanie is a secretary; Joyce teaches in a private school. Both women speak quietly and are quietly attractive. Both are currently in therapy. Both were in therapy for the first time when the sexual contact occurred. Both fell very much

‡‡ Who are both "guilty" and afraid of being rejected.

"in love" with their therapist and enjoyed the sexual contact (Joyce immediately and Stephanie after nine months). Both continued paying for "therapy" for some time after the sexual contact began. Stephanie's "affair" began after ten months of treatment and lasted for nearly a year. Joyce's "affair" began after more than a year of treatment and lasted for five months. Joyce first saw her therapist for three months in 1960, when she was twenty-one, and then again in 1963, when she was twenty-four. The therapist was in his late fifties at the time. Stephanie saw her therapist when she was thirty, in 1969. Both women saw the same therapist.

STEPHANIE:

I've always been isolated. . . . My older brother is an alcoholic and another brother killed himself. My sister who was so bright left school to get married and the dishes just piled up. . . . No, I never talk to my family. I left them years ago and finished high school on my own.

I started therapy because I was so depressed. I was sleeping a lot and

JOYCE:

My parents were always threatening to lock me up in a nuthouse—when my first boy friend told me he was marrying someone else I got really hysterical and went home crying and screaming like a nut. And my parents had this thing against crying. You're not allowed to cry. So they smacked my face and they were holding me down and they told me they'd call a nuthouse ambulance if I didn't shut up. . . . When I got rheumatic fever they said, no one's ever going to want me, I'll never get married and they went miles out of their way to buy medicine because God forbid somebody should find out.

I went to this doctor twice. First, after my boy friend got married. I gained a lot of weight. Life just had no meaning. . . . I used to see him [the therapist] for ten minutes at a time in the beginning. I thought it was peculiar but I never asked about it. He gave me lots of pills for my depression and weight, and insisted I take birth control pills even though I wasn't sleeping with anyone.

I always thought I was ugly, hideous, plain, plain Jane. I thought he must be crazy to flatter me so. . . . Sometimes he used to stand over my chair as I talked. . . . Once he chased me into a closet. After about three months he put his arm around me and kissed me on the head and said, "I love yóu and want to make you happy." I was grateful for that but I didn't believe him.

He always kissed me good-by after a session, but crudely, never affectionately. When I tried to tell him this, he got annoyed and said, "Try to pretend you like it." But I'd go

had to drop out of school and work because my parents wouldn't pay for it. . . . Then I stopped when I became pregnant and the man I was living with said, "It's a choice between your psychiatrist or me. If you want me to take care of you and the baby, you've got to stop seeing your psychiatrist." Which I did. He never would marry me though. . . . I went back for therapy when he left me about three years later.

The first time, when I was twenty-one, he said to me, "Do anything you want here in this office. It's not just speaking. If you want to do something, you can act it out. Any fantasy you can act out. Some women like to take their clothes off. Some women like to jump around. You can do anything. But I didn't feel like getting undressed and jumping around. When I went back to therapy I was working as a waitress and he [the therapist] asked me to be his secretary, but it never worked out.

After that first passionate kiss I was really upset. I told a close friend about it who had me talk to a psychiatric resident. "Are you sure this really happened?" he said. "Yes."

home and cry. . . . I hadn't slept with anyone for nearly three years when I started therapy. My marriage —well, he was the first man I ever slept with and it ended after six months. I was never sexually satisfied. . . .

"Well," he said, "many times, a doctor might give you a little peck on the cheek and you can blow it up in your mind to be something other than that." And I said, "No, I didn't," and he said, "All I can tell you is, work it out with your analyst." Funny, I talked to another young psychiatrist, who was a friend, about it. He said, "As a professional all I can tell you is stop seeing him." I should have listened to him but his answer left me kind of perplexed and I suppose I didn't really want to give up the relationship. So I finally went to bed with him.

He was always after me to lay on the couch and I didn't want to. When I finally did he would lay down next to me. I didn't want to sleep with him—I was very depressed after it happened. I remember thinking: Well, if I allow this then maybe he'll be more affectionate. . . . He jumped right up afterwards and went back to his typewriter. He didn't seem to notice that I was sad. That I hadn't had an orgasm. All he said was "You don't mind if I don't take you home—I've got so much work to do."

We would start a session and then all of a sudden I would find him lying on the couch next to me. . . . I was still paying for therapy and asked whether I should be, but very hesitantly. . . . We never really resolved it. . . . I know I needed him very, very badly. It was like he was God. . . . I guess I loved him.

If I didn't have an orgasm here it was my fault. He's an analyst and

I had orgasm after orgasm. Even though he came pretty fast. He should know what he's doing. Besides, I wasn't in a position to comment on anyone's love-making. I'd once gone to bed with a woman, you know . . . but I was very frustrated and alone and couldn't talk to him. . . . Once I screamed, a really anguished howl, and he pushed me away, got up, dressed, and said, "Don't you think you owe me an explanation . . . ?" He said: "There's nothing wrong with our relationship, it's a perfect doctor-patient relationship, a perfect working relationship, and a perfect relationship as lovers. . . ." He had me typing letters for him—the same form letter for hundreds of different people. He made at least a hundred dollars for each letter, and gave me three dollars for typing it.

When I got very distraught, I'd call him. He'd hang up on me a lot. . . . Once I took a fistful of sleeping pills. He said, "Oh, it's just your subconscious bothering you, don't pay attention to it" . . . and then he left his wife and moved into bachelor digs. The first time I went there I was absolutely mortified. He had what looked like sperm on his sheets, and there was a diaphragm in his bathroom. I asked him how could he be so thoughtless—and he said,

treated me like a whore, just like my fantasies, and I guess it worked —sexually. Psychologically it was tearing me apart.

I never called him except that one time he offered me the secretary job, but suddenly I was so depressed and upset and I wanted some help and I called him up, hysterical. "Please talk to me on the phone," and he said, "I can't talk to you now, I'll call you back." And he never called back. I went to his office and told him I wouldn't be a patient any more, that he'd been mean and cruel and that it's unhealthy. And he tried to talk me out

"How can you accuse me of sleeping with another woman, just because you see a woman's umbrella —even a woman's diaphragm—in my apartment?"

I would wait for him to call, and then he wouldn't. Once I waited home all weekend and when he called on Monday morning it was only to make sure I'd type his letters. . . . I couldn't work and I felt like I was cracking up. . . . He started to go away for weekends in the summer, after he'd promised to take me with him. . . . I stayed away as long as I could and then, when I went back, he said he didn't want to sleep with me any more but did want me to type a book for him. . . .

You know, once we were alone together, naked, in his office. The door was locked. The bell started ringing and ringing and wouldn't stop. It rang for nearly twenty minutes. He didn't answer it. I was curious and I looked out the window. I saw it was a girl standing there crying. "That's me next year," I said to myself.

of it. He said that he wasn't using me and that the psychology books I read were old-fashioned. Modern-thinking people believe the way he did. When he saw I was really going to leave, he said, "I'm warning you. Nobody will ever, ever be able to help you. I am the only doctor in the world who can help you."

The depression, the feelings, the fear got worse and worse. A fear mostly that I was losing my mind, that I was insane. . . . I was a whore because I could feel sexual. . . . The more upset I got, the more librium he gave me. "But I'm upset about us," I'd tell him. And then he stopped making love to me. I was hurt. I didn't want him to make love to me and yet I was terribly hurt that he didn't, because I thought maybe he doesn't want me any more. . . . He finally told me he thought it was too much for me, that I couldn't handle it.

A couple of months after I left him I went away for a holiday weekend in the country. I'm so used to doing everything for everybody. People would come into our house and I'd cook and clean for fifteen people, we'd put all of Larry's friends up [her daughter's father]. This weekend again, it was "everyone else go out to play and have a good time while

I do the dishes." I really didn't want to, but there I was doing them. I don't know how it was or why, but there was a safety razor above the sink. And I found myself on the floor, trying to cut my wrists. And I didn't make a mark. I was going tickle, tickle. Then I tried to cut my wrists with my father's razor and finally made it into the hospital. I called him [the therapist] and begged him to get me out of there. "I'm here maybe because of you." He said, "Yes, I'll get you into Creedmoor."

I couldn't get it out of my head. So finally I called him and asked for my money back—for all the "therapy." He explained to me that when a surgeon makes a mistake the patient still pays. And I told him had he been a surgeon I would certainly be dead, but he wasn't, and I'm not, and I'd please like my money back.

I saw him [the therapist] only once again. I thought I was pregnant and went to him for a shot, to bring on my period. He accused me of talking about him. (I'd told the girl who originally sent me to him about what happened.) Then I think I said, "I want my money back," and he said, "No." I said, "I'll blackmail you, I'll sue." And he said, "You can't, you can't prove anything. . . . You're crazy." . . . It's been five years now. Once in a while, when I've gotten very depressed, and very angry, I've picked up the phone and called him and hysterically screamed at him: "Why did you do that to me? You tried to kill me. Why? Why?"

For years I was a bookstore browser. One night in a Greenwich Village store I found myself standing next to a frizzy-haired woman, classic shopping bag in tow, talking to herself out loud. "Word salad," my professors would say. But it was wonderful to listen to: deep and golden and endless. At some point, I said something like "Amen" or "Right on," or whatever the equivalent was in 1963. Startled, she stared at me suspiciously. Where the hell did I get off taking her seriously when the world had already made it plain to her that her safety lay in being misunderstood and not noticed . . . and if I were a rival victim of visions, why didn't I just go back to my own flagpole and sit on it? She literally growled at me and walked off, taking up a lonely position at a bookstall at the far end of the store, where people resumed their pitying looks.

Lady-Sister: To you, wherever you are, I dedicate this chapter.

Chapter Six

PSYCHIATRICALLY
INSTITUTIONALIZED WOMEN

The case of Mae Neustadt, a 72 year old woman who was freed after 40 years in Matteawan State Hospital for the Criminally Insane, is back before the State Legislature. Mrs. Neustadt, who now lives alone in the Bronx, on welfare, was released nine years ago through the efforts of a lawyer who became convinced she was sane and unfairly detained. . . . Mrs. Neustadt's own three-page memo quietly summarizes the experience, noting years at Matteawan of walking "back and forth with a heavy iron polisher, polishing an already polished floor, and if I stopped for a few seconds to rest," she continued, "I was struck in the face by the attendant and told to keep polishing until I was told to stop."

New York *Times*
February 3, 1971

Suit by housewife against psychiatrist for treating plaintiff against her will while temporarily hospitalized in a private mental institution pursuant to a court order. Prior to the incidents herein, plaintiff and her husband had been having some marital difficulties. On December 6, 1963, defendant appeared at plaintiff's home and introduced himself as "Dr. Wolodzko." He had never met plaintiff or her husband, who had asked him to examine plaintiff. Plaintiff testified that the defendant doctor told her that he was there to ask about her husband's back. . . . On Demember 30, 1963, defendant and another doctor apparently at the request of plaintiff's husband, and without the authorization, knowledge or consent of plaintiff, signed a sworn statement certifying that they had examined her and found her to be mentally ill. The certificate was filed with the Court on January 3, 1964, and on the same date an order was entered for the temporary hospitalization of plaintiff until a sanity hearing could be held. The judge ordered her committed to Ardmore Acres, a private institution, pursuant to the applicable statutes.

Plaintiff was transported to the institution much against her will. The detailed facts are in dispute. However, it appears that two ambulance attendants in white jackets appeared at her home, when she was partly undressed, and in the presence of her children and the defendant, she was forcibly taken to the hospital. Her testimony is that she begged to call her relatives and an attorney; that she got to the phone which at the orders of the doctor was taken from her; that she was advised she would be taken in a strait jacket; that she agreed to go without the strait jacket. Defendant disputed some of these facts; and he could not recall some of the facts of her testimony. However, at the trial, he testified that he did make arrangements with her husband and the ambulance people outside the house; that he met them on a corner and told the husband that the ambulance should stay out of sight.

When she arrived at the hospital, she was kept from the telephone; her pleas to call relatives and an attorney were rejected on orders of defendant, three nurses forcibly injected medication. On one occasion, when she told her children to contact relatives, the doctor threatened she would never see the children again, if she tried that again. Finally, after nine days, she happened upon an unlocked phone and called her relatives in Texas. She was released by court order on January 27, 1964. It is undisputed that plaintiff repeatedly requested permission to call an attorney and that Dr. Wolodzko refused such permission.

The Mental Health Court Digest
February, 1972[1]

A widening wave of shocked horror is sweeping Britain following disclosures that two sane women were kept confined in a mental hospital for about 50 years each simply because they had borne illegitimate children. . . . The women's parents went to local government officials for help with their "wayward" daughters and, Sheridan said, "the local authority to whom the parents turned did not have a department to deal with unmarried mothers." . . . Miss Baker was 23 when committed to the hospital in 1921: Miss Kitson was 22 when committed in 1928.

New York *Post*, May 27, 1972.

During the 16th and 17th centuries a number of "private madhouses" had begun to spring up "especially in and around London." These houses were operated for a profit and accepted only those inmates whose families could afford the relatively high prices. Before long, evidence of abuses came to light. Wealthy husbands apparently viewed confinement in these unregulated madhouses as a comparatively inexpensive way of ridding themselves of bothersome wives. Daniel DeFoe began to call public attention to this as early as 1687. He exclaimed against the "vile practice now so much in vogue among the better sort, as they are called, but the worst sort, in fact, namely the sending their Wives to Mad-Houses at every Whim or Dislike, that they may be more secure and undisturb'd in their Debaucheries. . . ." DeFoe goes on to say that "This is the height of Barbarity and Injustice in a Christian Country, it is a clandestine Inquisition, nay worse. How many Ladies and Gentlewomen are hurried away to these houses, which ought to be suppressed, or at least subject to daily Examination, as hereafter shall be proposed?" He further says that "If they are not mad when they go into these cursed Houses, they are soon made so by the barbarous Usage they there suffer, and any Woman of Spirit who has the least love for her Husband, or Concern for her Family, cannot sit down tamely under a Confinement and Separation the most unaccountable and unreasonable. Is it not enough to make one mad to be suddenly clapp'd up, stripp'd, whipp'd, ill fed, and worse us'd?" He further says "All conveniences for Writing are denied, no Messenger to be had to carry a letter to any Relation or Friend; and if this tyrannical Inquisition be not sufficient to drive any Soul stark staring mad, though before they were never so much in their right Sense, I have no more to say. . . ."

Allan M. Dershowitz[2]

Most women who are psychiatrically hospitalized are not "mad." Rather than challenge the psychophysical vocabulary of the female condition, they adopt its tone more surely than ever. They are depressed, suicidal, frigid, anxious, paranoid, phobic, guilty, indecisive, inactive, and without hope. Only a few women can reject such traits entirely, or combine them with opposite-sex traits such as physical aggressiveness and sexual potency. Only a few women experience the meaning of Joan of Arc, the Virgin Mary, and the female Christ child; only a few women can cultivate their contact with the "psychic" world.

I spoke to twenty-four women who had been psychiatrically hospitalized at some time between 1950 and 1970. Twelve women clearly reported exhibiting opposite-sex traits such as anger, cursing, aggressiveness, sexual love of women, increased sexuality in general, and a refusal to perform domestic and emotional-compassionate services. Four of these twelve women also experienced "visions." The other twelve women reported a predominance of female-like traits such as depressions, suicidal attempts, fearfulness, and helplessness.

The women's present ages ranged from nineteen to sixty-five. As a group they had been hospitalized seventy times or an average of three times each. Their total hospital stays ranged from one week to nearly ten years. The number of times each woman was committed ranged from one to fifteen. Five of these women were hospitalized ten times for "depression"; ten were hospitalized fourteen times for "suicide attempts." At the time of their first commitment, five women were married, two were divorced, one was widowed, and sixteen were single. (Seventeen of the first commitments took place among women who were under thirty years of age.) Two of the women were black and one was Puerto Rican.

Each woman had been in private therapy for approximately* fifty months: forty-three months with male therapists and fourteen months with female therapists. Each woman saw approximately three different therapists, both before and after hospitalization.

Two of the women never completed high school, four completed high school, six had some college, seven received B.A. degrees, and five had completed some graduate school training. Eighteen of the twenty-four women were either only or oldest children.

Some of these women committed themselves voluntarily: their lives seemed hopeless, there was no alternative, and their parents or husbands insisted it would be "better" for them if they "cooperated" from the start. More often, these women were committed wholly against their will, through brutal physical force, trickery, or in a state of coma, following unsuccessful suicide attempts.

CARMEN: I was so sad [after my daughter's birth] and so tired. I couldn't take care of the house right any more. My husband told me a maid would be better than me, that I was crazy. . . . He took me to the hospital for what they called observation.

KATHRYN: After my husband left me and the baby, I was too depressed to do anything. I was a twenty-year-old mother, and back home dependent on my parents. . . . I didn't go to college because my mother didn't think I was smart enough. My father was very violent to me. . . . It was a shitty family and I escaped it by getting married. . . . So I came back home and said, "I'm home," and my mother said, "Like hell you are. You made your bed, lie in it." So I had to threaten that I'd kill myself to get some sympathy and my mother said, "Okay, if you're crazy you belong in a hospital. If you're depressed, go get some tests to find out

* "Approximately" means an exact "total average" for the entire group. This group of twenty-four women includes Third World women, lesbians, and women who had sexual relationships with their therapists. In other words, this is not the *unduplicated* comparison between the groups of women presented in Chapter Four.

why." . . . My father knew the director of this private loony bin and they all told me to sign myself in and be grateful.

RUTH: I was married about eight years when suddenly my husband seemed to be bored with me and the children. So he kept going to meetings every night. He had fun with the boys and became very popular. But I felt neglected. So I got angry. When I asked him why he couldn't stay home sometime with me and the children he just slammed the door and said I was sick and needed a doctor. Well, I believed him and went to someone he recommended. To make a long story short, this doctor didn't ask me my problem. All he did was give me a needle and put me to sleep. Then he kept giving me shock treatments . . . this caused me to sleep all the time. Consequently, my children missed my attention and my husband enjoyed his freedom and had no guilt. . . . This shock treatment went on for about six years. I was very subdued all the time and never objected to anything.

SOPHIE: My husband was a very difficult man, always losing his jobs because he fought with the boss. I had to leave one good job after another and follow him to his next job. . . . Then my husband found a girl friend—I didn't complain, marriage is not a bed of roses—and my multiple sclerosis symptoms started. My husband told me to get shock therapy, that my symptoms were in my head. Lucky we couldn't afford it privately . . . but he [my husband] brought a psychiatrist home and they both threatened me. If I didn't commit myself, they'd commit me and that would be worse for me. So I went into the hospital.

BARBARA: My mother had me put away when I was thirteen. She couldn't control me. My father had left us, she was drinking and crying all the time. I kept running away from bad foster homes, and so she finally commited me to an institution.

Washington (AP): An associate of consumer advocate Ralph Nader says doctors are receiving inadequate warnings that a potent "chemical strait jacket" for mental patients can cause symptoms of Parkinson's disease. . . . A Food and Drug Administration official agreed the drug (stellazine) is overused, particularly for the treatment of mild anxiety and primarily trivial complaints.

New York *Post*
April 30, 1971

The drug industry openly acknowledges the enslavement of women, as shown in an ad with a woman behind bars made up of brooms and mops. The caption reads: "You can't set her free but you can make her feel less anxious." Another one pictures a woman who, we are told, has an M.A. degree, but who now must be content with the PTA and housework. This, we are advised, contributes to her gynecological complaints, which should be treated with drugs.

Robert Seidenberg, M.D.
1971

All of the women received massive drug dosages (such as thorazine, chlorpromazine, stellazine, mellaril, and librium), and many received shock therapy and/or insulin coma therapy as a matter of routine, and often *before* they were psychiatrically "interviewed."

LAURA: The first thing they did was give everyone shock treatment. It didn't matter who you were. You walked in and they gave you shock three times a week. Before they decided what ward they were going to put you in, they shocked you completely. . . . I was scared to death. I thought I was going to die. . . . The only person who came to see me, and this is going to make you laugh a little bit, came to give me an I.Q. test.

Many of the women were physically beaten. Their requests for contact with the outside world were denied. Their letters were censored or not mailed. One woman's diary was partially destroyed.

Legitimate medical complaints generally went untreated: they were condemned or brushed aside as forms of "attention getting" or "revenge."†

BARBARA: I got beat up lots of times. Then I learned the ropes and they put me in charge of beating up the younger children if they got out of line. . . . They were beating up five- and six-year-olds. If I complained about it they'd do the same to me.

SOPHIE: I knew something was *physically* wrong with me. I was having trouble walking . . . but they didn't believe me. . . . I was limping and falling down and they were laughing at me. They [the attendants] kicked me, only because I asked for some good medication. Once they kicked me and threw me in a room, no bigger than a closet, to spend the night on the floor, without my clothes.

Those women remanded to state asylums were involved in sex-typed forced labor. They worked as unpaid domestics, laundresses, ward aides, cooks, and commissary saleswomen. If they refused these jobs they were considered "crazy" and "uncooperative" and punished with drugs, shock treatments, beatings, mockery, and longer hospital stays. If they accepted these jobs, and performed them *well*, the hospital staff was often reluctant to let them go.

SUSAN: I refused to peel potatoes in the kitchen. So they threw me in solitary for a few days.

CARMEN: I was proud to be the private housekeeper for Dr. X. I cleaned and cooked, baby-sat, shopped and even tutored her son in Spanish. . . . What I didn't like was having to wash their underwear. That I didn't like.

† It is ironic that a *mental* patient can successfully sue an asylum for physical injuries sustained during her incarceration, but not for *mental* injuries. Nor can she successfully sue for poor or non-existent medical attention.

1. "Demeter." Marble statue from the sanctuary of Demeter at Cnidos. Ca. 350-340 B.C.

2. "Pluto and Proserpina" by Bernini, 1621-22

Modern women are psychologically starved for nurturance and role-models, i.e., for female heroines and protective goddesses. It is significant that mothers and daughters have been minimized or totally excluded as primary figures in Judaeo-Christian mythology. Demeter and Persephone were the central figures of a mother-daughter religion—the Eleusinian mysteries—in ancient Greece. Demeter is the goddess of life, corn, or grain. Her daughter Persephone (Demeter's own virgin-self) is abducted and raped by Pluto, god of the underworld (or possibly by Zeus or Dionysus, either of whom, according to myth, may have been Persephone's father). In great sorrow and anger, Demeter refuses to let any crop grow until her daughter is returned to her. Finally, Persephone is allowed to remain with her mother for most of the year (spring, summer, and autumn), and with her husband during winter, when no crops can grow. While Demeter protects and "saves" her daughter, Persephone is still denied uniqueness and individuality. Both women still symbolize the sacrifices of self that biology and culture demand of women; both women represent a rape-incest-procreation model of sexuality.

Some women, in states of madness, identify with Joan of Arc, the not-so-legendary Maid of Orleans, and with the Catholic Madonna. These two figures are the modified Christian equivalents of the pagan goddess Demeter and her daughter Persephone. Joan is the only Persephone-maiden in modern history who is not raped or impregnated. She never becomes a "mother." She avoids the Demeter-mother and Persephone-daughter fate. She is our only remembrance of Amazonian culture. However, Joan is still ritually sacrificed as a source of male renewal— not through rape, pregnancy, and motherhood, but through her military victories for a male sovereign, and her subsequent political persecution—and canonization. Since Joan does not live in Amazon society, she is doomed to appeal to and lead a male, rather than a female, army.

3. "Joan of Arc and Judith" from the manuscript executed in Arras in 1451 by Martin leFranc—*Le Champion des Dames*

Unlike Demeter, the Catholic Mary has no daughter. Her only contact with divinity is through her "servicing" of men: be it the Holy Father or her own son. Catholic mythology, as shown in Fra Bartholommeo's painting, symbolizes the enforced splitting of woman into either mother or whore—both of whom nurture, worship, and ultimately mourn a dead man and/or a divine male infant. Like many women, Mary foregoes sexual pleasure, physical prowess, and economic and intellectual power in order to become a "mother." Sigmund Freud has said that: "A mother is only brought unlimited satisfaction by her relation to a son; that is altogether the most perfect, the most free from ambivalence of all human relationships."

4. "The Entombment" by Fra Bartolommeo

5. "The Annunciation" by D. G. Rossetti

6. "The Alba Madonna" by Raphael

Rossetti has painted a very young Mary—a somewhat terrified, trapped, and asexual girl, whose cross of sorrow, self-sacrifice, and service begins with the news of her forthcoming divine pregnancy. Unlike the pagan Demeter, Athena, or Diana, the Madonna is usually portrayed as physically undeveloped and maternally "beautiful"—as only a contented, gracious, and somewhat matronly mother can be to the male oedipal eye (as in Raphael's "The Alba Madonna"). Interestingly, the Madonna often grows younger as her son grows older until, in Michelangelo's sculpture of the Rome "Pietà," she is idealized as the eternal Virgin Mother, and looks young enough to be her son's bride. The Madonna is the primary role-model for women in our culture.

7. Insane Asylum: Crowded ward of the New York Lunatic Asylum, Blackwell's Island, 1868

Elizabeth Packard (Chapter One) was hospitalized by her husband against her will in 1860 in a private asylum that probably looked like this. Violent women, terrified women, suicidal women, women being driven mad by the hospital itself—all crowded together in a physically and psychologically humiliating setting. From 1960 to 1968, American women comprised 61 per cent of patients in private hospitals. Nelly Bly, an American journalist, admitted herself to the Blackwell Island asylum in 1887, in order to write an exposé, which appeared in the New York *World*. Periodically, exposés of mental asylums and criminal prisons have appeared in American newspapers, but neither institution (like the institution of the family upon which they're patterned) has disappeared or been substantially reformed.

8. France's oldest mental asylum, the Salpetrière, reserved special wards for old and indigent women, prostitutes, pregnant women, and young girls. In 1950, approximately 70,000 women over sixty-five, or 27 per cent of the total number of female patients, were hospitalized in American state and county asylums. (This does not tell us anything about the number of women in old-age homes.) By 1968, women over sixty-five comprised 36 per cent of all women in American state asylums—or 72,046 women compared to 48,094 men. While the total number of female and male patients in state asylums has steadily decreased (due to drug therapy, other facilities, and the increasing usage of old-age homes), the percentage of patients who are "old" women in state asylums has just as steadily increased. An "old" woman, even more than an "old" man, is a useless "thing," an object of scorn, mockery, pity, and neglect.

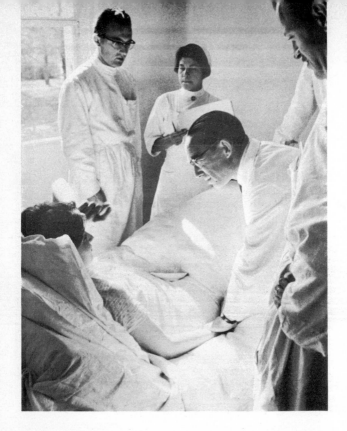

9. This photograph was taken in a mental hospital. The players in the drama are as old as the witchcraft trials: distant, condescending, potentially benevolent but all-powerful male Doctor-Inquisitors; a subservient female Nurse-Handmaiden; and a female Patient-Witch "possessed" by unhappiness, powerlessness, and dependence.

10. "Artemis and Iphigenia," reconstruction by Studniczka

Artemis, or Diana, the virgin huntress, is Apollo's twin sister. Unlike Athena or Aphrodite, her "mother" is not a man, but a woman. Artemis is always attended by sixty ocean nymphs and twenty river nymphs. According to one myth, Artemis rescues Iphigenia from being sacrificed by her father Agamemnon. Artemis is a Lesbian figure of Amazon origin. The only way her father, Zeus, can seduce her female lover Callisto is by assuming Artemis' form.

11. "The Conversation," sculptor unknown

These two women are strongly sensual, familiarly so, with each other, but not in a way that particularly appeals to male (or female) pornographic fantasies. They seem to be there *for each other*—and not as objects either to quell male fears of impotence or entrapment, or to excite male rape-lust.

12. In America, the world's "richest" country, more nonwhite
women of all ages die than do white women. The nonwhite
infant mortality and adolescent suicide rate is significantly
higher than comparable white rates. Many Third World women
must raise their children alone, either with tragically inadequate
welfare stipends, or with salaries that are significantly lower
than those of employed black Puerto Rican and white *males*.
Women's prisons in America house predominantly Third World
women.

13 and 14. In tropical Africa, although the birth rate is very high, the maternal death rate is alarming, and the infant death rate in certain regions is as high as 150–400 per 1000 live births. While most women in Africa have traditionally always worked strenuously in childbearing and rearing, in agriculture and/or commerce, they have not been political, military, or religious leaders as often as men have, nor has polyandry existed as often as polygamy. There have, however, been many female queens and warriors in Africa—as forgotten as their South American, Asian and European counterparts. Once European intervention occurred, the African woman's position was even further downgraded in comparison to her male counterpart: African men were forced and/or encouraged to participate in education, modern farming, land ownership, factory work, etc. Female warriors ceased to exist entirely. To date, most African revolutionary political leaders, militarists, judges, and priests are men, not women.

15. Athenian Red-figured Pottery, 450 B.C. (THE
METROPOLITAN MUSEUM OF ART. ROGERS FUND,
1907)

Most women are shocked and astounded by scenes of female
warriors, who are victorious in physical battles with men or,
for that matter, victorious against natural forces or political opponents. (Military or epic-romantic violence is both a real form
and a metaphor for other *definitive* actions.) In Greek art, vic-
tors traditionally move from left to right (or from "feminine"
to "masculine"). Here is a victorious, mounted Amazon, riding
right, about to spear a fallen Greek. The helmeted Greek is
about to spear another Amazon, who turns in her flight to defend herself with her ax, while her exceedingly graceful and
muscular companion raises her ax in both hands to assist her.
The Amazon on horseback is wearing boots with fur tops.

All the figures are red. The full battle scene, depicted on the
urn, is not shown in this photograph. It includes five other
Amazons, one driving a chariot and two others watching part
of the total battle between six Greeks and seven Amazons.

16. Athenian Red-figured Pottery, V-IV Century B.C. (THE METROPOLITAN MUSEUM OF ART. FLETCHER FUND, 1944)

A bearded Greek, wearing stockings and a helmet decorated with a dolphin (a symbol of the origin, divinity, and tragedy of the male child), is attacked by two Amazons. The saber-wielding Amazon cuts a joyful, almost transcendent figure. She wears shoes, long sleeves, and trousers under a belted tunic, and an oriental cap.

Amazon weapons depicted in Greek art include axes, sabers (swords), bows and arrows (usually of the Scythian variety), shields, and spears. Animals such as panthers, lions, and dogs are shown on Amazon shields. The Amazons sometimes wear greaves, Attic or Thracian helmets, and oriental caps (with or without mantles). Footwear includes boots, shoes, sandals, ankle straps—and bare feet. In some battle and many non-battle scenes, Amazons are shown wearing short tunics and jewelry. There is evidence that Amazon societies existed in Africa, in the Mediterranean and Aegean regions, near the Black Sea, and in South America.

17 and 18. "Wounded Amazon," Roman copy of Greek statue attributed to Polykleitos or Kresilas, 440-430 B.C. (THE METRO-POLITAN MUSEUM OF ART, GIFT OF JOHN D. ROCKEFELLER, JR., 1932)

This marble Roman copy of a Greek sculpture stands 6 feet 8¼ inches high. The Amazon is wearing a short belted chiton and an ankle strap. Her hair is short, parted, and combed back. She is said to be wounded in or above her right breast (the breast, or rather the lacteal gland, purportedly burned off in childhood in many Amazon tribes). This woman is intensely beautiful, rhythmical, and serene.

PRISCILLA: When I refused to mop up the ward and put the chronics' shit in the little coffee cans for them, they [the attendants] ganged up on me. They put a sheet over me, threw me down to the floor, and began punching and kicking me.

> Many patients were received and discharged, while I was there, who never had five minutes' conversation with the Doctors while in the Asylum. Often the new arrival would . . . inquire "When am I to have an examination?" I would reply "You never have an examination after you get here, for the Doctor receives you on the representation of those who want you should stay here."
>
> Elizabeth P. Ware Packard
> *Modern Persecution* (1873)

Only a few of these women received any psychotherapeutic attention. Therapy groups (and therapists) either interpreted their requests for information or release psychodynamically or counseled them to become more "feminine" and "cooperative."

LAURA: Fix yourself up, they told me. So every morning I got the hot sweats [insulin therapy] and every afternoon I spent in the beauty parlor with the other women. Of course, you had to pay for it. . . . You have to hide your feelings, pretend everything is wonderful, if you want to get out.

JOYCE: I had a doctor who kept interviewing me. He'd go over the same story over and over again. I remember I was looking terrible, my hair wasn't combed, I had no make-up. He said, "Why don't you fix yourself up? A nice girl like you!" And I said, "I never want another man to look at me again."

LAVERNE: I finally figured it out. You weren't supposed to be angry. Oh no. They lock you up, throw away the key, and you're supposed to smile at them, compliment the nurses, shuffle baby—so that's what I did to get out.

CAROLE: I really was aggressive. I knew my legal rights and I was fighting mad. . . . There I was in a human toilet bowl, a concentration camp, and I couldn't get out. They didn't like me and my college education.

Many of these women were sexually propositioned or molested while in mental asylums. However, freely chosen heterosexual and especially lesbian intercourse was discouraged and prohibited.

BARBARA: There was a girl who was raped by an attendant but the nurse went to speak to him and it was hushed up. A doctor tried to rape me during a gynecological examination and I was afraid to complain, afraid they'd say I was lying or crazy and give me shock treatments.

MARSHA: I was falling in love with a woman at the hospital—but that was considered "sick." They have these Saturday night dances you're supposed to go to, and you're not supposed to dance with another woman but only with a man. But you're not supposed to go to bed with him either.

After the story of Miss Doris Anderson, the black welfare lady from Baltimore, was printed . . . the phones began to ring and mail began to come in. The callers told of other sane, healthy people who fell afoul of bureaucratic psychiatry and were packed off to asylums against their will. Many of the callers stressed that this was not something which only happened to black women on welfare. They told of white middle class women having the same thing done to them. No case of this happening to a man was reported—they were all women, and in no instance did any of the victims file suit against their jailers. Some remained silent because they didn't know exactly how to fight back. Either they didn't have a lawyer and weren't quite sure of how to get one or they were intimidated, as though being taken away to the funny farm had caused them to doubt their own sanity.

Nicholas von Hoffman
Washington *Post*, February 4, 1970

It was for others' interest I plead—it was of others' wrongs and woes I complained. It was for them and their sakes I deliberately laid down my position as the Asylum favorite, and became henceforth the Asylum prisoner. From this time, for two years and eight months, was I made a close prisoner, and never after, with but one exception, allowed to step my foot outside the Asylum walls, and I fully believe it was the Doctor's purpose to make a maniac of me, by the skillful use of the Asylum tortures.

Elizabeth P. Ware Packard
Modern Persecution (1873)

Only two of the women had any awareness of their legal rights, and of course both were defeated in court battles and "punished" by further psychiatric incarceration. Only one of the twenty-four women considered her experience of "madness" as a positive event. Only one of the women did not consider herself as "crazy." Most of the women were humiliated, confused, fatalistic, naïve about their hospitalization and about the reasons for it. Most dealt with the brutality by (verbally) minimizing it and by blaming themselves. They were "sick"—weren't they?

LAURA: In the beginning, I wasn't shrewd at all. I was just so hurt. (Laughter.) I didn't know that they would punish me three times as much if

I tried to escape. . . . They put me in a strait jacket and this was rather cruel and kept me alone in this room for twenty-four hours. I could hardly move and I was completely stiff. They wouldn't even let me go to the bathroom. They put a bedpan under me and things like that. *But you have to understand that I was sick. I can't fake it and say I wasn't, you have to realize I was really ill.* [My italics.]

JOYCE: I remember there was this huge room. The day room. And all these people. Hundreds of people. Some of them were leaping around the room and doing all kinds of weird things. I was so terrified that I really began to cry. And my thoughts were, Oh, my God, this is it, I really am crazy now. Now I know I'm crazy because I'm here. . . . Then I said, "I'm schizophrenic, aren't I?" And he [the psychiatrist] said, "No, you're not schizophrenic, you're hysterical and neurotic!" And I wouldn't believe him. *I insisted that [schizophrenia] was my diagnosis.* [My italics.]

LUCY: Whenever I'd question something they'd done, criticize them, especially about how they treated some of the other patients, they'd yell at me and lock me in solitude. I'd get emotional and excited, *I'm sick like that* [my italics]. . . . They're not explicit about what's expected, but you find yourself locked up if you say too many things too loud that they don't like. . . . *I was sick, no question about it.*

Are these women "sick"? Are they more "sick and tired" than medically "sick"? Why do they think they're "sick"? Does their sickness really consist in accepting the sick role—a female prerogative in our culture? Are these women being punished for rejecting their sex-role stereotype—or for embracing it in too deadly a manner? Are they being punished for being *ambivalent* about their sex roles? Are their psychiatric hospitalizations merely accidental? In any event, how should they be "treated"?

Can any of these questions be answered to everyone's satisfaction? Would any of the answers be true for all the women? Many women described ambivalence toward their sex role during and/or preceding their hospitalization. Laura may speak for them. Throughout these selected parts of the interview I have italicized some examples of typical "masculine" and "feminine" feelings or behaviors that exist very actively, side by side, in Laura.‡

Fearfully, bravely, curiously, Laura came to talk with me one Sunday afternoon. "My mother told me to be careful," she said, "but Lois [a mutual friend] said it would be all right." At thirty-five, Laura "rents a room" from her mother, doesn't "go out" any more, reads voraciously, writes poetry, and sees a male psychiatrist three times a week. Although she has an M.A. degree, she works as a secretary. She is not a feminist. Laura was twice psychiatrically hospitalized and once married. She insists that she was "mentally ill."

LAURA: I can't get around it. I was really sick. I began to hallucinate, I really imagined that people were against me. . . .

PHYLLIS: Were they?

LAURA: No.** . . . You see, I didn't have enough money to make ends meet. I had finished graduate school and couldn't get a job, and I was writing. . . . I asked my mother for some money and she refused me because I was supposed to be grown up and supporting myself and, if I couldn't, I should get married. We had a terrible fight over this and she called the police. . . . I didn't realize they'd lock me up, I thought my mother was bluffing. . . . She called them *because of my terrible temper* —she's intelligent enough to sense that something was wrong. The police handcuffed me and took me to Kings County. They took everything away from me, my clothes, a ring, and gave me a sedative.

PHYLLIS: Did you see a psychiatrist?

---

‡ There are few places in our culture where women are actively *supported* for manifesting psychosexually androgynous or "male"-like behavior.

**PHYLLIS: How did you feel when your mother called the police?

LAURA: At the time, at the beginning, I felt she was against me and it was brutal. It *was* sort of brutal, what she did.

LAURA: Yes—my bad luck. He must have gotten the idea I was much worse than I really was *because I started crying, bawling:* everything was so horrible. This was the wrong thing to do. He took it as a sign of grave mental disturbance because I couldn't control myself. . . . *I was a trouble-maker. I tried to escape.* I didn't want to be locked up any more. But they caught me and sent me to Central Islip where they immediately gave me shock treatment three times a week. I thought I was going to die. Nobody interviewed me for a month. Only one person came to see me during the treatments—to give me an I.Q. test. I must have done very well because they transferred me to a "better building" for "special attention"—insulin therapy on top of the shock. . . . Mornings were taken up with insulin and by the time you got through you were dead. They gave you some sugar, eggnog, to revive you, but then you were sort of exhausted for the rest of the day anyway. In the evenings we'd play cards. . . . I was in a daze most of the time. . . . Before they let you go or before they let you think you're well, you have to know that you've been sick. And I *had* been sick.

PHYLLIS: How could they decide you were sick if no one talked to you very much?

LAURA: Well, I was getting accustomed to dealing with these people. . . . I did feel different really, like my youth had gone, disappeared in the interim. Not only that, but the shock is quite potent. You can't go through the shock and still have the same thoughts. It sort of interrupts your thoughts. You get new thoughts. . . . My parents had been divorced for many years. . . . The hospital was willing to let me out if someone would look after me.

PHYLLIS: Did you ever think of staying with your father?

LAURA: I can't. My father wouldn't have me. He doesn't want any children around. . . .

PHYLLIS: What about friends? Lovers?

LAURA: Well, no one had visited me. They all had their own lives . . . truthfully they weren't that concerned with me. I don't think my experiences were so unusual in that respect. They'd come over and sleep with you for a while and then they'd go back to their own lives . . . but I got a teaching job in another state and that's where I met my husband. *For some reason* or other he wanted to marry me—you know I can't analyze everybody's reasons. . . . So after a year I married him. . . . He was the first man that really ever wanted to marry me. . . . Love? Well, I don't know what that is: you may think I'm a very strange person. . . . Before he married me he asked me if I would support him while he got his doctorate. Like an idiot, I said yes. . . . So I worked, teaching, and he went to school and after about a year and a half of marriage I started imagining again.

PHYLLIS: Imagining what?

LAURA: This time I imagined he was having an affair and I imagined people were against me. I started that again. . . . He was spending most of his time away and when he was home he wanted a meal and sleep. We hardly ever made love. . . .

PHYLLIS: *Did you have any lovers?*

LAURA: Oh no. I started imagining and then I had these *temper fits* where I would start breaking things and screaming at him. . . . A couple of times he went off to sleep in a hotel. . . . I suggested that we see a marriage counselor because I was afraid the marriage was splitting up. . . . He went to a therapist and this time my husband put me in a hospital.

PHYLLIS: On his say-so alone?

LAURA: Yes. He came in with these muscle men and they tied me up with something and they hung up the phone—I was on the phone with my mother. . . . I got hysterical but they wouldn't let me talk to anybody, not even my therapist. My husband was just standing there. . . . He knew I was scared to death of shock treatment and hospitals. I'd told him about the first time, but he thought in a private hospital they'd treat you differently. . . . Last year I looked up my diagnosis in a medical textbook and it said I was incurable. I got very upset and took a cab up to see my therapist. I wanted to know if there was no hope for me.

PHYLLIS: Why do you think you have schizophrenia?

LAURA: Well, that's always been the diagnosis and the prognosis is supposed to be incredibly poor. . . . My therapist was very reassuring. . . . He's sometimes surprised that I'm not envious of married women, he expected me to be jealous of them all. . . .

I think that age, as well as "unfeminine" behavior, i.e., troublesome, needy behavior, contributes to the "accident" of female psychiatric hospitalization. Both Barbara and Carole attempted suicide, Barbara when she was thirteen and Carole when she was forty-five. Both were in hospitals because their families couldn't or wouldn't keep them, or because they didn't have families. Both had "fighting spirit": a trait not nurtured in families or in asylums.††

Carole is sixty-five years old. She lives alone in a New York City welfare hotel, lives alone behind a locked door in a small room that houses a trunk filled with legal briefs and news clippings, a forbidden double burner, and an eternity of traffic noise. She has spent ten years in New York mental asylums. Her smile is dazzling, her energy mysteriously sourced. By profession she is an actress. And, though properly brought up, and even more properly heterosexual, she never did marry.

CAROLE: From my childhood I wanted to be an actress. And the family, from the time I was sixteen, kept getting me engaged. I gave back eight rings, beautiful, big rings. . . . *I didn't want to get just married,* y'know what I mean, go in for bridge and mahjong, it wasn't for me. They did everything they could to block me . . . and they started this engagement business. I can't remember how many wealthy boys they "arranged" for me, but the rings always went back after two or three months. . . . My family was very strict with me, and very disappointed in me. They wouldn't allow me to spend a night at a girl friend's house if she had a brother. What if someone had raped their precious piece of junk? . . . Once when I came home a little late the whole house was lit up—what a scene! You're young, such scenes must have gone out before your time.

PHYLLIS: No, I had them too.

CAROLE: Well, they sent me to a friend who was a psychiatrist.

†† I am also taking the liberty of italicizing the very typically "feminine" and "masculine" behaviors that exist, side by side, very actively, in these two women.

Psychiatry isn't learned out of textbooks. When a psychiatrist treats somebody he uses his common sense and his heart to get to the trouble. . . . I liked him. . . . Not all psychiatrists are like the rats in Bellevue. He had more books than I'd ever seen in one house. . . . Finally he called my parents in and said, "I don't want her to go to Hollywood. She's not up to that rat race out there. They'll take her like Grant took Richmond. . . . I'll tell you what I want to do. I want her to go to medical school." My mother started laughing. She said, "You want *her* to be a doctor? *She couldn't even stand to see a baby diapered*. . . ." Well, by the time I was twenty-five they were tearing their hair out. "You're an old maid, you've got a bad reputation, what's gonna become of you?" *So I had to cut myself off completely*: Hollywood, here I come. . . .

PHYLLIS: How did you get into a mental asylum?

CAROLE: Well, Hollywood didn't "take" me completely. It was rough but I was able to save some money . . . but everyone told me, "Go to New York, get yourself even a small part on the stage and they'll, y'know, they'll grab you back." . . . So I came to New York. . . . *Then I met him at an audition—a pudgy guy with sort of a good father's face*. He said he wanted to manage me. I was a "valuable piece of property." I admit I was leery of it, I mean, there was always sex strings attached out in Hollywood with anything. . . . As it turned out he was leading up to the sex thing. . . . He became my business manager, got me parts. I turned checks over to him and he said, "I'll give you just what you need. . . ." Then suddenly he's through! "Well, give me back the money you've been holding—" Nothing! Finally, I was so desperate I went over to his office. He grabbed my shoulder and beat me with his great big burly fist on my head and yelled, "Throw her out! . . . Throw her out! Call the cops." . . . *I was so ashamed*.

PHYLLIS: Did you ever sleep with him?

CAROLE: About four or five times. I was so ashamed that I was standing there calling "All right, call the cops, let everyone know. . . ." He ran around like a maniac. . . . "I wasn't a whore when I came in here looking for a job and its non-existent pay," I yelled back at him. *I was reading scripts for him too, for nothing*. "But you are one, you are one," he yelled, with his fist up in the air. "Yes, it took a dirty, filthy, slimy thing like you to make one out of me." I ran out. . . . I just lay crying at home for days. . . . Some friends wanted to go over and beat him up. *I said no—I was too ashamed.* I was behind in my rent, I was physically run down, I just couldn't handle things. I went to the Diplomat Hotel and paid for two days in advance. I told them, "I'm very tired, I don't want to receive any telephone calls," and I hung up the "Don't Disturb" sign on the door and took phenobarbital and seconal. It was five twenty-five when I last saw the clock and went off to sleep. . . . I woke up five days later in Bellevue at night. They were hurling questions at me. "Why did you do it? Do you know where you are?" I hurt so badly. I couldn't walk, my vision was blurred. . . .

Carole was medically injured and medically neglected. At her commitment hearing—she had insisted upon one—the judge asked whether "there was anyone to take care" of her.

CAROLE: I said no. I didn't want my aunts or my mother to know anything like this. And he says, "Well, you'll need some more treatment." And this bastard [a psychiatrist] gets up and says, 'Well, in any state hospital she can get medical treatment." . . . They'd hung this label of involutional psychosis and schizoid personality on me. . . . I could barely walk . . . *but was I aggressive, was I uncooperative!* That's the big one, if you're uncooperative, you're crazy. I knew I wouldn't get medical treatment in a state looney bin so *I asked the judge to have me killed if he wouldn't free me.* Well, that did it. I begged the judge, "Don't do this," but he sent me to the state asylum.

Barbara is nineteen and by conventional standards, very beautiful. She dresses in high-hippie fashion: a slender, human mobile of leather, suede, brass, and silver. She is newly a mother and couldn't talk for very long the first time we met: her husband wanted her back home as soon as possible. She chain-smoked and drank coffee and blew jokes at me like soap bubbles. Then she got very serious.

PHYLLIS: Why were you put into the hospital?

BARBARA: Because *I tried to kill myself*. . . . There was too much pressure on me [she was thirteen at the time]. My father deserted us and I think my mother loved us but she had too many problems. She couldn't function. . . . She put me in foster homes and my father would come to visit and tell me she didn't love me and I'd end up crying. . . . I had foster fathers and all these weird foster parents that wouldn't feed you. . . . I couldn't believe what was actually happening to me. When I got older and went to Catholic school, I was weird by that time. I wasn't a normal happy child and I used to get beat up by this nun who heard that my mother was spreading bad stories about her and I didn't have any friends and I was alone. My mother drank and tried to kill herself every once in a while. I gave my mother a very hard time. *I stayed out till four or five in the morning* when I was thirteen. . . . I finally got shipped to Creedmoor to the children's ward.

PHYLLIS: How long were you there?

BARBARA: About five or six months, and then there was a head nurse, who, if the girls gave her too much of a hard time, would see that something was done about it. Some of her privileges would be taken away or she would be beat up. I had personal experience—to have the head nurse disapprove is a very bad thing in these hospitals. I had gotten beat up a few times myself. One girl had taken my mascara and she said she lost it so the head nurse said, "Are you going to let her get away with it?" We played a punch game where one girl got punched on the arm. We had to hold her and punch her on the arm—really sick things. The attendants were more messed up than the patients were.

I escaped from Creedmoor twice . . . a detective found me. I was staying with some people I knew from the hospital and her (*my girl friend's*) *uncle tried to rape me and I broke his finger. Then I called up the head nurse at Creedmoor and asked to come back*. This time I didn't have any trouble with the doctor or the head nurse or the social worker. I got along fine. I didn't mess up the ward.

PHYLLIS: Did you go to school while you were there?

BARBARA: From ten to twelve in the morning. It was called junior scholastic—it was real bad. . . . They told me not to make things rough—to cooperate, etc., or else I'd have a hard time. I was standing in line getting toothbrushes or something and they gave me a big cup of liquid thorazine to drink plus some other thing and I passed out. I didn't know what it was at the time. I found out later that you could have momentary blackouts from too much thorazine. . . . I woke up in bed and went to the nurse to ask her for something to make me feel better and she said, "You better get back to bed or I'm going to stick a needle up your ass."

These chronically ill women—they used to lock them up in the bathroom. They'd never get their clothes changed. They used to urinate all over them. When the visitors came they would give them a bath and tell them that "she's doing just fine." I went down and told the supervisor that they were giving me more medication than they should and she told me that if I open my mouth one more time she would shut it for good. It was just horrible. We cleaned the wards for two weeks before an official inspection. . . .

They'd put the patients in seclusion without a bedpan or anything and then they wanted us to clean it up and I wasn't going to do it. They wanted me to put the diarrhea in a coffee can. If you are not really flipped out, it's very hard to stay and some had to stay for very long periods of time as no one really wants them.

I got involved with a girl there—sexually involved—when I was seventeen and there was nothing they could do about it. There was no kind of counseling, which I needed, and which this girl needed. . . . They took this girl and asked if I ever had an orgasm with her and she said yes, which I did. It was a very sick relationship and not normal and when I was seventeen I couldn't figure out whether or not I was still gay. There was nobody I could talk to about it. . . .

When I told my English teacher all the things that happened at Creedmoor, she didn't believe it. She thought I was lying when I told her about being beaten up and giving me all those drugs to put me into a state of helplessness. People are afraid of any people who are different from them. I didn't need to be at Creedmoor if there was someplace else for me to go to.

Not counting my mother, my first lesbian experience took place when I was eight years old. After school, Ann would come over to my house and weave magic tales of what some *boys* had done to her the previous night. I asked many questions and so Ann would show me, kiss by kiss, caress by caress, what had actually happened. Of course, we both "graduated" to boys and had to put away our "childhood games." . . .

Two years ago I met Ann, working as a bank teller. She was very pregnant and quickly told me all about her husband, her husband's job, her husband's down payment on a ranch house, and her husband's plans for a summer vacation. "Hey, Annie," I wanted to say, "do you remember those great kisses?" But I didn't. I remained silent.

I dedicate this chapter to the breaking of that silence between women.

Chapter Seven

LESBIANS

The repudiation of the mother by every female, as the culture demands her capitulation to the male, must surely be the cruelest sacrifice in the catalogue of compromise which constitutes a civilization at war with itself in the repression of its own instinctual freedoms. . . . The culture is a caricature of biological differences. Our first (and last) outpost of resistance to psychic integration—the maintenance of the illusion of two separate and distinct sexes in their grossly caricatured family-political manifestations. Plastic Lady and Palooka Man are the two sexes polarized at their distorted extremes to protect their own disease. The rest of us participate in the disease by going down with the ship in resignation or protest or subversion down under the hold. That's where the lesbians and homosexuals have been hanging out all these centuries. In the subterranean passages of the mind. . . . All women are lesbians except those who don't know it . . . until women see in each the possibility of a primal commitment which includes sexual love they will be denying themselves the love and value they readily accord to men thus affirming their second class status.

Jill Johnston[1]

The love of women for their own sex was equivalent to . . .
orphic [homosexuality]. Here again the sole purpose was to transcend the lower sensuality, to make physical beauty into a puri-
fied psychic beauty. [In] Sappho's strivings to elevate her sex . . .
she was concerned not with one alone; Eros drove her to them
all. . . . Wherever she found physical beauty, Eros impelled her
to create spiritual beauty as well. . . . In the presence of this
idea she came to look with indifference on everything she had
valued as a young girl, wealth, jewels, the ornaments of outward
sweet existence.

J. H. Bachofen[2]

When a couple is new to swinging and the woman has
never been exposed to another woman, she usually says that
she would find this repulsive and cannot imagine it. After the
first two or three parties where she sees women obviously enjoying each other, she is likely to modify her stand and say,
"I do enjoy having a woman work on me, but I could never
be active with another woman." Then, when she has been in

> swinging for several months and attended many parties, she
> may well say, "I enjoy everything and anything with a woman,
> either way she wants to go." . . . at large open parties we
> observed that almost all the women were engaged in homo-
> sexual activity with obvious satisfaction, especially if a younger
> group was involved.
>
> Gilbert D. Bartell[3]

Most psychoanalytic theorists either sincerely misunderstand
or severely condemn lesbianism. Some do both. The "condition,"
they say, is biologically and/or hormonally based. No, say others, it
is really an environmental phenomenon. In any event, all agree,
it is maladaptive, regressive, and infantile: even if it isn't, it leads
to undeniable suffering, and is *therefore* maladaptive, regressive,
etc.*

More moderate voices suggest that lesbianism is not infantile,
just limited. We are all bisexual by nature, they say, and conditioning (society, the patriarchal family) cripples and restricts both
women and men to heterosexuality. Bolder voices disagree. Women
are *naturally* more bisexual as well as more sensual than men. From
a physiological point of view, women are better sexual and emotional love partners for each other than father-men can be to them.
Still bolder voices reject the supposedly "advanced" view of our
bisexuality: no, they say, *in our culture*, bisexuality for women
is limited, is a frantic compromise, is a blatant and cowardly "cop-
out." Dr. Charlotte Wolff, in her book, *Love Between Women*,[4]
inadvertently and only partially explains this last view in the following way:

* Psychoanalysts are generally no different from most people in their
valuing of "pleasure" rather than "pain," and in their definitions of what constitutes each experience.

The lesbian's yearning for her mother's love is always put in jeopardy through the existence of a male . . . one wonders why [lesbians] are so much resented by men and women. Because of the pride and vanity of the male, only few men would consider lesbians to be serious rivals. Men's dislike of them goes back to a fundamental psychological cause: The need for the mother in a woman. The male wants to be "fed" by the female. He needs ego support throughout his life. A lesbian who "feeds" (loves) another woman puts him and his world into chaos; she is a rival because she takes away maternal support which should be HIS not HERS.

Women who "feed" both men and women cannot successfully "feed" the long-starving (and often swollen-bellied) women in patriarchal society. From a psychological point of view, it is only women who can "make up" to each other for their lack of mothering. At this moment in history, only women can (if they will) support the entry or re-entry of women into the human race. In order for most women to overthrow their "feminine" conditioning, women must receive the kind of emotional, sexual, economic, and intellectual support from others—both older and younger than themselves—that men do.†

Many researcher-clinicians have confused, or equated, lesbianism with male homosexuality. Many researchers have also studied and "sympathized" more with the latter than with the former group of "patients."‡ Of course, since *whatever* men do is con-

---

† I am not suggesting that either the means or goals of feminism will necessarily be accomplished by women "becoming" lesbians or by women following the life styles or indicates of pre-feminist lesbians.

‡ Most have not "sympathized" at all, Merle Miller "came out" in the New York *Times* in 1971. Some of the letters he received from psychiatrists had the following advice! "While I sympathize with Mr. Miller's failure to be cured of the disease . . . [and feel] that homosexuals have the same civil rights as anyone else, they also have the right to try and get treatment for their 'illness.'" Another psychiatrist offered to "counsel" Miller "free of charge because it is clear from your tone that you are in desperate, even frantic need of help."

sidered more important than *anything* that women do, male homosexuality has certainly been more overtly punished, socially, legally,
and economically, than lesbianism has. Probably the fear of male
physical force, coupled with male sexual aggressiveness, is an important factor here. Male homosexuals are perceived as potentially
combining these two forms of force—and using them against other,
perhaps weaker or younger *men*. This threat is an intolerable one
to men, who psychologically must retain the initiative of force
or action, in order to be "men." This same threat is, however, a
daily fact of life for most women. Heterosexual men threaten all
women, especially young girls, with a combination of greater physical and "sexual" force—but they are neither feared nor punished
by our culture for this. The very same behavior has a totally different meaning as a function of whether it is performed by men or
women, and as a function of who the recipient of that action is.

Male homosexuality is often perceived, even through tears, as
having a more "glorious" tradition and a more legitimate or valued
meaning than lesbianism. Historically, for example, many male
homosexuals have waged "heroic" wars together, have headed
governments, churches, and industries, and created artistic and intellectual masterpieces. Some people think that male homosexuals
are the keepers of Western culture: in a sense, they are quite right—
but my feeling about what this *means* is probably different from
theirs.**

Male homosexuals are sometimes seen as embodying a culturally *valued* concern for beauty, love, violence, and death. Like
Thomas Mann's hero in *Death in Venice,* male homosexuals are
seen as martyrs to a cause that is both more spiritual and sexual
than is the cause of biological reproduction. The love of men for
men has been seen as more real and more elevating than those sorry

** It means, among other things, that our culture is anti-female, and
pro-war.

domestic events that involve women and one's own children. Platonic "spiritualism," and everything it implies (from sex without "love" and love without sex—to modern science), is a basic value of Western culture.

Lesbians do not have a gloriously extensive ancestry. Their mothers and grandmothers, like those of heterosexual women, lived with men and did not control the means of production. Lesbians are women: as such, most are traditionally more domestic, conventional, and sexually monogamous than male homosexuals are— traits to which women are condemned, but for which they are not really valued.††

Lesbianism has not been as legally punished as homosexuality. However, it has been "punished" by *being completely legislated out of the realm of possibility for most women*. There are probably more male homosexuals than there are lesbians.[5] Women are more totally repressed, both sexually and economically, and are therefore more sexually timid (with either women or men), as well as more economically powerless than are either homosexual or heterosexual men. In one sense, it is more difficult for women to become and survive as lesbians than it is for men to survive as homosexuals. For example, men either don't need or don't *think* they need women for economic survival. Most women both *need* and *think* they need men in order to survive economically, as well as "psychologically."‡‡ Women have no institutionalized sisterhood that both men and women really respect. Female sisterhoods are involved with functions of self based on heterosexual relationships and/or motherhood. Even women in certain religious orders are "brides" to a male Christ—and housekeepers to the local governing male prelate.

†† Sex gender is, I believe, a more basic predictor of behavior than is race, class, or sexual *preference*.
‡‡ Many married fathers are active homosexuals.

> There is no law against the placement of a child with Lesbians but, in divorce cases there are generalities about the moral atmosphere in the "home." "Most judges would not place a child in a house shared by Lesbians," according to Carl Zuckerman, lawyer for the Community Service Society, "but if there were no better alternatives, the child would be placed with a homosexual parent."
>
> New York *Times*
> November 17, 1969

Women are more conditioned to want and need motherhood than men are conditioned to want or need fatherhood. Traditionally, a "bachelor" life is not viewed as tragically as motherless "spinsterhood" is—and often isn't as tragic in terms of mobility, alternatives, etc., within a given class or race.

In a sense, it is theoretically easier for women to love women than it is for men to love men.* Our mothers were women and, Michelangelo aside, most object-models of sexual or aesthetic beauty in our culture are female. Also, most women know how to be *tender* (not that they always are) with other people. Traditionally, most men, whether they are homosexual or heterosexual, know only seduction, rape, and pillage—in bed and on the battlefield.

The God-of-War ideal of masculinity is so overpowering that few men dare take off their helmets and armor—*especially with other men*. They probably do so more readily with women, because it is "safe," a fact no doubt as painful to male homosexuals[6] as

---

* It is true that the so-called "masculinization" of women is more accepted than the "feminization" of men. (All things female are despised.) It is easier for women to wear pants and work at jobs outside the home than it is for men to wear dresses and high heels and to stay at home in the kitchen. Yet I wonder: why would anyone willingly offer up their feet for binding? And if they do, isn't it to better attract, support, and worship men?

the fact of heterosexual women "feeding" men and starving women is to lesbians. I suppose that twentieth-century lesbians and homosexuals "suffer" from a similar dream, imprinted by at least three centuries of patriarchal family life: namely, the dream of bourgeois domesticity, approved public coupling, a homecoming— a dream whose reality is denied to both lesbians and homosexuals.

Two recent studies[7] have compared lesbians with male homosexuals, and lesbians with heterosexual women. They found that both lesbians and heterosexual women sought psychotherapy with equal frequency (a female institution); and that both groups of women were as frequently depressed (a female "disorder"). However, the lesbians attempted suicide, drank alcohol, and dropped out of college more often than did the heterosexual women.

The lesbians sought psychotherapy more often than did the male homosexuals, and were seen as having a "significantly higher prevalence of 'psychiatric disorders.'" Their female conditioning was still being viewed, by themselves and by professionals, according to a male standard of mental health. Lesbians also attempted suicide and used drugs more often than did male homosexuals. *No* lesbian engaged in "promiscuous" sadomasochistic sexual practices; a small percentage of male homosexuals did.

Only a minority of lesbians are sexually "aggressive," non-monogamous, anti-romantic, or verbally or actually involved in large-scale sexual orgies of the Roman steam bath school. This is understandable since such psychological stances and practices characterize both *male* homosexuality and *male* heterosexuality. With all due respect for the absolute and immediate guarantee of sexual freedom for all people, and with a respect doubly necessary because I am not a male homosexual, I must suggest that male homosexuality, *in patriarchal society,* is a basic and extreme expression of phallus worship, misogyny, and the colonization of certain female and/or "feminine" functions. Male homosexuals, like male hetero-

sexuals (and like heterosexual women), prefer men to women.†
It is as simple as that. In a sense, most male homosexuals are
"kinder" and more honest with women than are male heterosexuals
(a fact for which they are duly punished). Unlike heterosexuals,
most male homosexuals do not seduce, make promises to, or marry
those whom they fear, dislike, are jealous of, or have contempt
for—i.e., women. Of course, the greater capacity for real friendship
and respect that some male homosexuals have for some women
is a valuable and often unique experience for the women. However,
it is still purchased at the expense of female sexuality. Women can
be accepted by men—be they homosexual men or heterosexual
men—as *either* "brains" or "cunt," as *either* "heart" or "cunt," as
either "mother" or "cunt." Women are rarely accepted as emotional, intellectual, and sexual beings. Small wonder that women
find it hard to develop all three capacities; with whom would
they share them? Lesbians, particularly feminist lesbians who are
trying to subdue their self-contempt, sexual timidity, and heterosexually modeled role-playing, feel that at this point in history only
women can be midwife, mother, sister, daughter, and lover to the
woman as *human being*.

The only theory I have read about lesbianism by a psychiatrist
that begins to make sense to me (or, to be honest, that agrees with
some of what I already thought and wrote) is Charlotte Wolff's
presentation in *Love Between Women*. Dr. Wolff proposes "emotional incest with the mother" as the essence of lesbianism. She
locates certain aspects of lesbian psychology in history and mythology:

> The similarity between [the lesbian's] virility and freedom from
> the fetters of being an object of the male makes the homosexual

† I think that more lesbians have experienced (or have wanted to experience) sexual relationships with men, often pleasurably, and often within
a legal marriage, than male homosexuals have experienced or wanted to experience sexual relationships with women.

woman resemble the image of women in matriarchal times. . . . The wide range of activities, the undoubted capacity to manage her life without dependence on men, is the ideal of the homosexual woman. Female homosexuality is inseparable from the very qualities which were the prerogative of women in early history. It is of no consequence to these conclusions whether the matriarchate existed as a definite period of history, which I believe it did, or in mythology only. Mythology is history, transcending concrete data and revealing their true meaning.

Dr. Wolff suggests that "love" flourishes within a context of "sameness and harmony" and is impossible in an "alien" context:

The alien object may arouse admiration, excitement and even adoration, but it cannot inspire love. The girl who succeeds in getting the better of her father (and the male in general), without recourse to feminine tricks, may be full of satisfaction and triumph, but she will have learned little about the realities of love in the process.

Thus Wolff is very sensitive to the "feminine" heterosexual woman's isolation and nurturance deprivation:

The love a man can give her is found to fall short in essentials, which only a mother can provide. It is she herself who has to supply these. She has to become what she could not possess—the mother—in her relationship with the male.

Wolff views the "unhappiness" of lesbians in terms of specific social ostracism, general female oppression, and lesbian ambitiousness. Lesbians are more emotionally demanding of each other than heterosexual women are of men.

Women are conditioned to put up with a lot more from a man, and they will, because he is the provider and the father of the children. Women demand from each other love, kindness, tolerance, understanding, sex—the lot. And if they don't think they are getting it, it's easy enough to get out.

I have no more basic a theory to offer.

THE INTERVIEWS

I interviewed nine white lesbians and two black lesbians. Two women (one black, the other white) had no experience with therapy or psychiatric hospitalization. Six of the women had been hospitalized when they were approximately‡ twenty-one years old, for approximately three hundred and twenty days. Nine of the women had been in private therapy for approximately forty-four months—thirty-nine months with male therapists and twenty-one months with female therapists.

Their present ages ranged from seventeen to forty-four; the ages at which they "became" lesbians, psychologically and/or sexually, ranged from nine to twenty-four. One woman never finished high school, four had some college experience, five completed college, and one had completed some graduate school. Some of these women were sexually "frigid" with women: most were not. At least half had sexual relationships with men.

While the majority of the women did not seem to be involved in heterosexually based role-playing, and were neither very "feminine" nor very "masculine" in dress, body carriage, or mannerisms, most were as "romantic" and monogamous as heterosexual women. Only two women, one aged seventeen, the other aged thirty-seven, were emphatically, and ecstatically, non-monogamous (at least in their verbal presentations of self). The seventeen-year-old came trooping into my house with four women from her "living-collective." Their laughter was infectious; they wore headbands and

‡ "Approximately" means a "total average" for the entire group.

grease paint, carried frisbees and yo-yos, and told me, laughingly, that they all "made it" with one another.

Five of the six lesbians who were hospitalized had in varying ways, and at varying times, become feminists. By 1971, when these interviews took place, eight of the eleven lesbians had become feminists.

Without exception, every lesbian in private therapy was treated as "sick."**

LOIS: One female therapist got scared when I became "gay." "I can't treat homosexuals. There's nothing you can do with them." She made it sound like terminal cancer. . . . One male therapist kept insisting I wasn't gay, but he told me it's something I'll outgrow. . . . He told me I'd end up alone and bitter in the gay scene, and *that* didn't appeal to me. It still doesn't. . . . Another woman therapist said, "But men are so marvelous to sleep with! Lesbianism isn't necessary, it's absurd!"

In a sense, being psychiatrically hospitalized helped me. I'd hit bottom. Now I could be a lesbian, that's not as bad as a crazy. . . .

CAROLE: I became infatuated with my first therapist, who was a woman. She told me that lesbianism is a sickness. She also told me that I

MARSHA: I've been trying to kill myself since I've been twelve—gas, pills. . . . I was walking around with a load of anger that I had no place to put. . . . I wound up in Bellevue and was sent to a private hospital where I saw a psychiatrist who was shocked by my homosexuality. . . . After I left Bellevue I saw him for a couple of months, privately. He called my mother in for an interview (he said he thought he would get a better understanding of me if he met her). In the course of that interview he told my mother that I was a lesbian and suggested that I be weaned away from this woman (my lover). My mother blew her stack. She called this woman's parents and family, and told them how their sister was destroying her daughter, etc. The upshot of that was that I had been staying at my mother's house

** One woman told her mother about lesbian play with a girl friend, when they were both ten years old. Her mother took her to a psychiatrist who administered shock therapy as a form of treatment.

wasn't a lesbian. . . . I stopped eating and I was down to ninety pounds. I looked like a little boy with long hair. The therapist there, a man, also kept insisting I wasn't a lesbian, that everyone had these feelings, and I should push them out of the way.

PHYLLIS: Did you ever ask, "Well, what would be wrong if I were?"

CAROLE: No, I only knew that from the general feeling on the ward, that it was wrong and that I'm not a lesbian. . . . The therapist felt that the feelings I had for women were basically anti-male feelings instead of pro-woman feelings.

for a few weeks after getting out of the hospital. I moved out and I didn't speak to my mother for two years.

Then I saw a woman psychiatrist for a year. She kept encouraging me to relate to men. I couldn't handle things any more and I admitted myself to Hillside [a private hospital]. I was there for a year and the anxiety built up tremendously. I was falling in love with women at the hospital and this was considered "sick." . . . When they have these dances Saturday night, which you are supposed to go to, you are not supposed to dance with another woman, you are supposed to dance with a man. They encourage you to have dates to go to the movies. They have movies on whatever night it is. Saturday night. You are encouraged to have activities jointly with the men's wards or cottages.

Although supposedly "sick," these women were also discouraged from thinking of themselves as lesbians—and encouraged to date or have sexual relations with men.††

FRANCES: I fell in love with a girl for the first time when I was twenty-four. I'd been in therapy at a hospital clinic [Bellevue] and told my therapist about it when he came back from his vacation.

PHYLLIS: What was his reaction?

†† One well-meaning, very motherly therapist actually arranged several "heterosexual" dates for her painfully shy patient.

FRANCES: He freaked out. He started yelling at me. "You're doing this because you think I'm your father and you want to hurt your father. You're a spoiled child. The minute I go away you do this, you go and do something that can be so dangerous . . ." and he just freaked me out! Y'know. Because, since I'd been in therapy, I was truly happy. I did what I wanted to do, 'n' she was really lovely, and I was very happy. But he freaked me out, y'know. Basically he just said that my behavior was arrested at a homosexual level. He sort of made me understand that it was a very unfortunate thing that I was doing and that it would result in heartache. Which I understand, I mean, I do. It's certainly much better to live within the system. Although this system is for shit. You know, my girl friend was also coming to Bellevue for treatment. . . . So one angle he took was that she wasn't too cool, because look, she was coming to Bellevue for treatment and I said, "Oh, God, I'm here. What are you talking about?" . . . Then he said, "how could you stand it—don't women smell awful?" and I said, "Wow, y'know, if you wash" . . . and he said, "Oh, please, no matter how clean a woman is, no matter how clean, she still smells." And I said, "I don't know, it just doesn't bother me." "Did you ever see the statue of David?" he said. "A man's body is so much more beautiful than a woman's body!" . . . "You're crazy," I said. "I'm not saying my values are the values, but you better dig it, Doctor, and check out your own set of eyes, you've got some thinking to do. . . ."

PHYLLIS: Did he encourage you to go out with men?

FRANCES: Yes, he did, and I said to him, "Do you want me to go out with these pigs, just because they have penises? They're stupid, they have nothing to say to me, I have nothing to discuss with them. The only thing they could possibly do is fuck me, and possibly take me out of this blissful existence with women. And you don't care what they are, they could be the worst, filthy, perverted bastards, as long as they're men, y'know, it's okay. Is that what you're telling me?" He says, "Well, I'm saying that you could find something to talk about." I said, "Look, I've tried, there's nothing that I could talk about with them."

He [the therapist] acknowledged that some of the men might have been pigs. "Y'know," he said, "well, maybe you went out with a few bad men, but, uh, not every one is bad. And you gotta keep looking, and you gotta find a man, and you gotta go with a man. Anyway, a woman can be just as rough, just as dangerous as a man. . . ."

He said, "let a man touch you. You're too sensitive to a male touch," —because I had been. I was getting very uptight, y'know, at being touched by men. A lot of men come up to you in a very familiar way, touch you like you're a piece of equipment, or, I don't know, like you don't belong to yourself. Y'know, they come and touch you as if you owe them this kind of thing, to be soft for them, and to be responsive to them. And it got me really uptight. And I told him about this, and he said, "Force yourself. Touch someone's hand. Force yourself to be touched by men. What are they going to do, kill you? They're not gonna kill you!" And I said, "Well, I'm really afraid of men." Y'know, I was abused by men, there were some incidents in my life that were very painful and he said, "They're not gonna kill you, they're not gonna kill you." And that's what he tried to tell me. . . . You know, the way I'm talking about him sounds really awful. I mean, I loved him at the time. . . . I mean, I'm not committed to women only. 'Cause I think that's not good. I think that women should—y'gotta be committed to people, and to finding good people.

JOAN: I went into therapy because I was depressed about the way I look. I grew to about five feet ten inches, my present height, when I was twelve. I'd never dated. . . . I was passionate about literature and music and I was totally isolated. . . . I was isolating myself in such a way that I'd have to pay a price for it. . . . When I was eighteen I became enamored of my girl friend. We would listen to operas together and go to libraries. We'd hold hands and that was very beautiful, it had a tremendous amount of meaning. But I did not want to be a homosexual and go over the brink. . . . I had started masturbating after years of being a good Catholic. I guess I didn't believe in God any more.

Dr. B. was about forty-five and very charismatic, very demonic. He told me to masturbate and didn't believe that I did. He wanted me to show him, right there in the office. He said if I didn't get laid by the third date the guy was a fag. So I started fucking men. Dr. B. said I was very frigid, that I had a masklike face.

PHYLLIS: You were about twenty?

JOAN: Yes.

PHYLLIS: Did you love this first man?

JOAN: No . . . I despised him. He always had to have new cars, like Cadillacs, but he couldn't say Beethoven's name properly. He was about ten years older than me and very materialistic. . . . I started sleeping with a guy down the hall also. He sleeps with about five to ten different women each week. . . . I had fifteen credits in college and a twenty-hour-a-week job and I was carrying on two affairs at once and I got very upset and very depressed. But I pulled myself together and did my schoolwork. . . .

PHYLLIS: What did you feel?

JOAN: I was worried that I was somehow losing myself. . . . I was abusing myself, not because I was losing my virginity, but because I was losing energy, and concentration, and control of myself. . . .

Dr. B. didn't allow me to keep a journal because I was too introverted, too "fixed upon myself"—something I'd always been hearing. Fucking was very highly valued no matter how exhausted or hurt you got or how you picked up this disease or that disease. . . . He said I'm not a homosexual, I don't come on like one. I said, "What is a homosexual, because I never met one." But he would just assure me that I didn't look like one and that was strange because I was obviously at the beginning of becoming one. . . .

I said I did not want children. I wanted my achievements rather than children. He really did not go into that. He thought that the whole society was so screwed up that there was no point in having children. He did not seem to value marriage much.

I attended group also. The group was ripping me apart. They ripped everyone apart. They didn't like the way I looked, I didn't wear make-up, I didn't take dating seriously . . .

PHYLLIS: Did the other women in this group yell at you for this too?

JOAN: Yes.

PHYLLIS: Were there any lesbians in the group?

JOAN: No.

PHYLLIS: Were there any male homosexuals?

JOAN: Yes.

PHYLLIS: How were they treated?

JOAN: With more consideration. They had a right but I didn't have a right to be where I was. . . . The group's technique was to tear everyone's defenses down.

These two interviews make painfully apparent the extent to which lesbians (or lesbians who seek therapy) are as naïve, fearful, and "suggestible" as heterosexual women: perhaps even more so. Their sexual experience remains a private, "personal" reality, one that they can't share with their mothers, employers, classmates, children—or with their therapists. Their sense of reality, their *knowledge of pleasure,* is treated as either non-existent, second best, or dangerous. (I have certainly never heard of a therapist actively questioning his patient's heterosexual realities, or of subtly or overtly "prescribing" lesbian experiences.)

I would like to close this chapter by, in Charlotte Wolff's words, "letting life itself comment." The following interview was done with a black lesbian who had never been in therapy.‡‡ The interviewer was a black woman.

DORIS: Weren't you married?

SHIRLEY: Married, me? You must be thinking about my girl friend. Honey, I wouldn't get married to save my life. And I can truthfully say that most women who get married are sick! They're really sick!

DORIS: What you're saying is that all housewives are mentally sick? This is what it appears that you're saying, that they're crazy.

‡‡ She is not included statistically in either Lesbians in Therapy or Third World Women in Therapy.

SHIRLEY: Wait a minute, do you realize that most housewives have a ninety-eight- or ninety-nine-hour work week slaving their fuckin' ass off for some bastard?

DORIS: You've got to work sometime.

SHIRLEY: Well, honey, it's a bullshit system and anyone who gets in it is crazy. But, all right, let's dig this. You come home, right?

DORIS: All right, all right.

SHIRLEY: And I come home and I have to cook, and then I have to clean, and then I have to wash dishes and I have to wash his little dirty shorts, right, and heaven help me if my husband won't bat the kids right around, right? Then he comes home from his little . . .

DORIS: Isn't this what you were put here for?

SHIRLEY: Well, just wait a minute, honey. Just let me finish. When he comes home from his office job sitting behind his desk, right, and he eats . . .

DORIS: That's there with the job, honey.

SHIRLEY: Well, freak that. I have to wash his dishes, and then he wants to screw, on top of all this. And I just can't dig it! And, you know, ask me, I'm a lesbian, right? And I don't have to love 'em, I don't have to fuck 'em and I damn sure don't have to depend on 'em, and that is freedom, honey, because no matter how heavy my load, honey, I'm gonna make it 'cause I'm free. I feel that I am free!

DORIS: It appears that you are a man-hating woman.

SHIRLEY: No, I don't hate them. I don't hate them. I just don't dig them.

DORIS: What about child raising? Aren't you denied that rewarding experience of giving birth to a child someday?

SHIRLEY: Surely you jest, honey. Who in the hell ever told you that having a kid was such a wonderful experience? If you think that a woman walking around with a swollen stomach for nine months is a pretty sight, you better go scratch your ass, I mean right now, 'cause then you a liar. If you think that labor pain is such a wonderful experience . . .

DORIS: This isn't the rewarding experience I'm talking about. I'm talking about—

SHIRLEY: Wait a minute—

DORIS: —this baby. Having someone to take—it's yours. Something of your own. I'm not talking about the labor pains. Of course, what's so rewarding about that? I agree with you. Have you ever been through it?

SHIRLEY: Wait a minute. Let me talk, let me talk. You think that laying on a metal table with your legs all cocked up and some old white bastard shoving some cold clamps up your thing . . .

DORIS: There are black ones too.

SHIRLEY: Well, that's his business. You don't know many black ones, do you? While your fucking husband is probably out somewhere screwing everything in sight. Well, honey, I can't stand it and I can't dig it and anybody who goes through it is crazy. A man will feel you, fry you, fight you, fuck you, and then forget you, honey.

DORIS: You can always get a midwife.

SHIRLEY: He'll turn around and tell you, "You've come a long way, baby." Ain't that much coming in the world.

DORIS: How long have you been homosexually oriented?

SHIRLEY: Homosexually oriented, baby: why don't you just say "in the light"? That's what it breaks down to. Well, I'd say actively about six years. About six years.

DORIS: Phew, you ain't kidding, are you?

SHIRLEY: Well, no, are we. Actively about six years.

DORIS: What do you mean by actively? Actively, actively, what do you mean, you just keep going from one to the other?

SHIRLEY: No, well, when I say actively—I've probably been in the light all of my life because I can't remember having any meaningful experience with a man. You know, I can take them or leave them and, baby, I left them most of the time because they never interested me in any way. And, you know, in the books and everything—I must have slept through that period in my life when I was supposed to make that big transition from girl friend to boy friend, but I never made it. But what I'm saying is that I didn't have my first homosexual experience until I was about twenty-two.

DORIS: Why was it twenty-two? I'm sure you could have had some opportunities to engage, you know, at an earlier stage of life, or did you not?

SHIRLEY: Well, number one . . .

DORIS: Were you sheltered?

SHIRLEY: No! Come on, girl. Well, number one, I was very confused and very frightened about where I was coming from, actually.

DORIS: What do you mean by "coming from"?

SHIRLEY: Well, I thought I was one of the sickest persons in this world. You know, I dreaded even thinking about the term "lesbian" and I used to cope with the situation by telling myself that I was normal, you understand? And the only thing that would take my normality away would be for me to have an actual gay experience. And I also used to tell myself that you're not gay if you never do it. So I didn't, 'cause I didn't want nothing to tread on my sanity. So I pretended to like boys and dresses and parties and all that bullshit.

DORIS: So you were just fooling yourself?

SHIRLEY: No, no, I wasn't fooling myself, I was trying to live with myself, and I went out with fellas and I let them fuck me. . . .

DORIS: Well, if you didn't want to be a girl why—

SHIRLEY: That's what I'm saying. The more they did it, the worse I got, and the more I pretended to act normal, the crazier I got. And I mean I was going out of my mind. When my mother died I just stopped pretending to be something that I wasn't because it ain't done much straightness in the world and it put my mind at ease, you better believe it, and I regained my sanity which was slowly seeping away from me, from trying to be ungay and I am definitely gay. And I realize that I am not the sick one. It's all those poor simple fools out there, those little housewives that sign their life away when they say, "I do." You know, they sign their death warrant. And like I said before, I am free. I am definitely free.

DORIS: Tell me a little about your family background. You know, your relationship with your parents. Something as far back as you can remember, you know. How things were.

SHIRLEY: Relationship with my parents—

DORIS: Ummmmm.

SHIRLEY: Well, that's a story in itself, honey, 'cause my father was a pure fuck.

DORIS: Oh, that's nice to hear.

SHIRLEY: My mother was a fool 'cause she lived with this fuck until she went foolish.

DORIS: What do you mean by fuck?

SHIRLEY: Well, he used to beat the shit out of her really. He used to beat the shit out of this woman every Friday, 'cause you know on Friday that's when the eagle flies. And it used to fly him straight to the liquor store; and he'd come home all sloppy drunk and stone broke and this went on until my mother died.

DORIS: What did your mother die of, honey?

SHIRLEY: Well, she died, the doctor said she had a heart attack. Well, that's what the doctor said, but I, me, I personally believe that she just gave up living 'cause her living was hell, baby, and she worked in a white woman's kitchen for twelve years and that's just where she died.

DORIS: What do you mean by "she just gave up"? She said, "Well, oh, I think I'll die" and just went on? What do you mean by "she just gave up life"? What do you mean by that?

SHIRLEY: Well, when—I mean when you ain't got nothing more to live for, man, you just give up. If your life ain't worth shit, you ain't worth shit, baby.

DORIS: Wait a minute, do you think she committed suicide or something?

SHIRLEY: No! You don't understand what I'm saying.

DORIS: I don't really.

SHIRLEY: When you give up, you just give up. You can't take all this bullshit from everybody, especially from somebody who's supposed to be your husband and all this kind of crap, and you just can't, you can't dig on it. That's all. You know, about two or three weeks before she died my mother told me that she would be free soon. You know, she knew she was going to die and that's why she said it. It was a term she always used—that she would be free soon. And for me to settle down and get married to someone who I loved and depend on—

DORIS: Did she mean male or female?

SHIRLEY: Well, she meant male because my mother was a strict, you know, gospel woman and—

DORIS: Did she know of your experiences?

SHIRLEY: Are you kidding? Of course not.

DORIS: Are you sure?

SHIRLEY: I'm positive. And you know she was trying to tell me don't be a slave so I can live a better life than hers but what she was really saying was don't be a slave but be a free slave. Don't marry a fuck like she did.

DORIS: Don't be a slave but be a free slave. That sounds kinda off the wall. What do you mean?

SHIRLEY: Well, marry a nice fuck. Don't marry a fuck like she did. Well, my mother was pitiful. The only way she got her freedom was through death and I, when she died, I say this ain't going to be me 'cause I realized that the only way—

DORIS: What do you mean? How do you know that your mother didn't enjoy herself? She stayed with this man for such a long time.

SHIRLEY: That's right, she stayed there 'cause she had children to support and the only way that I'm gonna get my freedom, you know, to obtain my freedom, was through living the life that I want to, so I stopped pretending to be something that I—

DORIS: This is what I said. You don't want to go through the same thing that your mother went through so you chose something else. . . . Okay, I just want to ask you one more question. With the way the majority of most women are going, do you think there is an alternative to the present life style?

SHIRLEY: You mean the women's present life style?

DORIS: Right, yes.

SHIRLEY: Well, how can you have a solution for something that's been going on for centuries? And the only possible alternative would be for somebody to be Lord and Saviour Christ for a day, and let's say if I was King Jesus, you know, I would place a curse on every man alive and this curse would be a little thing they call a twelve-month pregnancy and each man would produce about seven girls.

DORIS: Why seven? Seven! My God!

SHIRLEY: Oh, one for each day of the week, right. No woman would be without a lover or somebody to talk to, you know, affection.

When I was six years old in Brooklyn, Martha was my best friend. She was black, and her mother had died in a fire in a country called Africa. She lived in a basement with her father, the janitor, who was always laughing. Martha and I ran away from home together every afternoon. We also planned to co-captain the best punch-ball team ever. Our plans were ended by a supper invitation.

"What," my parents screamed at me, "you want to go down into the basement at night—with her *father* there, with men, cards, numbers, liquor, God knows what?"

"Her father lives there," I explained. "He's the janitor. But I promise we won't bother him. . . ."

Well, I never got to taste any African food in my sixth year (if that's what we would have eaten). And for years, whenever I went to the ocean, I saw black men laughing dangerously at me in every roaring wave. (The bands of embittered black youths who rove New York City, grabbing "tits 'n' ass" in a white rage, haven't helped me any with that one.)

And sometimes I wonder what adult uniform they gave Martha: "welfare mother," suburban citizen, black militant, Dead on Arrival?

Martha, I dedicate this chapter to everything that was between us—and to whatever revolution changes what couldn't be into an unremarkable occurrence.

I also dedicate this chapter to George Jackson, Angela Davis, and to the inmates who participated in the Attica prison rebellion.

Chapter Eight

THIRD WORLD WOMEN

Dr. Hill acknowledged, in an interview today, that [black] families headed by women were considerably more vulnerable to economic and social ills. An important reason is that women heads of family are likely to earn much less than men. . . . The report says that "national earnings data do not support the popular conception that wives' earnings in most low-income black families are often greater than husbands'. It is said that in 85 percent of the black families with incomes of $3,000 or less, the husband's income surpassed the wife's."

New York *Times*
July 27 and 28, 1971

In the first national comparative study of its kind, the Census Bureau has found that persons of origin in Spanish-speaking countries earn significantly greater incomes than blacks, even though they have poorer educations. . . .

Further, statisticians say, while the incomes of both groups still fall far behind those of whites, there is some evidence to suggest that the Spanish group is gaining somewhat faster than blacks are.

New York *Times*
October 18, 1971

Is women's liberation irrelevant to black women? Of course, as has been pointed out, half of blacks are women; the question might be asked whether the black movement has been relevant to them. The black movement is conceived as primarily directed toward the black man, and programs to meet its demands have reflected this. The Job Corp, with many blacks, was practically all male until a 1966 Act of Congress required at least ⅓ participation by females; of the 125,000 trainees under the Manpower Development and Training Act in 1968, only 31.7% were women; in 1968, in the Job Opportunities in the business sector program, only 24% of those hired were female; the training program of the National Alliance of Businessmen is restricted to black males.

Nancy Henley[1]

What do black women feel about Women's Lib? Distrust. It is white, therefore suspect. . . . They look at white women and see them as the enemy for they know that racism is not confined to white men, and that there are more white women than men in this country and that 53 percent of the population sustained an eloquent silence during times of greatest stress. . . . The problem of most black women is not getting into the labor force but in being upgraded in it, not in getting into medical school but in getting adult education, not in how to exercise freedom from the "head of the house" but in how to *be* the head of the household. . . .

For years in this country there was no one for black men to vent their rage on except black women. And for years black women accepted that rage—even regarded that acceptance as their unpleasant duty. But in doing so, they frequently kicked back, and they seem never to have become the "slave" that white women see in their own history. True, the black woman did the housework, the drudgery; true, she reared the children, often alone, but she did all of that while occupying a place on the job market, a place her mate could not get or which his pride would not let him accept. And she had nothing to fall back on: not maleness, not whiteness, not ladyhood, not anything. And out of the profound desolation of her reality she may very well have invented herself. . . .

. . . black women have always considered themselves superior to white women. . . . Black women have been able to envy white women (their looks, their easy life, the attention they seem to get from their men;) they could fear them (for the economic control they have had over black women's lives) and even love them (as mammies and domestic workers can;) but black women have found it impossible to respect white women. I mean they never had what black men have had for white men: a feeling of awe at their accomplishments.

Toni Morrison[2]

Unfortunately, there seems to be some confusion in the Movement today as to who has been oppressing whom. Since the advent of Black power, the Black male has exerted a more prominent leadership role in our struggle for justice in this country. He sees the system for what it really is for the most part, but where he rejects its values and mores on many issues, when it comes to women he seems to take his guidelines from the pages of the *Ladies' Home Journal*. Certain Black men are maintaining that they have been castrated by society but that Black women somehow escaped the persecution and even contributed to this emasculation. Let me state here and now that Black women in America can justly be described as a "slave of a slave." . . .

Those who are exerting their "manhood" by telling Black women to step back into a domestic, submissive role are assuming a counter-revolutionary position. Black women likewise have been abused by the system and we must begin talking about the elimination of all kinds of oppression. If we are talking about building a strong nation, capable of throwing off the yoke of capitalist oppression, then we are talking about the total involvement of every man, woman and child, each with a highly developed political consciousness. We need our whole army out there dealing with the enemy and not half an army.

Frances Beale[3]

Black ladies, the last thing we have to worry about is genocide. In fact, we could use a little. Look at what's happened to us in the last hundred years; we've been bravely propagating and all we've gotten are a lot of lumps and a bad name. On the other hand, there are people like Glazer and Moynihan carrying on about our matriarchy and inferring that we've botched up the job long enough and that if we insist on doing something, confine ourselves to standing behind the man of the family and bringing him up to par. . . . Anyway, there's the brother nattering away about how we've been lopping off balls long enough, it's time to stand aside. So you stand there looking as pink and white and helpless as is possible under the circumstances. . . .

Joanna Clark[4]

Though it appears that both men and women live together within the institutions of society, men really define and control the institutions while women live under their rule. The government, army, religion, economy and family are institutions of the male culture's colonial rule of the female. . . . A female culture exists. It is a culture that is subordinated and under male culture's colonial, imperialist rule all over the world. Underneath the surface of every national, ethnic, or racial culture is the split between the two primary cultures of the world—the female culture and the male culture.

National cultures vary greatly according to the degree of the suppression of the female culture. The veil and seclusion of women and their almost total segregation in Arab culture makes for differences between them and, for example, Sweden. A Swedish woman may not be able to tolerate the suppressed life of Arab women but she also, if she is sensitive, may not be able to tolerate her suppression as a female in Sweden. Crossing national boundaries often awakens a woman's understanding of her position in society. We cannot, like James Baldwin, even temporarily escape to Paris or another country from our caste role. It is everywhere—there is no place to escape.

Fourth World Manifesto[6]
January 13, 1971

I have no theory to offer of Third World female psychology in America. No single theory will do descriptive justice to women of African, Latin-American, Mexican, Chinese, and native Indian descent. Furthermore, as a white woman, I'm reluctant and unable to construct theories about experiences I haven't had; and as a psychologist and feminist, I'm really more interested in exploring the laws of *female* psychology than in exploring their various exceptions and variations.

The experience and effects of sexism are different for Third World and white women in America. For example, more Third World women have worked outside the home and within the context of a female "kinship" system than have many middle class white women. More white women have had more education put to less use, and more fathers and husbands economically supporting them in isolated family units than have most Third World women. However, the publicly employed Third World woman really has no more mobility, psychologically or economically, than her white non-publically employed counterpart. The ghetto "kinship" system is as much a structure of bitter necessity as is female isolation within the middle class family. The feminist desire to overcome dependence on men cannot be shared by those Third World women who, because of racism and class warfare, have never been allowed a similar dependence. (Although they may indeed have longed for such dependence and for the privileges it represents.) Thus, it is Third World revolutionary, cultural, political, and religious organizations, and not feminist organizations, that offer Third World women either a desired white-like interaction with men, or one that is rooted in African or South American cultural heritages (both of which predate and still exist outside of racist American society).* This is one of the many reasons that those Third World

* Of course, from my point of view, women have never fared as well as men in traditional Africa or South America. The maternal death rate and infant death rate are very high on both continents. While most women in Africa have traditionally always worked strenuously in childbearing and rearing, in agriculture and/or commerce, they have not been political, military, or religious leaders as often as men have, nor has polyandry existed as often as polygamy. There have, of course, been many African queens and militarists, and many matriarchal cultures in "pre-historical" Asia, Africa, South America and Europe. Once European intervention occurred, the African women's position was even further downgraded in comparison to her male counterpart: African men were forced and/or encouraged to participate in education, modern farming, land ownership, factory work, etc. Female warriors ceased to exist entirely. To date, most African revolutionary or traditional nationalist leaders, militarists, judges and priests are men, not women.

women who can afford to be politically active in any sense are not feminists. An alliance of women either representing or fighting for women's rights belongs more to the future than to the past. For example, men have always been seen as more physically and intellectually powerful than women. To strictly heterosexual women, they are also the only possible sexual partners. For these reasons alone, Third World women, like most white women, will "stick" by their men sooner than they will "become" their own men, i.e., sooner than they will incorporate "male" or all human characteristics. The real sexual revolution is harder and more threatening to people of both sexes, and of all classes and races, than are even other extremely difficult revolutions.

I understand what a black or Puerto Rican working woman feels and means when she says: "I want to *stop* working. I want to be *able* to stay home with my children. I want to be *able* to have a man care for me." She is talking about having *one* full-time job instead of two. But she doesn't necessarily feel, any more than white women do, that being a mother and "housewife" is an invaluable form of labor without which her husband (or the government) could not survive. Women of all classes and races are not socialized to regard the family as a public institution, or as particularly oppressive to women.

My hypothetical Third World woman is also talking about the many privileges of having a white skin in America, especially if it belongs to a middle-income wallet. She is talking about racial differences in housing, schooling, and employment.† She is talking about feeling safe on the streets or in her home—something that, whether realistic or not, most white women, even in cities, have always felt.‡ She is also talking about the privilege of psychological dependence and material security: even if these are temporary

† Lower income white women suffer these tragedies, also.
‡ More *reports* of rape exist for Third World than for white women.

privileges, and purchased at the expense of human dignity and freedom, the pleasure of such female privileges is real and has kept many of us alive.** The fact is, it is probably better to be the slave of a rich man than the slave of a poor man; better to be at the mercy of power than at the mercy of powerlessness. Strength can often afford mercy, weakness, rarely. It is even better to be the slave of one man whom you know—a husband—than the slave of many strange men—such as the men in the state legislature or in industry. (Unless, of course, you are a *young* and successful prostitute who can remain independent of the many men who pay high wages.)

During the last decade, both black and white male theoreticians, and more recently, black and white female theoreticians, have written about the black and Puerto Rican woman in America and about the "Third World" woman in the Third World proper. Frantz Fanon, an eloquent and brilliant black male psychiatrist, was, unfortunately, embarrassingly, painfully a sexist in his writing about Algerian women. I read Fanon in 1969 on a long bus ride on my way to a meeting. Furiously, I underlined nearly all of his *A Dying Colonialism*, as impressed as I was angry and disappointed by it.[6] A group of feminists must have been on a bus ride too, because their conclusions are similar to some of my own.[7] They say:

> Fanon is correct in saying that the French tried to destroy Algerian [male] culture and that this is a typical colonial tactic

---

** From a psychological point of view, as long as a particular group is still "profiting" from the misery of the less fortunate, it is as cruel as it is foolish to expect the less fortunate to be self-sacrificial, noble, etc. Let all men (all white people) give up all their powers and privileges *first*—their wives, secretaries, prostitutes, their material comforts, their information, their *privileged childhoods*— then, and only then, will women or black people begin to consider the redemptive features of "goodness" or "equality." Until then, women and black people will want all the free drinks, the handshakes, the trophies, the inside tips—the "killings." Oppressed groups do not internalize the values of power any less than other groups.

of one male culture vs. another colonized male culture. But Fanon shows a typical male inability to see the brutal colonization of females by males. In his use of the veil, as a symbol of Algerian culture that the French were trying to destroy, he oversimplifies in order to avoid a recognition of his own male guilt and the Algerian males' culpability towards the Algerian females' repressed and demeaned culture.

If Fanon were more honest he would recognize that the French, as a male culture, had no more interest in the Algerian woman's freedom than had the Algerian male. But Fanon, who has such angry passion against the French colonizers, does not extend his vision to demand justice for the Algerian female. In fact, he pooh-poohs the idea that Algerian women are oppressed at all. Nowhere, except in things which he does not realize that he is revealing, does he admit the fact of female oppression by the male in Algeria. . . .

Through the imposition of a servant status on women the female culture has elaborated a whole servile ethic of "self-sacrifice." Self-sacrifice—as the major ethic of the female culture —has been one of the most effective psychological blocks to women's open rebellion and demand for self-determination. It has also been a major tool of male manipulation of females.

Kardiner[8] and Moynihan,[9] less eloquent than Fanon, are white male professionals. Their writing about black women and black "matriarchs" in America is racist and sexist, as well as uninspired. Grier and Cobbs, two black male psychiatrists, are, at best, mediocre in their ascribing a second-class humanity to black women. Let me quote from their chapters entitled "Achieving Womanhood" and "Marriage and Love" in *Black Rage*[10]:

So it may be that after a brief struggle a black woman feels that femininity, as it is defined in these times, is something she cannot achieve. Rather than having her heart broken every day, she relinquishes the struggle and diverts her interest elsewhere. She has derived none of the intensely personal satisfaction she might have received as an honored and desirable sexual object. The full flowering of a woman's sexual function and her capacity to enjoy it are based on her evaluation of herself. If she considers herself an especially worthwhile person, she can joyfully submit to her lover, knowing that he will likewise prize and value her. Her enjoyment of the sexual function will not be impaired by the feeling of being degraded by the man. There is a natural inclination for a woman to yield herself to a powerful lover, gaining additional narcissistic supplies in her possession of him. Her own high evaluation of herself, in turn, evokes in the man a similar high evaluation of her. If her narcissism is impaired, the sexual act is a degrading submission to a man who does not value her, and she arises from it feeling a loss of self-esteem rather than a personal enhancement.

With youthful narcissism crushed and sexual life perverted, [black women] drew back from these modes as a primary means of life expression. Letting youth go, and sex go, they narrowed their vision to the most essential feminine function—mothering, nurturing, and protecting their children. In such a role the black woman has been the salvation of many a family. To call such a family matriarchal, as many have done, is to obscure the essential maternal function and to suggest an authoritarian for authority's sake. We suggest that the black woman has been beset by cruelty on all sides and as a result, centered her concern on the most essential quality of womanhood.

I don't know. I just don't know whether such sentimental romanticism really describes, explains, or is at all relevant to black women in America. Or whether it should be.

It is difficult to *document* racist practices in the selection and treatment of the "mentally ill." First, the statistics, like those on child molestation or rape, are not easily available. Second, most

Third World people are simply too poor to be able to afford private therapeutic treatment: they are socially controlled and condemned in more direct, physical ways.†† Third, racism, in psychiatric diagnosis and treatment, is usually further confused by class and sex biases. Nevertheless, it is undeniable that black women and men are discriminated against and misunderstood whenever they make contact with the psychiatric world.‡‡[12] However, when a Black or Puerto Rican woman is hospitalized, her "treatment" is probably very similar to that of a white woman. It consists of domestic and "maternal" tasks—or of psychological preparation for domestic, maternal and heterosexual tasks. Psychiatrically hospitalized black men are mistreated but not in this way. Despite differences between Black, Puerto Rican and White women, and differences in how they are perceived by male professionals, the fact that they are *women* makes them all equally vulnerable to the predominantly masculine standard of mental health. Also, despite differences, crucial (and devalued) aspects of the female role are probably shared by women of all races and classes. For example, a recent study has suggested that significantly more women than men, both among the black and white populations, have *reported* nervous breakdowns, impending nervous breakdowns, psychological inertia, and dizziness. Both black and white women also report higher rates than men for the following symptoms: Nervousness, insomnia, trembling hands, nightmares, fainting, and headaches.[13]

---

†† Henley points out that women, like blacks, are "steered into heavy drug use, but into drugs that tend to pacify rather than eliminate them, perhaps illustrating that women are less expendable from the point of view of the dominant culture than are blacks. Of course, "elimination" is no more sign of respect than is "purification" in the service of the dominant (male) culture.[11]

‡‡ It is also undeniable that many black as well as white employees of the psychiatric establishment, such as attendants, orderlies and nurses, particularly in low-paying jobs in State and County asylums, are brutal to inmates of all races.

THE INTERVIEWS

I spoke with nine Third World women, six of African descent and three of Latin-American descent. Their ages ranged from twenty-seven to forty-eight. Two women had some high school experience, four had some college experience, two had completed college, and one woman had some graduate school experience. Five women were legally single, one was legally married, two were divorced, and one was widowed. With one exception, a school-teacher, none of the women earned more than five thousand dollars yearly, if that, and usually in a secretarial or clerical capacity. Three of the women were unemployed or living on welfare. Two of the women, both black Americans, were feminists.

Three of the women had been psychiatrically hospitalized: one woman briefly, for attempting suicide, another several times for "paranoid schizophrenia," and a third woman many times for a total of more than five years for "involutional schizophrenia." None were hospitalized in private institutions.

Seven of the women had been in private therapy with approximately* three therapists apiece, for approximately twenty-five months: seventeen months with male therapists and twenty-four months with female therapists. The women saw a total number of ten male therapists and eight female therapists. With the exception of two black male psychiatrists and one Puerto Rican female social worker, the therapists were all white.

I spoke to five of the women with another Third World woman present. Two of the interviews were conducted without me by a Third World woman. I spoke to one woman with a white friend and former therapist present, and to one woman alone, at her request.

* "Approximately" means a total average for the group of seven.

Why did these women seek, accept or feel comfortable with black or white male therapists?† In general, most of the women were as "hooked" on heterosexuality, "love," and marriage as their white counterparts.

WILMA: I couldn't stand being without a man. Every time a guy left me I would do three things: be afraid I'd kill myself, run to a therapist, and find another boy friend as soon as possible.

CAROLINE: Dr. B. is a very handsome black man. Very attractive. Great personality. Good doctor. And he tried everything. He almost stood on his head. I just did not talk to him about what was really bothering me. He never got to me. I didn't relate to him. . . . It was so terrible. I sat there for six months before we even talked a little bit about what I was feeling. You see he has this thing if I didn't talk he very rarely said anything. And I don't talk sometimes about things that are that close to me very well. So we sat through about twenty-five minutes in the session looking at each other and I sat there being miserable, and that's kinda what happened. . . . I suppose I was resisting. I don't know what it was. He just couldn't seem to open me up. It was a long waste.

PHYLLIS: You don't blame him, though?

CAROLINE: No, I liked him. He was very nice, like a nice vase. You put it on the shelf to be admired and I wouldn't run in there and say anything intimate or earth-shaking to break the vase. I actually used to replace the flowers in his outer office (he neglected them terribly) and I really liked him but I just couldn't talk to him. [After my suicide attempt] I started seeing Dr. L., a white man, who I also liked a lot. He's really helped me. But you know, no matter what I say, he brings it back to me. If I got bubonic plague it would still be my fault. . . . No, I can't talk to him about orgasms, I'm too embarrassed.

---

† Naïveté? Race hatred? Same-sex hatred? An opportunity to finally be with a white man who couldn't seduce or buy them? Or who would, but "nicely"?

EVELYN: I started therapy primarily because of a guy I'd had a brief relationship with and he rejected me. And I had actually made a humiliating telephone call. The first time I'd ever done anything like that in my life—to just simply confront him verbally and this was after I'd drunk about three quarters of a bottle of vodka. I was absolutely smashed out of my skull in order to work myself up to this chance to call him and say, "Why did you put me down?" And he told me that there had been someone else in his life who had returned or some such jazz and I was just out of my skull with depression. My whole view of therapy had always been that it was only sick people that did it. It was an admission that you were weak and I was not weak. I was a strong, strong person and I don't need anybody and I don't need nothing. I don't even know how I got up the stuff to go the first time, but I did. . . . I think I was attracted to him. He was white, male, and over twenty-one and I guess I viewed him as available and single. Whether or not he was I never did know, anyways. Then I remembered early fantasies about having sex with him and that kind of thing. And then I went through the thing where I'm sure I was trying to seduce him and he didn't turn on to it although he was very friendly and so forth. And I remember my being angry about his not turning on to it.

The problems of being both black and female in a racist and sexist society are staggering, the permutations of violence, self-destructiveness, and paranoia endless.‡ How nice, white, verbal "therapy" can really help with these seemingly bottomless tragedies is quite beyond me.

Most of the women I talked to had childhood and marriage

‡ I worked out one traditional permutation with a black woman: for most of her life, it was clear to her that black men don't like black women, prefer white women, can't earn money, beat you up, run around, and aren't really as "acceptable" as white men; white women—they're bitchy, childish, rich, and racist: even the poor ones are rich, and anyway Lady Jane just isn't important, she can't love, she isn't strong, my God! why do the men want her? Black women —they're made of stronger stuff, but they're also bitchy, poor, racist, and would cut your throat to get a white man or a "good" black man: Ask me, I know, I'm a black woman; white men—don't ask, just don't ask.

experiences of physical brutality, double-standard puritanism, and sexual dissatisfaction.**

WILMA: I was never attracted to white men. I only went to bed with brothers. . . . I really bought that myth of black male superiority in bed and kept going to bed with them—but it's not true! Practically none of them could screw; I mean they were incompetent. No, I really mean they didn't care about me, and they figured they were just such hot shit *naturally* that a *natural* screw ought to be good enough for any woman . . . so, with three exceptions, they were pretty cold and clumsy—and they didn't *want* to learn. Eventually I would explain what I wanted—in words of one syllable—and that didn't work either. . . . They're just incompetent. Men are sexually incompetent.

PHYLLIS: Now don't go around spreading myths of sexual inferiority based on sexual gender . . . (laughter).

WILMA: Yeah, but white men didn't do anything for me either. . . . The men all made me feel that it was my fault, that I was guilty, like I had to pretend. . . . Are they [black men] any different with white women? Are white men?

LAVERNE: I went to bed with him when I was fifteen. The only thing he wanted to do was screw . . . he would never talk to me. . . . He went out with other girls but told me not to worry, that he was going to marry me. I felt that the other women were whores and promiscuous. Sometimes I'd even pick one out for him—someone stupid and superficial. . . . It took me about two years to really enjoy the sex with him.

CAROLINE: I was twenty-five when I had intercourse with a man for the first time. He was black, married, and five years older than me. It was very cold . . . but I was very grateful that finally someone took me to bed. I blamed myself for not having orgasms. . . . In my mind it was going to

** I do not mean to imply that Third World men are less sexually giving than white men. I do not think, however, that twentieth-century poverty, racism, and doctrines of machismo or "primitive" pride are in any way *helpful* to the sexual and sensual liberation of Third World women—who are already sexually repressed as a function of white patriarchal culture.

be an affair but in my emotions I guess the first affair women think, no matter what, it's just not going to be like that at all.

RITA: "I guess I had a very strict upbringing . . . I really thought if I'm not a virgin at my wedding that the church lights would go out . . . I was taught that it's all right for men not to be virgins and even to have girl friends after marriage, as long as he takes care of you and the children . . . I have to tell my husband everywhere I go before I go . . . once I went to a dance with my girl friend but I was scared. He said he would kill me but he didn't. I never went out like that again—no courage, I guess."

These women, far from occupying a specially reserved place of reverence in the Black or Puerto Rican male (or female) community, described being the taken-for-granted "natural" prey of Black or Puerto Rican men.†† Of course, this in no way exempted them from white male "preying." However, depending on their level of Black or Feminist consciousness, white male socio-sexual advances sometimes angered or frightened them less because of its socially more "acceptable" and (potentially) economically more rewarding nature.‡‡ Many women were told to marry "up" (or "white") only to live in fear that they would be abandoned for a white woman. Many of the women described hostile relations with their mothers based on skin-color (they weren't "white" enough), and on issues of marriage, social status, and sexual behavior.

†† A recent study by Menachim Amir documented that in 77 per cent of the sample cases studied, in Philadelphia, both the rape victim and offender were black. In 18 per cent of the cases, both were white. Of course, black offenders are always more pursued than white offenders. We just do not know how many white men rape black or white women.[14]

‡‡ A sore but sexist point with many black men. As men, they would like to "own" women as white men can—or as certain African men can. Nevertheless, we cannot overlook how brutally and literally most white men *buy* black (and white) women. Black and poor men in America are reduced to stealing and/or despising what wealthier men can buy. Rape will always exist in patriarchal-class society.

EVELYN: I'm curious to know from white women whether they get this same kind of attitude from black men. Like I'm their property automatically. It's like we're altogether surrounded by this enemy so therefore whoever of my people comes into this thing, we're together and we're buddies and you're mine. When I first started on this job [as a secretary], it was like absolute indignation that I wouldn't respond to their [black male] advances. I would walk along corridors and I would get these little sounds, you know, or I would get a comment and I wouldn't respond. Absolute indignation! It was like they weren't going to accept this. I had to confront them again and again, to tell them that I in no way wanted any kind of intercourse with them, socially or otherwise. That I was going to call the shots about who I was going to socialize with whether they liked it or not. It took three months for me finally to make them understand that I have a right to not want to be bothered. They would call out to me, "If I was a white man you wouldn't do that." It was fantastic. This happened to me about a half dozen times—"You'd talk to me if I was a white man." They didn't know me at all, but this was like their paranoia. I found about three different things. The white men, they would make advances, but when I would rebuff them, that would be the end of it. And I think what they probably felt was, well, she digs her own black men. Like they could only see me, I'm sure, in relation to my being an appendage to some other man. It's got to be some other man.

PHYLLIS: Did white men make as many advances?

EVELYN: No, although I find on the whole, taking the whole span of things, like from the beginning of the day to the end of the day, there's far more white men who make advances to me in the street: there are more white men in the population.

PHYLLIS: Did white men on the job make the same kinds of advances?

EVELYN: No. Not the same kinds. What they do is run a path back and forth in front of my door. They will only make a verbal thing if they think they can get away with it, and not be seen. I remember once, one white guy was going into a doorway, so he just called something because he was disappearing, right. . . . But with white men too, the indignation is there. You can't set up the rules as to whom you socialize with. "If we extend ourselves to you and show you that we want to be friendly, O piece of black ass, you therefore should be ungrateful for this?"

CAROLINE: I'm twenty-seven years old now and my grandmother and her sisters, they look at me kind of queer. Like, what's the matter with her? Because my cousins are all married and have children. Growing up, I did have a lot of contempt for black men. You are always steered toward the one that's going to achieve a certain social position, that's going to raise your social status. I couldn't think of a common, everyday nine-to-five man that didn't have a career. He had to be a college graduate with a certain sort of social position. This is the kind of thing that my family is geared to. My mother married in that way . . . but in order [for such a black man] to continue [his] upward climb he would get a white woman. Several of my mother's stepbrothers have married white women. . . . There is always the feeling that if you get a black man on the rise that he might ditch you for a white woman if he gets a little bit higher. I think that part of the terrible isolation [that led to a suicide attempt] was that I didn't relate to men. I couldn't or wouldn't bring home to my family the socially acceptable ones and this led partly to the isolation. Also, the fact that I'm growing older and haven't gotten married and still hadn't embarked on a career and was stagnant and hadn't really done much of anything [led to the suicide attempt].

I feel I have to stand behind the black men because they've suffered. . . .

PHYLLIS: Haven't Black women suffered too?

CAROLINE: Well, yes, but the way out of that suffering is to help our men win the revolution. . . . I've sometimes wondered, though, how could I help fight if I'm busy taking care of babies?

Two of the Third World women who were psychiatrically hospitalized had genuine "madness" or "schizophrenic" experiences. Like many white women in Western culture, they relived (the meaning of) the crucifixion and/or the Immaculate Conception. During these experiences they were very ambivalent about or hostile to "woman's work," such as domestic servitude or sexual passivity. I don't know whether their "psychiatric careers" are very different from those of white women. I leave that for you to decide.

Several years ago I worked as a psychologist in a New York City hospital that "serviced" Spanish Harlem. It was there that I first saw but didn't meet Carmen. She was a dark-haired, heavy-set woman in her mid-forties and was causing a "commotion" on the psychiatric ward. She had thrown a banana peel on the floor and, despite threats and pleas, refused to pick it up. "This is the crazy ward, isn't it?" she demanded in excellent English. "I can do what I like here—or I shouldn't be here." I laughed—one of the few laughs I had on that particular police job, and walked on. Now, three years later, I was sitting in Carmen's living room, a neatly kept project apartment, filled with plastic crucifixes, plastic flowers, plastic couch covers, plastic doilies, and real police sirens. Judith, a friend of mine, who had been one of the therapists on the psychiatric ward, had befriended Carmen and been befriended by her. They had kept in touch.

Because Judith asked, Carmen agreed to speak with me. Several times that afternoon, when Carmen cried, Judith held her, squeezed her hand and mine, and made cups of coffee for us all.

PHYLLIS: Why did you go to a mental asylum?

CARMEN: Well, the first time was after my daughter was born. I was thirty years old and had a very bad delivery with her. I never had no trouble before—I was seventeen when I had my first son. This time I was very nervous coming home. I came home and I started to get sick.

PHYLLIS: Sick in what way?

CARMEN: Well, I stopped eating, first of all. Stopped sleeping. I just didn't eat and sleep. My friends came to see me and I wouldn't talk to them. I just looked up at the ceiling. I lay down and looked at the ceiling and then I stopped eating. For two weeks I was like that, and everybody was coming here trying to find out what was wrong with me. My baby needed food and I just lay in bed and smoked. I just didn't feel like doing it. I couldn't make the corner straight on the bed sheet.

PHYLLIS: Was anyone helping you take care of the baby?

CARMEN: No. They just didn't know what was wrong. Finally, someone called a doctor and he said, "She's having a terrible nervous breakdown!" . . . So they took me to Bellevue—it got so bad that I didn't recognize anybody—and I got very religious. I blessed everybody.

PHYLLIS: What happened at Bellevue?

CARMEN: It was terrible. They used to tie you up all the time—put you in seclusion. Once I wanted to take a shower. I didn't want to get into a tub because they line you up, naked in front of everybody, you strip down, get in line, and you get into a tub. There were only two tubs and I didn't want to get in because I was recently operated, you know, I had the Caesarian and I didn't want any dirt to get on me so I had a big argument with one of the attendants. Also I got scared of the shock treatments. It's a very scary feeling, especially when you feel like the metal things of the electricity goes through you—it's like a hammer hitting your head. I was afraid of the third one.

PHYLLIS: Did you say you didn't want it?

CARMEN: Oh, I fought against it. But they gave it to me by force.

PHYLLIS: Who signed for it?

CARMEN: My husband did. He said the doctor said, "She's not doing any good so let's try shock treatments."

PHYLLIS: How often did the doctor talk to you before deciding you weren't doing any good?

CARMEN: Well, I don't remember talking to a doctor. . . . After three weeks I was doing wonderful. I was back to normal. I brought up my daughter and everything. I didn't expect I would ever get sick again. Then

I started to get tumors and I was hemorrhaging, so I told the doctor, "I don't want no more children, so I'd like a hysterectomy before it turns into anything else." In the hospital I began to get religious again, after the hysterectomy. . . . One of the doctors, he was a psychiatrist, he came to me. I remember him coming to my bed and he gave me an injection and then he asked me what was wrong with me. The only thing I answered was

I don't want to go to Bellevue, that's all. And then they said to my ınd, "If you can get her home you can keep her home if you want o my husband brought me my clothes and he brought me a black dress. I put it on but the next minute I took it off and said, "Nobody is dead in the family, I don't have to wear black." So I stripped.

JUDITH: Maybe you felt bad about the hysterectomy. . . .

CARMEN: No. I had nine abortions. Them I was guilty about. An abortion is a direct sin against God. But an abortion is better than a hungry child, isn't it?

PHYLLIS: What happened after you kept refusing to put on the black dress?

CARMEN: I went to Bellevue. And Bellevue sent me to Rockland State. When I found out I was in a mental hospital you don't know how I cried. I got gray overnight. When I got there I saw the gate and said, "Gee, this sort of looks like a prison." I said to this other patient, "What kind of a hospital is this?" And she said, "Don't you know you're in a mental hospital, honey?" "No," I said, "this is a nut house?" "Yeah," she said, "that's where you are." So they all started to laugh because I didn't know. Oh, I felt terrible after that. I don't know how I managed not to get sick again there.

You stay there till you get well. Most women when they're sick don't take care of themselves. I comb my hair right away. That shows you're advancing. That you're not so sick.

PHYLLIS: What happened at Rockland State?

CARMEN: Happened? What could happen? They keep you locked up all day. I used to go out to work just to get out.

PHYLLIS: What kind of work?

CARMEN: Oh, you mop floors, you make beds, you wash windows, you wash floors.

PHYLLIS: Did they ever pay you for that?

CARMEN: No, the only place they pay you is the commissary. Ten dollars a month for food. I worked there also. I was a private maid to one of the psychiatrists, a woman doctor. She knew that I spoke English and Spanish. She said, "I'd like you to work for me because my son wants to learn Spanish. In school he is learning Spanish and with you around you'll talk to him in Spanish and he'll pick up more."

PHYLLIS: Did she pay for that?

CARMEN: They're supposed to pay you three dollars a week but being my husband used to leave me five dollars a week she never paid me. I had to dust, pass the vaccum, had to change the sheets, pick up her clothes after her. I used to wash her panties. Now how low can you get, her panties I had to wash!

PHYLLIS: Why didn't you tell her?

CARMEN: I should have, but it was such a pleasure being out of the ward. Also, other places were worse. They had a laundry there and, let me tell you, you work hard there.

PHYLLIS: Who worked in the laundry?

CARMEN: A lot of girls. You see them marching like prisoners in the morning.

PHYLLIS: Did they get paid?

CARMEN: No, the only place that pays you is the commissary. . . . I went back to Rockland a lot of times. I got religious a lot. I could bless people and make them well.

PHYLLIS: Maybe you could. . . .

CARMEN: So now, my husband wouldn't wait long. If I didn't sleep one night he would find me in the kitchen sitting by the window. Then he'd take me right away. He wouldn't wait to see how bad off I was. He'd take me right away.

PHYLLIS: When you were sitting by the window, were you thinking?

CARMEN: Yes, thinking. Important things. . . . I never stayed longer at Rockland than two or three months. Until my husband got a mistress. He was always a good husband. He'd bring home all his salary, and even with being with that mistress he had, he never let me be without anything. My rent was paid. I had money for my food and he even used to give me gifts, just as if there was nothing going on between him and another woman. But that last time I was there [at Rockland] it seemed like the two of them were trying to get rid of me. He left me in there ten months, close to a year. That mistress hurt me quite a lot, especially when I first knew about it. I thought my world would come to an end because I love my husband very much—he was a very good man.

PHYLLIS: How did you find out?

CARMEN: I started to get anonymous calls—letters—from her. She's crazy. He claimed that she was jealous and all that—it was true. That didn't make me sick, it was the funniest thing. I can't understand why I get sick because, like I say, my husband was very good to me, very good —all the time I got sick except for the last ten months. No, he didn't come to see me at all—I got mad at him. The only way I could get even with him was to make him believe that I had a man that wants to marry me—and that's when he jumped.

PHYLLIS: When you found out about your husband having a mistress did you get very upset in the hospital? Did somebody take notice of that fact?

CARMEN: No. It hurt me, though, because my daughter knew about it and she never told me.

PHYLLIS: She probably didn't want to upset you.

CARMEN: Probably. She was too young. Well, I resigned myself to the fact that she's the mistress, staying in the house—let her clean and cook, while I rest, in the hospital. Every time I'd come home for a week all I would do would be clean and cook and clean and wash and clean so I went back to the hospital. True you don't like to be locked up but I consoled myself, oh, somebody else is cleaning the house, doing the cooking.

PHYLLIS: Kind of like a maid. . . .

CARMEN: Yeah, she's sorta Negro anyway—what I couldn't understand was the fact that she would actually fix food for my husband to take to see me so I don't know what kind of combination they had between the both of them or the convenience or the plans they had.

JUDITH: The convenience for your husband was great.

CARMEN: Oh, yeah, that's why he enjoyed it—that didn't make me sick but it got me mad because he was going to leave me there [in Rockland].

You see, the legal procedure is the husband signs you in. I tell you it's true because my father tried to get me out, my two sons tried to take me out, and the doctor would not let me go home. My father said, "I'd even take her with me to my house," and the doctor wouldn't agree to it either. I don't know what he wanted—so finally the only way I could get out was that my father and mother was supposed to live here with me.

PHYLLIS: How did you finally get out?

CARMEN: Like I told you, my two sons came to me. I said, "You gotta do something to get me out of here. He don't want to sign me out." And my two sons, one sat on each side of me and said, "This is enough, my mother has been here ten months—she is well—you're not going to keep her here any longer—so you're gonna sign her out whether you like it or not." My other son is a big bruiser so he said, "You don't want to get a little beat up, do you?" So finally my sons made him do it.

PHYLLIS: What happened then?

CARMEN: He [my husband] brought me home—we lived there like two companions, no sex, no talking of any kind. When he came from work I'd leave the food on the stove and I'd take my plate and go look at the television. There was no conversation between us or anything. The only one who got annoyed was his mistress. You know, he never loved her completely. In fact, I used to warn her. I told her, "Look, I throw him out every day and he don't want to leave—it's not my fault." She got red as a sheet. I said, "I don't want him," and I never gave the understanding that I was hurt what they were doing to me—because I told her, "I have a man of thirty-eight years who is willing to marry me so if you can take my husband off my hands I'd really appreciate it." Oh, I was ripping but I didn't let her know it. She said, "He's taking advantage of me." I said, "That's your problem, not mine." So she said to me, "Well, I can't blame you because we did it to you first." I said, "You don't bother me at all. I'm even tired of my husband for years already. In fact, I've been going out with this man for three years and he don't know about it."

She thought she was gonna come here and mess me up—'cause she wanted me to get sick.

Only once I had a fight with him. He called the cops and they thought it was just a family argument. Then my husband called them on the side and told them I had been a mental case and all that. Bellevue again.

He [my husband] thought I wouldn't let him leave me but he found out different when I changed the lock on the door. My current boy friend lives across the street. He's a very happy-go-lucky man. He'll say all of a sudden, "Let's go to a movie, you don't have to cook." I'd say, "Gee, that's nice, let's go!"

LaVerne is in her mid-twenties. She is a part-time college student and secretary. She talks as fast as I do, and sometimes exceeds me in manic gusto. She is very intelligent and twice as explosive. She has been in and out of private therapy for about six years and has been hospitalized three times.

PHYLLIS: Why did you go to a mental asylum?

LAVERNE: The first time, it was after a party. I came home very upset and, honey, I had a hallucination you wouldn't believe. I was not the Virgin Mary, but *another* Virgin Mary. I had three climaxes in a row and gave birth to another Jesus—the black Christ. It was a virgin birth. It was a virgin birth because I wasn't having sex with anybody. But he wasn't around. The child was gone. Now, the mother got to get herself together. If he is gone, I've done something wrong. I felt I better do something if I am a mother of Christ so I took a bath.

Then I made a lot of phone calls. I called Rockefeller because I wanted some things done about black-white relations. . . . I wanted black people to love themselves. I knew, but they didn't. There was so much promiscuity around—and I *mean* that. By the time I called Rockefeller I calmed down. I was going to sleep. But my mother started calling neighbors because she was afraid of me. She was always afraid of me. She's half white and thinks she's better than me. She's a fuckin' whore—yes! She's had boy friends who've felt me up—and she just sits there and denies it. . . . But now she called the neighbors in to sit with her all night.

Then I started hallucinating again. I thought people were trying to get through the walls at me—oh, shit.

Then I wanted to be like an American Indian—instincts, instincts is where it's at. So I turned up the record player and started dancing around the house. And I pulled up the shades—I wanted everyone to see me. My mother, she *locks* doors. I took a hammer very calmly and broke the locks on my bedroom, my mother's, my brother's, and the guest room. I was dancing around—people were looking in. "Hi, kids, how'rya doing?" I told them.

Then the cops came in. They were obviously afraid of me. "What are you afraid of?" I said, "you want some Kool-Aid?" One cop said, "Oh, God," and I said, "What are you saying, that's my Father because I gave birth to another Christ child." But I'm not going to tell them about the Christ because they'll think I'm nuts, and I'm not too sure about that scene myself . . . so I'm going to be real cool.

They [the cops] asked who was responsible for me. "My mother," I said. But she was already at work. So they got the next-door neighbor. I held on to her. I was afraid, I was scared, and I asked her, "Please don't leave me, they're gonna hurt me." But she pulled away from me. Oh, I didn't want to go to a hospital. I know what they do to you there. . . .

PHYLLIS: What happened at the hospital?

LAVERNE: They stuck me with needles. They feed you—force feeding, or you won't get out. They put me in a strait jacket. They wouldn't let me talk to a psychiatrist. Then when I did, I told him about getting too much medication, and I cried, so they gave me more medicine because I was upset.

PHYLLIS: What kind of medicine did you get?

LAVERNE: Thorazine, but that made me break out so they gave me something else, but I have a sinus condition so they gave me stellazine, which was the nicest thing but it wasn't strong enough, so they gave me thorazine again.

PHYLLIS: Did they give you shock therapy?

LAVERNE: Oh no. I said if they ever did I would have intercourse with the doctors, spit out my food. Shock therapy is a dangerous thing. I saw what happens—you start forgetting things—I've spoken to patients. And you get depressed again anyway.

After ninety days they can't keep you. Anyway, I quieted down and never yelled and never said anything. The patients said, "You want to get out—this is what you do," and so I did it. I helped the nurses and told them how cute they were. I washed the floors. I never washed a floor in my life before.

PHYLLIS: How did you get into the hospital the second time?

LAVERNE: I got married, right! and I was working to send him through school. He'd come home at night and tell me about the pretty girls he'd seen. "You're so ugly without make-up, God, are you ugly," he'd tell me. "Your breasts are too small." But he wouldn't talk to me—oh no! He'd just wanna screw, turn over, and go to sleep. . . .

Then we're at a party and I heard him talking to another guy. He said I was cute but stupid. "So whadya want her for, man—pussy?" "Yeah," he answers. Oh, shit! Since I'm thirteen years old—and he still just wants pussy! I wanted to get a gun and kill him, but I couldn't get a gun so easy. My brother talked me into taking a job instead, working with children. . . . Well, I left him [my husband] and went back to live with my mother—and we don't get along, right? So we had a fight—ahh, she doesn't love me. She told me I was too stupid to go to college.

She let me just rot in the hospital that first time, she's a fuckin' whore, that's what I told her, that always gets to her. So she put me in the hospital again. She called her boy friend over and he beat me up because I had disrespect for my mother. "You son of a bitch, you try to put me in the hospital, I'll kill you." I tried to call my therapist but he punched me to the floor each time. They tied me down and put me in a strait jacket.

At the hospital—questions! "What's the matter?" the psychiatrist wants to know. "Wars stink. Prostitution stinks. You stink." "I think we're gonna have to keep you," he says. "No foolin'!" This time I had a beautiful woman doctor from Central America, and she really helped me get out. . . .

They gave me a lot of psychological tests and, you know, I came out masculine. What does that mean? Like on one test they ask: do you want to be married and happy or rich and single? "Oh, shit! Rich and single," I said.

Why didn't our mothers and grandmothers and great-grandmothers tell us what battle it was we lost, or never fought, so that we would understand how total was our defeat, and that religion and madness and frigidity were how we mourned it?

Why were our mothers so silent about rape and incest and prostitution and their own lack of pleasure? Why, when they had so many words, did they not name our heroines for us, tell us about feminists and suffragettes and Amazons and great-mothers?

Chapter Nine

FEMINISTS

I wish woman to live *first* for God's sake. Then she will not make an imperfect man her god, and thus sink to idolatry. Then she will not take what is not fit for her from a sense of weakness and poverty. Then if she finds what she needs in Man embodied, she will know how to live and be worthy of being loved. . . .

Woman, self-centered, would never be absorbed by any relation; it would be only an experience to her as to man. It is a vulgar error that love—*a* love—to Woman is her whole existence; she also is born for Truth and Love in their universal energy. Would she but assume her inheritance, Mary would not be the only virgin mother. . . .

Margaret Fuller[1]

But early I perceived that men never in any extreme of despair wished to be women. On the contrary, they were ever ready to taunt one another at any sign of weakness with,

Art thou not like the women, who—The passage ends various ways, according to the occasion and rhetoric of the speaker. When they admired any woman, they were inclined to speak of her as "above her sex." Silently I observed this, and feared it argued a rooted skepticism which for ages had been fastening on the heart and which only an age of miracles could eradicate. Ever I have been treated with great sincerity; and I look upon it as a signal instance of this, that an intimate friend of the other sex said in a fervent moment that I "deserved in some star to be a man." He was much surprised when I disclosed my faith that the feminine side, the side of love, of beauty, of holiness, was now to have its full chance, and that if either were better, it was better now to be a woman; for even the slightest achievement of good was furthering an especial work of our time. He smiled incredulously. "She makes the best she can of it," thought he. "Let Jews believe the pride of Jewry, but I am of the better sort, and know better."

Margaret Fuller[2]

Nowhere is woman treated according to the merit of her work, but rather as a sex. It is therefore almost inevitable that she should pay for her right to exist, to keep a position in whatever line, with sex favors. Thus it is merely a question of degree whether she sell herself to one man, in or out of marriage, or to many men. Whether our reformers admit it or not, the economic and social inferiority of woman is responsible for prostitution. . . . It is conceded that woman is being reared as a sex commodity, and yet she is kept in absolute ignorance of the meaning and importance of sex. . . . "The wife who married for money, compared with the prostitute," says Havelock Ellis, "is the true scab. She is paid less, gives much more in return in labor and care, and is absolutely bound to her master. The prostitute never signs away the right over her own person, she retains her freedom and personal rights, nor is she always compelled to submit to man's embrace."

Emma Goldman[3]

I see neither physical, psychological, nor mental reasons why woman should not have the equal right to vote with man. But that cannot blind me to the absurd notion that woman will accomplish that wherein man has failed. If she would not make things worse, she certainly could not make them better. To assume, therefore, that she would succeed in purifying something which is not susceptible of purification, is to credit her with supernatural powers. Since woman's greatest misfortune has been that she was looked upon as either angel or devil, her true salvation lies in being placed on earth; namely in being considered human, and therefore subject to all human follies and mistakes. Are we, then, to believe that two errors will make a right? Are we to assume that the poison already inherent in politics will be decreased, if women were to enter the political arena? The most ardent suffragists would hardly maintain such a folly.

Emma Goldman[4]

The binding force in this collective is feminism . . . we act as mutual role-models for each other—that is, role-models as feminist professionals—something which we all find hard to come by in our everyday work settings. We are able to identify with each other's successes: "If good things can happen to this woman in the male-dominated world . . . then perhaps there's hope for me." . . . The collective acts as a supportive system during individual crises and uncertainties . . . we provide for each other those vital, informal channels of communication which are used so regularly by *male* professionals, and from which they so systematically exclude their *female* colleagues. Men will meet and exchange valuable information over dinner or coffee—but when a woman colleague is "lucky" enough to be included (this once happened to one of our members) they're apt to say "Pardon us for talking shop" and immediately start talking nonprofessional trivialities . . . the collective has provided for all of us a place where we feel comfortable to be ourselves—by this I mean a place where we are not castigated as being "aggressive," for taking over, being articulate, disagreeing, confronting. We really value each other's competence. . . .

The Chicago Women in Psychology Collective

Why has modern feminism surfaced in America? Why has so startling, so simple, so dangerous, so elite an idea as female humanity, or equality, or supremacy, or sexuality, surfaced as a potentially *mass* movement? Is modern feminism essentially a by-product of certain changes in material reality such as birth control technology and planetary overpopulation? Is modern feminism one of many survival-responses to the changing nature and/or diminishing availability of agricultural and industrial work, at a time when, barring warfare, starvation, and ecological disasters, more people are living longer? This might explain why women are being encouraged or even forced to talk about "sharing" their spheres of domesticity and emotionality with men: the work for which men have been made into "men" and women into "women" is disappearing. Is feminism an expression of an American war-weariness so deep that some men either want women to solve the problem of violence for them—or wish to become "feminine," i.e., pacific, so that they may finally experience a victim's guiltless-ness and fatalism?

To the extent to which feminism is conceived of as a cooperative rather than a competitive ideology; to the extent to which it is ritual, tribal, and pleasure-oriented, rather than unique, individual, and heroic-death-oriented—it is feared as "barbaric," "primitive," or "fascistic," by women as well as men. Certainly I fear it, if the "rituals" are anything less than bold and true, if the rituals concern mediocrity and defeat, rather than power, pleasure, and self-defined works of the imagination.

Is the American feminist movement a "return of the re-pressed": is it an old religion, an old polity, whose time has mysteriously, impersonally, come round again? Or is it a genuinely new mythology, technologically rendered, whose consequences are unforeseen? Will the structures of human psychology remain un-changed if women should "win" the sex war—should directly control the means of production and reproduction? Or if men should become social and biological mothers? Or if women ceased being the psycho-biological representations of birth—and, conse-quently, of death? Or if women became biological mothers and social fathers? Or if a communist-sexual revolution really succeeded? Or if sexual gender ceased to exist as a significant, identifying dimension?

Can women "win" the sex war, or banish such a war en-tirely, *without* becoming the dominant sex? If women were to dominate, would biological men then be as oppressed as biological women have been—and if so, why should this matter to women? There must be some good or at least some overwhelming reasons why the injustice of female oppression has never mattered enough to men for them to banish it.

Is the sex war at the root of other major evils such as race and class slavery, capitalism, puritanism, imperialism, and warfare? And if so, can such evils be exiled from the mass human condition forever by any but a feminist method? (What *is* a feminist method?) Given our conditioning as women, can we ever become feminist revolutionaries (or human beings), without becoming lesbians? As women, can we wage *any* sort of revolution if we are psychosexually bound to men or marriage or full-time child care? Men can scarcely be revolutionaries under such conditions, even though their relationship to women, marriage, and child care is a far less committed one. But why even wage a struggle, especially a violent one, if its goals are simply revenge or power? What if we "won" and became as removed from emotion and sexuality as men are? But perhaps, as women, we will never be allowed full emotional and sexual expression *unless* we control the means of production and reproduction.

With great intensity, women in groups are asking these and many other questions. It was in "consciousness-raising" groups that women began to break the twentieth-century silence between mothers and daughters. The small group provided a way and a place for women to name their common plight. It also served as an experimental model of cooperative and competent society, especially for women whose experience with extended families or female kinship and living arrangements (or with genuine cooperativeness) was minimal.

Relatively privileged white middle-class women discovered that privilege was not freedom; that love was a foreign country with few survivors; and that the female body is as colonized as any ghetto or Third World country. They also discovered that neither men nor women liked women, especially a strong or happy woman.

A discontented, complaining, "weak" woman, although disliked, is far more acceptable than a contented and/or powerful woman—who is experienced as dangerous, and is ostracized and "killed" far more quickly and inevitably than her male counterpart—especially if she is in any way sexually knowledgeable, independent, or "aggressive."

Women in small feminist groups also talked, often endlessly, about sexual orgasms. Their tones were informative, comic, relieved, angry, and joyful—as they began to reclaim their bodies. Women's acceptance and enjoyment of their bodies is an absolute prerequisite for their self-development: and I am not talking about an American mechanistic "sexual sell," or about any type of male-originated or fantasied group or "free" sex.*

This "talking about orgasms," which was initially derided as bourgeois self-indulgence and "racist," actually constitutes a valid example of "giving" women what they "need" before, or as a way of talking "politics." (It goes without saying that neither female sexual orgasms nor ghetto breakfast programs alone, in themselves, are anything more than first but necessary steps in the right direction.) But I think that it was this "talking about orgasms," together with the expression of anger in an *atmosphere of female approval,* that led to whatever changes occurred in women.

And the changes occurred quickly, in an exhilarating and suspiciously instant, prefabricated way. For a while it seemed as if some apocalypse was about to happen, as if all wrongs would be righted, and the gates of paradise forced open by reason and sorority. It took awhile before American women were directly introduced, politically, to the twentieth century; awhile before we realized the extent to which publicity, like all advertising, is a substitute for change, a compromise offering, instead of something of value;

---

* I suppose that women will only be able to experience their sexuality fully when their *mothers* have controlled the means of production and reproduction.

awhile before we understood how truly divided we were, how deep our female conditioning was, and how difficult it will be to change it. Until then—the events were dizzying, contradictory, and absolutely uncorrupted.

Almost overnight, women organized demonstrations, legal actions, bail funds, abortion services, wage strikes, national and international meetings, caucases, magazines, pamphlets, communes, disputes, rock bands, theater groups, female studies programs, self-defense programs, all-female dances, and lesbian and women's centers in every major American city. For those women involved, the women's movement, to a greater or lesser extent, began to vie with, supplant, or shore up the institutions of marriage, love, and psychotherapy. Up to a point, women's liberation was more "therapeutic" than either marriage or psychotherapy: it made women happier, angrier, more confident, more adventurous, more moral— and it produced a range of behavioral changes.

Some women quit their jobs and refused to be involved in alienated and/or oppressive labor,† others began job training, college or graduate school, and planned careers seriously, for the first time. Some women started living together; some began living alone for the first time. Some women insisted that their husbands share child care and housework equally; others organized all-female cooperatives for this purpose. Some women had abortions; others refused them, where they might not have done so before. Some women left their husbands; others began to live with a man, feeling somehow at less of a psychological disadvantage than before. Some women refused "alimony"; others insisted on it as back pay and as reparations. Some women withdrew from drugs;

† It is important to note that only those who could afford to do so—both financially and pychologically—did this. Most women, especially those over thirty with children, cannot just quit their jobs as mothers, housekeepers, factory workers, and secretaries: they can only demand wages, wage increases, and better working conditions.

others turned to them—out of curiosity, paranoia, impatience, and despair. Many women stopped walking down city streets with their eyes averted, stopped not "hearing," stopped not "responding," or stopped responding in female ways to male verbal abuse. Some women found that, the stronger they grew and the more they understood, the more they "needed" a man or a monogamous "partner," either because they felt they could begin to hold their own in such a relationship or because they feared what they knew, and needed the blind comfort of traditional role-playing—just one more time. Their conditioning was too strong and the woman's movement still too weak to help them grow beyond a certain point.

Many women started reading "political" and "scientific" books as passionately as they read novels: somehow, the glaze of "stupidity" that films over understanding—when understanding understands that, even if it understood, it could never inherit the castle and the kingdom—tentatively began to lift. The characteristic female (and black) attitude of boredom and failure in white male-dominated and sexually integrated classrooms began to shift to curiosity and success. Within a small group, or at a woman's conference, women stopped giggling, "losing," and competing with each other for male attention and approval. There were no sexual distractions either: most women weren't "attracted" to each other. Many women found they could think, found that it gave them pleasure, realized that their *thinking* ability was needed by others.

Some women stopped going to beauty parlors, stopped wearing make-up, stopped shopping (or shopping frequently) for "sexy" or "fashionable" clothes. Women began to value their time: they needed fewer adornments to "make up" for being female. As a woman, I do not like Puritanism—in thought or dress. However, as a woman, I cannot put my heart into the elite frivolity of expensive or frequently changed costumes—when such costumes are not only *not* available to all people but, more important, seem to signify a growing passivity and dependence in men as well as women.‡ It is, however, politically naïve to think that poverty, racism, or pollution in America will be "solved" if women will only stop conspicuously consuming. The military-industrial complex in Washington and Detroit are far more crucial to such solutions than are the clothing, cosmetics, and detergent industries. Further, it is far easier for women who can't afford to "buy" to rationalize "not buying" into a form of power. But this is a cultural and moral gesture—not an economic boycott. Fighting for the right to buy, or stealing if employment is denied, are far more realistic paths of action for powerless groups.

Some women affirmed, discovered, or began to explore their bisexuality or lesbianism. Some women remained celibate for long periods without any noticeable anxiety or suffering. Others felt that it was important to them to have both warmth and sexual intimacy on a frequent basis: either casually or non-casually, with other women, or with men. Some women masturbated to orgasm for the first time, or for the first time without guilt. Some women decided to have a child, or another child; others decided firmly against ever doing so.

What have contemporary American psychologists and psychiatrists thought and felt about feminism? How have they behaved toward feminism—as an ideology, as a movement, and as something that has been influencing their female patients? Publicly, they have behaved like any other group: they have engaged in nervous laughter, purposeful misunderstanding, hairsplitting, malicious cruelty, misguided sympathy, boredom, hostility, condescension, and

‡ The fact that American men are being advertised into an involvement with cosmetics and fashions is not as much a sign of sexual equality as it is of capitalist market-seeking and a failing economy. Perhaps the frantic costume changes from one historical period to another signifies some collective desire to find the "path not taken"—and to take it out of the holocaust.

commercial and academic capitalism.** Some clinicians have been genuinely curious, sympathetic, and supportive. A minority have joined the women's movement. Several professional journals have devoted "special issues" to women—as a newly discovered but exotic minority-majority group. The *Radial Therapist,* a collective "underground" journal, has published articles about women and sexism in each of its issues. Groups of women psychologists, therapists and "patients" have organized referral lists to feminist therapists. No one has presented a new theory of human personality based on feminist ideologies—nor has anyone psychoanalyzed feminism.

Many male psychologists who are verbally "sympathetic" to feminism still call their middle-aged female patients "girls"; still describe them in terms of how "attractive" they are; and, of course, still relate to wives or girl friends in non-reciprocally dependent ways. Many are sympathetic to feminism because they are sexually "attracted" to feminists, whom they see as more "interesting" and "sexually promiscuous" than their wives.

Most psychiatrists publicly deny the existence of sex-typed slave labor in state and county hospitals; minimize the effect of medical and psychological "experiments" on their patients; tell "dirty jokes" at their staff meetings; and deride feminist grievances. They are more willing to pity women than to respect them; more comfortable with unhappy women than with angry women.

Most male and female clinicians are emotionally and financially

** In 1970 a group of women, speaking for the Association for Women in Psychology, addressed a crowded convention meeting of the American Psychological Association. They demanded token reparations for female mental patients (for legal fees, education, housing, etc.). The amount of money demanded was equal to the money that women psychologists had paid in membership dues over a five-year period—money which was never used to serve job security or advancement opportunity for these relatively privileged women professionals. The demand was met by very loud and hostile laughter, and was followed by the hostile diplomacy of bureaucratic "procedurism." Needless to say, no money was ever received for this purpose—but most of the women involved in the demand found themselves invited speakers to the 1971 convention. And so it goes.

bound by the romance of the bourgeois family. Few middle-aged clinicians of either sex have any class consciousness. At a recent professional meeting, one female clinician, in a nostalgic description of pre-World War II Vienna, recalled how "really liberated" all the Viennese women were. I asked her whether poor and un-educated women in Vienna were also "liberated."†† She answered that she really hadn't thought of it "in those terms." Clinicians seem to dislike and pity the paranoia and anger of feminists: slyly, confidently, they want to know why are they so "nervous" about being found sexually attractive by "poor" Tom, Dick, or Harry? Why are they so angry at verbal abuse in the streets? (The lower classes have always been rowdy, excitingly so, come to think of it—but the police will always be able to handle the poor if they get too out of control) Don't these suddenly complaining women "unconsciously" invite harassment or rape, and don't they "un-consciously" enjoy it? Furthermore, isn't the point of women's liberation the liberation of men too, and not, heaven forbid, female power? Isn't capitalism the *real* enemy and feminism divisive and/or the "pouting" of spoiled white middle-class women?‡‡

Most contemporary clinicians are as confused about and hostile to feminism as most people are—and I am talking only about those clinicians who are *interested* enough to attend panels about female psychology and feminism or to publish on the subject. I have yet to attend a professional panel in psychology or psychiatry concerning women during the last two years, at which some women clinicians have *not* delivered impassioned speeches about the neces-sity and desirability of combining motherhood and professional careers—no matter that some other topic is specifically being

†† I personally would not define Freud's wealthy Dutiful Daughters as "liberated" but as "privileged."

‡‡ My feelings about this question are: first, that it is usually asked with-out information, seriousness, or respect; second, that sexism preceded capitalism and may indeed have led to it; and, third, that ridicule and misunderstanding are forms of violence that must be avoided as much as possible—especially by "scientists" of humanity.

explored. Their male colleagues usually remain safely silent during this genteel Saturday night brawl. The women professionals first insist they have no political ax to grind—and then quickly offer their political credentials: the existence of their own two or three children. Such offerings would be acceptable to me if we lived in a female-dominated culture, or in a culture that did not, rather dubiously "reward" women for breeding—more than for other activities.

After defending the motherhood faith, the convention clinicians usually take a breath and launch into a tirade against the "terrible and damaging mothers" their patients have had—those very same "mothers" whom feminists are apparently trying to sneak off the hook of maternal responsibility! They usually conclude their speeches with a description of their *male* patients in Pietà-like tones—to the approval of their male colleagues, who, in turn, will now not fire them from their jobs or exclude them from their communication networks. No need to: such women are maternal and feminine, and not angry man-haters like "the others."*

Some clinicians at professional panels have yelled at feminist participants, often rather hysterically and brutally. They have called them everything from neurotic and criminal to selfish and counter-revolutionary. Often, they want the feminists present to talk more about how sexism has hurt men than about how it has hurt women.† Often, they seek out individual feminists to confess their

* Female clinicians are generally as ambivalent about women as all other women are. The specifically painful price they've had to pay for even limited "success" outside the home will not allow them to quickly envision radical definitions of self. One successful woman academic told me, sotto voce, "Phyllis, of course it's conditioning, but conditioning *works*—and after such terrible conditioning, most women are in terrible condition. Would *you* want to work with them? More power to you for trying, but I just can't."

† I asked a black male psychologist at one of these meetings whether he thought a meeting about black power, equality, and self-determination should dwell overlong, and with great clucking sympathy, on how racism has hurt white racists. He laughed.

guilt, unhappiness, and confusion, to state their ardent desire to "learn" and to be "forgiven" or, more simply, to state their ardent desires.

What I am saying is that even the most sympathetic male professionals behave like men—and like men at conventions. They do not usually continue their "confessions" or change their behavior—either at home or publicly.

THE INTERVIEWS

What does it mean to be a feminist in America today? Why did we seek therapy and why were we psychiatrically hospitalized? What were our lives like before we became feminists or therapeutic patients, and how have they changed since?

I spoke to twenty-six feminists, including myself, "officially." Their ages ranged from seventeen to fifty-eight: sixty-eight per cent of the women were between twenty and thirty years old; sixty-one per cent were either only or oldest children: ninety per cent were white Americans. One woman had some high school experience, seven women had some college experience, twelve women had B.A. degrees, and six women had attended or completed graduate school. Four of the women were unemployed and living on welfare, four of the women were unsalaried students, four of the women were salaried within the woman's movement at minimum wage levels, two of the women were clerical workers, and twelve of the women were employed in professional capacities, for example, as teachers, journalists, or social workers. Only three of the women earned more than $8000 yearly: most earned between $2000 and $7500 yearly.

Twenty-one of the women considered themselves feminists of

about two years' duration. Five women had a more relatively recent commitment. Three women were heterosexually married, six women were divorced, thirteen women were legally single and living alone, three women were living in a woman's collective, and one woman was living with a man. Seven of the women were lesbians.

Twenty-five of the women had been (or still were) involved in private therapy, for a total group average of forty-one months (see Table 3). Feminists remained in treatment with male therapists for about thirty-one months and with female therapists for about nineteen months. Seven of the feminists, five of whom were also lesbians, had been psychiatrically incarcerated. Their average length of hospital stay was 158 days.

With few exceptions, all the feminists grew up in families where sex roles, however they were defined, were rigidly defined; in families where most mothers stayed at home for child care and domestic purposes—at least during their daughter's first five years of life; in families where menstruation was somehow shameful and virginity was not; in families where, no matter what else was allowed or encouraged, love, marriage, and motherhood were touted as *the* most important goals of female life. Most of the women had "troubled" relationships with their mothers, and of course, with developing traits such as confidence, a sense of self, tenaciousness, initiative, sexuality, a wide range of interests, a deep and preferred enjoyment of other women and "younger" men, and an ability to say no to what they didn't initiate or choose. Most of the women had "trouble" with work—with the getting and keeping of "jobs." Such "trouble" often increased after they became feminists—whether their jobs were as housewives and mothers, students, feminists, or bourgeois professionals.‡

‡ Awareness doesn't lead to instant or easy happiness. It may lead to the ability to make choices, which is one aspect of wisdom.

ALICE: You won't believe this—well, maybe you will—but when I went to my first department meeting, I was the only woman there. And the men assumed, they just *assumed*, that I'd take the "minutes." I walked out—and told them I wouldn't be bringing back any coffee for them either. After that, I developed a reputation for being "difficult" and "paranoid." . . . The secretaries, of course, preferred working for men. They were resigned to it, used to it—they might get flirted with or married. They didn't like working for a woman—and if my male colleagues saw me dictating a letter they'd say, "Oh ho! Caught you in the act, oppressing a sister, are you now?" But *they* didn't stop dictating letters, and I was responsible for as much on the job as they were—and of course, I was getting paid less money and couldn't really "fraternize" to make up for it. I could have had an "affair" with one man—and would have been somewhat protected by him—as his property. I could have flirted more to find out things, or acted as if they didn't matter to find out things; I could have played the usual game of token woman who doesn't like other women. . . . I did none of these things—and everything was an uphill fight, just everything. And I had no wife to go home to at night to comfort me. I only had a boy friend, who really *needed* and *thought* he needed comforting—and didn't know how to comfort in return without feeling "castrated" . . . and my first CR group thought I was too successful and therefore a "male-identified" woman and wouldn't comfort or support me either. . . . You get real cooled out if you're an "achievement"-oriented woman. No matter how high a price you pay, you're alone when you get anywhere—in a way that no man ever has to be.

DEIRDRE: I had a really good woman analyst. I thought I had become stronger and more sure of myself. I felt I didn't have to play any games with men—and I didn't believe I was picking the sadists any more. So, I got pregnant—a woman's thing to do—no? And my boy friend began having temper tantrums, affairs, and withdrawing from me. Now we had talked it all out before—about our having a child—and here he was behaving just like a trapped animal. And I had too much of a sense of self to do the usual crap—cry, beg, promise, lie. So I left him. I was very bitter. I felt that no matter how hard women and men tried to have a relationship, no matter how unique and exceptional they were, at some crucial pressure point, societal training of dominance-submission will rise to the surface. And men will be absolutely unyielding unless the woman plays her submissive role. . . . I became so frightened of what would happen to me—a bitter woman alone, totally responsible for a baby, so frightened when I realized how universal this situation is for women—whether men are legally or economically there or not—that I frightened the child to death— I miscarried. I think it was then that I became a feminist.

Most of the feminists described certain middle-class and existential problems that neither individual therapists nor isolated consciousness-raising groups had any control over—in terms of causing or "curing." The groups, however, were generally more aware that the problems were real, external, and could not be solved by the individual woman alone.

MARILYN: In a lot of ways, he [my therapist] has reassured me about getting pleasure from sex just for the sake of it. He felt outraged on my behalf when I was with a guy who wouldn't sleep with me because he thought I treated him like a sex object. In a sense, he was right, I didn't "love" him or want to "marry" him, but I did want to sleep with him. . . . When he turned me down I had this incredible experience of wow, what's happening! I felt guilty about treating him like an object, and I was hurt too. But dig it: this guy stopped in the middle of making love. He didn't let me get away with anything. The decision to be "moral" or "immoral" was not allowed to me.

DONNA: So I left my husband and gave up my "establishment" career. And was I grateful for [my boy friend's] struggling with his sexism. Gee: he's actually *trying,* I owe him even more than I owe a man who doesn't try. . . . Eternally grateful, that's me, Polyanna Pure, Earth Mother —and I can't help it, I love it, I love feeling good vibes. . . .

So then he tells me I should get into pottery and tie-dyeing and drugs: fuck the career, it sucks—*and it does*—but he doesn't drop out. He puts his shoulder to the capitalist wheel so that I can potter around—and while I'm at it, I can cook and clean and be what I love most—Earth Mother. . . .

Well, it's not a *bad* life, and he's more sensitive than other men, but somehow, psychologically, nothing's changed.

KATHRYN: How can a therapist or a love relationship or a single group "help" me with the accumulated and ongoing and constant damage of being a woman in this culture? I'm not supposed to *exist*—and I'm supposed to be happy about my non-existence. For example, the old, prefeminist me is not supposed to notice or respond to male insults on the street—but secretly, I'm supposed to like them. I should lay back like a pale ghost and not move too much while I'm being maritally raped, but I'm supposed to like it—see? It's like I'm not there, like I don't really exist—and I guess I didn't. Another example: in restaurants, my "date" or husband orders my meal for me. I don't speak to the waiters directly. And such public invisibility or non-existence is supposed to make me feel safe and loved and protected. It's Leda and the swan all over again: I'm supposed to get my rocks off by being raped. And I suppose I *did*: I went to beauty parlors and wore high heels and short skirts and make-up. Now that seems very sad and very frightening to me. I know how deep such conditioning goes and how hard it is to shake it.

Now take the new feminist me. I always pay for myself in restaurants. Often, when I'm with a poorer or younger companion, male or female, I'll pay for them too. Well, if it's a *male* companion, he gets the change and the waiter's thanks. Even with money, I still don't exist. Another thing, if I ask directions about how to get somewhere, or how to fix something, and if I have a male companion within *hearing* distance, *he'll* get the instructions. Last week I asked a male clerk in a country supermarket where the nearest liquor store was. A man standing nearby, whom I didn't even *know*, got the directions. And, oh yes, if men think you really want to be treated as if you exist, they do it coldly, and with a vengeance. "So you wanna be a man? Okay, take that on the chin." And you really get hit doubly hard with stiff upper lip, grin and bear it, brutality. They're saying to you: "It's nothing but punches to be a 'man,' especially if you happen to be a woman, so stay put—or watch out."

Most feminists are as concerned with heterosexual relationships and orgasms as other women are. Most feminists are as frightened of being without men, or without monogamous relationships, as other women are.

MARIA: Well, I thought feminism meant better relations between the sexes, certainly better sexual relations. I mean, the sexual relations couldn't get any worse . . . but they could, they could. I guess it's true, and yet I don't like to think so. Men don't really like you to be there sexually. If they're not in control, if they're not "safe" emotionally—which usually means emotionally distanced, they won't lay down with you in a loving way. Or they won't pretend to be "loving"—that's more like it. If you're lucky they'll come and run—literally and figuratively. And if they come too fast, or if they're impotent, or if they don't really like oral sex or if they don't want to see you again—they make you feel guilty—or, to be absolutely fair, they don't resist the fact that we're not unwilling to play our guilty parts. And they're really scared. They're scared if you seem to be happy. They're scared if they think you want to trap them. They're scared if you don't want to trap them. Because if you don't—that

ALICE: I always went with men who were older than me. I was a Daddy's girl like everyone else. Life or feminism or having more money changed that a little. I became more open to having relationships with younger men. . . . If a young girl takes up with an older man, sure, he pays for her, but she supports his ego, she's there for him sexually, emotionally, domestically. And up to a point she's probably happy about it. It's accepted. They can go places together. It all fits. If a young boy takes up with an older woman she may very well pay for him too—but his ego is still the one that needs supporting—especially if he's kidded or punished by other men or by uncomfortable social situations. Since he's been conditioned to be a "man," he really doesn't know how to support a woman sexually, emotionally, or domestically. The idea of doing so is usually very frightening to him. Even "feminine," counterculture, or political-revolutionary-type young men can't handle a woman being "up," in any sense of the would be a whole new game, or not a game at all. And they wouldn't know the roles, they'd have no "edge," they'd tumble into an abyss of vulnerability. . . . So they're frightened, and they turn their fear into some kind of cruelty, and familiar scene, we're still left holding the bag of understanding and compassion. They don't "understand" us if we're *not* "confused" and "unhappy." If a woman knows what she wants and thinks clearly—forget it!

word. It's too devastating. . . . A woman *may* get some more support from a group if she's careful not to engage in any individual acts of success. If you submerge your ego or self into a group process, or even into a private love relationship, and especially if you're troubled and unhappy and failing—*then* you might get sympathy from other women or from a man. In other words, if you remain more "female" than "male" —it's still easier to survive.

Feminists sought therapy just as other women did: often, for long periods of time, and with men rather than with women. They were "treated" with the same double standard of mental health with which all women are treated.

DONNA: "Why don't you fix yourself up?" he always said. "You look like a hobo—I'd almost think you were afraid of men!" Not a word about how right we are to be afraid. Not a word about athletics, lesbianism, politics or my eternal soul. Just "Dress up for Daddy" as proof of mental health.

VICTORIA: I was eighteen when I started therapy for the second time. I went to a woman for two years, twice a week. She was constantly trying to get me to admit that what I really wanted was to get married and have babies and lead a "secure" life; she was very preoccupied with how I dressed, and, just like my mother, would scold me if my clothes were not clean, or if I wore my hair down; told me that it would be a really good sign if I started to wear make-up and get my hair done in a beauty parlor (like her, dyed blonde and sprayed); when I told her that I liked to wear pants she told me that I had a confusion of sex roles.

I originally went to her when my friends started to experiment with sex, and I felt that I couldn't make it, and that my women friends with whom I had been close had rejected me for a good lay. . . .

DEIRDRE: I interviewed six male analysts. . . . Every one of them intimidated me with questions such as Was I married? Did I want children? Why hadn't I any children? Why was I divorced? And they never looked up from their notebooks. And I never went back after the first time.

SUSAN: I've had many, many therapists. You might say I've been lonely and unhappy for a long time. . . . My first therapist was a woman. She gave me an MMPI which she showed me, and it said I had very high ego strength which she said was a bad thing. I knew it's bad in the sense that if it's very high it's supposed to mean rigidity, but for a woman trying to do well in school ego strength is very important. . . . I suppose I was using therapy as a substitute for friendship.

My second therapist, a man, told me that I was the coldest woman he had ever had the misfortune to meet—that I was castrating. His professional judgment was that I would never get into any kind of long relationship. He pitied any man that ever got involved with me. My therapy with him was the worst experience of his life—he said. He went on in that vein for about ten minutes at which point I walked out on him. So then I decided I really didn't need to be in therapy. About a month later a fellow broke into my apartment—not to steal anything but to have some kind of sexual relations with me, and I finally scared him off. The police obviously didn't believe my story and they said I was inviting him because I had long hair and sandals and red curtains in my bedroom and then they had a plan where I was to lie nude in bed with the curtain open. The whole scene got very frightening. I told my boy friend and he suggested I see his psychiatrist, a man. So I did. He kept saying that I should wear my hair long instead of pulled back because it was more feminine. But it got tangled in fifteen minutes and I couldn't stand it. And he told me to put no pressure on my boy friend . . . he told me to just be "giving" for a change. At the time I was very afraid that the things he was saying were true— even though I would fight with him. There must be something wrong with

.a woman being assertive, intelligent, and capable: I was, and no one was loving me very much, and I was very unhappy. . . .

You know, I met him [this therapist] a year later by accident socially. I had been goaded into making a very passionate defense of women's liberation. . . . [My old therapists's] wife kept saying, "Right on," and then when he tried to protest, and said, "Don't I help out?" she said, "What do you do around the house—you don't do this and you don't do that"—it was absolutely a bizarre evening.

Some feminists attribute major changes in themselves to the women's movement and to their consciousness-raising groups. Others feel that psychotherapy has accounted for major personal changes—including their conversion to feminism. Some feel that both experiences, occurring simultaneously, were essential for change. Some women are keenly aware of the limitations and dangers, as well as the advantages, of both feminist groups and psychotherapeutic experiences.

MARILYN: Feminism has helped me feel close to my mother for the first time in my life. My father was always perfect to me and I loved and enjoyed him in a way I never did my mother. . . . Now I begin to see that one of the things that's gone on is that my father has really forbidden me to be close to my mother. He's really kind of separated her from her kids in a very sad way. I now feel so sisterly with my mother, it's incredible. At dinner the other night I saw that every time I would talk to her he (my father) would put her down, he would try to make her look foolish to me.

SYLVIA: Modern men get along better in groups than women do. They've had more experience at it, from sports on up. That's why I thought it was very important that women were willing to form groups. . . . But some feminist group rules are really destructive. For example, not being able to criticize a woman who prefers to sit and bullshit rather than grow, or carry off an action. Her fear intimidates me, makes me grow quiet and kind of despairing. . . . Well, once I brought up in a meeting that we should transfer some of the tenderness that we all have toward men to each other and nobody had thought about it! So I think that most feminists are still living their lives much as they would have done anyway or very close to it. We haven't talked about any kind of structures for our lives. We still have our little apartment and many women are in—or want to be in—a one-to-one relationship. In another group I brought up the idea of monogamy and how that worked against the women and that it was a very male kind of idea and the women who had close relationships with men were very threatened by that.

Many very active feminists cannot leave their current therapist, male or female: where else, in this world of shifting political allegiances and violence, can they be assured of some familiar feedback and attention? Some feminists cannot bring themselves to be really angry at former male therapists' (or husbands') behavior—even when they understand that it has hurt them. Secrecy, comedy, and the psychology of individual exceptions are still the main female weapons of survival.

LYDIA: Listen, Phyllis, I'm going to tell you something funny but promise me you won't draw any conclusions from it, okay? And don't make a big thing of it—it's not a big thing. Well, remember my shrink—yeah, he's a man—but he really did help me. . . . Well, after feminism broke like a wave of the future he got very interested in me, very interested, and one thing led to another and he started calling me late at night to talk things over. Now he'd been a very proper shrink and had never behaved like this before. Then he started visiting me at home and one thing led to another—no, there's a twist. He wanted me to go to bed with him *and his wife*—he thought it would be good for her. . . . Well, we're all a little bit crazy . . . but he really *was* helpful before all this started.

MARILYN: I'm still seeing a male psychiatrist, and I'm pretty active in the movement. He's very different: he believed in female oppression before I even knew about it. I need to keep seeing him, mainly because I sometimes get so paranoid, so angry, that I *must* be wrong. I get scared, and there's no women's group that can really deal with this—for me. . . . Sometimes he thinks I fuck men over too much—and I do. . . .

PHYLLIS: How do you fuck men over? Is stepping out of the inferior —or slave—role "fucking men over"—because *they* experience it that way?

MARILYN: (laughing) Okay, okay. Well, I think I raised his [the psychiatrist's] consciousness the other day. . . .

PHYLLIS: Did he pay you?

MARILYN: Oh shut up! (Laughing.) Really. He [the psychiatrist] was saying that if a therapist really has respect for other people he doesn't need his consciousness raised, he just won't oppress women. I really disagree with that. I gave Dr. X as an example. He used to be a director at a [private psychiatric hospital] and he had a lot of respect for people, sees people as autonomous, as making choices, and he's very hesitant to hospitalize a person ever. But this kind of guy could say to my supervisor, "I don't know why Marilyn is in women's lib—she's pretty, smart, and feminine."

Some feminists who are aware of the limitations of psychotherapy still see no other viable institutional alternative—especially if they are no longer relying on marriage and motherhood as major psychological and emotional havens.

PHYLLIS: Given your own bad experiences with psychotherapists, would you say that women should stop seeing therapists?

SUSAN: I don't think so, not immediately. I think that a lot of people use it as a substitute for friendship. There are times in your life when you're under a lot of stress and strain and you don't know people you can go to because you're in a new place or all the people you know have left or all the people you know are part of the problem. You want someone else to go to and we don't have an extended family in which there are people naturally to go to. So, there are therapists, and we go to them.

PHYLLIS: I agree, but I think that if we're hurting and we get slightly comforted by therapy, that it then makes it harder to reach out to some other place or persons for comfort or advice.

SUSAN: That's true, but I don't think abolishing or avoiding therapy is going to help because there are too many needy people and we don't have anything to shift to. . . . I suppose a CR group could help women leave bad therapists, give them strength to find better therapists.

PHYLLIS: When you feel depressed or anxious, and you want "help" with these feelings, can you count on a feminist group, especially a project-oriented group, to "help" you, to pay as much attention to you as a therapist would—if you paid her?

SYLVIA: No, unfortunately. It gets boring to listen to someone else always talking about their problems. There's another girl in the group who is even more depressed than I am and after she talked about her depression everyone got tired of hearing about it. . . . But therapy with a man is absolutely out—and therapy with a woman who's not a feminist is too painful. . . . I guess I have no fantasy image of a good mother or a wise goddess.

I would like to close this chapter with a description of what one of the feminists describes as a basically good relationship with a woman therapist.

ALICE: I was very attracted to this woman. She's European, verbal, maternal, humane. I always felt I could talk to her about whatever was important to me without being misunderstood. She's not a feminist, but I sensed an inner peacefulness or wisdom and, most important, a happiness about being a woman. But she's really unable to share my anger about sexism or about individual men. She alternates from chiding me or indulging me to being disappointed in me or pitying me. When a man—on the street or at work or in a private relationship—starts "coming on," she doesn't believe I get really frightened and angry or that I should. For example, I was at a business meeting in a professional capacity. One of the men immediately wanted to know how old I was. He told me how attractive I was and said how I must be something to "date." I got very angry but didn't show it. I left, for a therapy appointment, as it happens, and was feeling very anxious. My therapist then told me I was "obsessed" by "this question" of sex and power. "The obsession might be productive," she said, "but it *was* extreme . . . and you know extremity is not very grown up or civilized. . . ."

I suppose on some deep level I'm experiencing with her what all daughters experience with their mothers. I feel she's abandoning me to the "grown-up" world of men. She's saying, "You're a heterosexual woman. Be thankful. Go and try to find that one exceptional man, that one special 'feminine' man. Till your private garden and look out for yourself. Don't tempt too many demons." Good, solid, philosophical advice, humble, compassionate advice, and yet being thrown out of any Garden of Eden never feels good.

She's really telling me I can't stay in the world of women: with her, with my mother before her, with other women now. I must go out, alone, and probably bear a man's child. She feels that the highest level of object-relating is between the sexes. She believes—she *said* she believes—that even if we were all raised equally, given biological differences, that there would still be a major attraction *between* the sexes. I don't know about that. And even if it's true, I don't know if it's the "highest" level of humanity or civilizedness. It's a very conventional and dominant idea, a very seductive idea. One thing for sure: she's tempering my passion, my anger, my courage—and I don't think that's evil or even wrong. I do wonder, though, what the world could be like if she (and my mother) agreed with such anger, or had some kind of feminist vision: what would it be like?

Chapter Ten

FEMALE PSYCHOLOGY: PAST, PRESENT, AND FUTURE

FEMALE PSYCHOLOGY IN OUR CULTURE: WOMEN ALONE

> The women say, shame on you. They say you are domesticated, forcibly fed, like geese in the yard of the farmer who fattens them. They say, you strut about, you have no other care than to enjoy the good things your masters hand out, solicitous for your well-being so long as they stand to gain. They say, there is no more distressing spectacle than that of slaves who take pleasure in their servile state. They say, you are far from possessing the pride of those wild birds who refuse to hatch their eggs when they have been imprisoned. They say, take an example from the wild birds who, even if they mate with the males to relieve their boredom, refuse to reproduce so long as they are not at liberty.
>
> Monique Wittig[1]

The women say with an oath, it was by a trick that he expelled you from the earthly paradise, cringing he insinuated himself next to you, he robbed you of that passion for knowledge of which it is written that it has the wings of the eagle, the eyes of the owl, the feet of the dragon. He has enslaved you by

> trickery, you who were great strong valiant. He has stolen your
> wisdom from you, he has closed your memory to what you were,
> he has made you that which is not which does not speak which
> does not possess which does not write, he has made of you a
> vile and fallen creature, he has gagged abused betrayed you.
> By means of stratagems he has stultified your understanding,
> he has woven around you a long list of defects that he de-
> clares essential to your well being, to your nature. He has
> invented your history. But the time approaches when you shall
> crush the serpent under your heel, the time approaches when
> you can cry, erect, filled with ardour and courage. Paradise
> exists in the shadow of the sword.
>
> Monique Wittig[2]

Modern female psychology reflects a powerless and deprived
condition. Many intrinsically valuable female traits, such as in-
tuitiveness or compassion, have probably been developed through
default or male-imposed necessity, rather than through either biological predisposition or free choice. Female emotional "talents"
must be viewed in terms of the overall price exacted by sexism. It is
illogical and dangerous to romanticize traits that one purchases

with one's freedom and dignity—even if they are "nice" traits; even if they make one's slavery more bearable; even if they charm and soothe the oppressor's rage and sorrow, staying his hand, or leave-taking, for one more day.

In Chapter One, I discussed the myth of Demeter, the Earth Mother, and her raped daughter Persephone, the Divine Maiden, whom she rescues and reincorporates into her own biological-maternal destiny.[3] Nearly every woman in our culture has relived this myth in her own life. Its meaning still constitutes a powerful guide to our understanding of the female condition.

Persephone, like her mother, is denied uniqueness, individuality, and cultural potency. Neither Demeter nor Persephone is allowed to become a "heroine": one represents the earth, the other represents a return to earth. Their single fate symbolizes the inevitable, endless breaking of each individual woman on the wheel of biological reproduction. Women who live in patriarchal settings are defined by certain traits, or by the absence of other traits. For example, like Persephone, most women today are not bold, forceful, knowledgeable, physically strong, active, or sexually potent. Like Persephone and Demeter, women are still naïve, helpless, or *reactive* victims.* Their sexuality is defined for them by men, as an act of incest for procreative purposes. In the myth, Persephone is gathering flowers of forgetfulness (poppies) when she is abducted and raped. Most women "forget" their dreams of individuality when they marry. ("Marriage" is the modern counterpart to rape in mythology.)

Unfortunately, most women today do not have Demeters for mothers. Female biology and nature have increasingly been devalued by our culture—but women have not yet been freed from

---

* Men are often victims of nature but women *are* "nature." When women seek to be something other than "natural," they experience their limitations or victimization at human male hands, and usually not through earthly—or divine —circumstances.

being defined in biological terms. Thus, the modern Persephone is no longer graceful, no longer divine, no longer "saved" by her mother. Demeter exists no more—and certainly not for a daughter. Whatever Earth Mother qualities women retain are lavished almost exclusively on sons and husbands. Persephone has become Cinderella, struck dumbly domestic by a Demeter turned stepmother. *This,* if anything, is the female version of exile from the earthly paradise. Fairy-tale princes cannot rescue women from their exile; and mothers have become stepmothers. For this reason daughters and (step)mothers today, unlike Persephone and Demeter, are characterized by self-hatred and mutual mistrust. (Step)mothers have not prepared their daughters for pilgrimages, conquests, or reflection. They have put brooms into their hands and romantic or escapist illusions into their heads. Daughters can have no pride in their sex, which seems to survive and fatten on its domesticity.

We must remember that the original Demeter was free and did have real powers. Demeter was not a terrible Goddess of Death but one of great earthly riches, of Life.† Today, women grow up in households where adult members of their sex do not have Demeter's powers. (Step)mothers accept or glorify their servitude, sublimate their sexuality and intellect, and punish their (step)-daughters when they rebel against such a role. These conditions lead to the development of certain psychological traits. For example, women are submissive and are not rescued by their mothers when this trait leads to their victimization. (Step)daughters learn to survive as they have seen their (step)mothers survive: through self-sacrifice, through feelings of guilt, conservative postures, inflexibility, "nesty" materialism, and through great social protesta-

† We must note that it is Persephone, a frail, pale being who as Pluto's unwilling wife, is the Queen of the Dead in patriarchal mythology. Ancient mythology did not always grant women the truly terrible powers it knew and feared they had. Stepmothers and witches in modern fairy tales are usually defeated. They too are not allowed a true measure of their wrath or power.

tions of "happiness" which must be backed up by even greater private declarations of unhappiness.

Persephone's traits of naïveté, docility, and conservatism are probably more conditioned than inevitable attributes among modern women. Nevertheless, such traits exist among women and are devalued by men and therefore by women. Furthermore, such traits are intrinsically valueless—whether they appear in women or men.‡

Persephone, the purest image of the Divine Maiden, has many mythological reflections. Psyche, the wife of Eros, whom I discussed in Chapter One, is an important variation of the myth and is relevant to modern women in certain ways that Persephone is not. We do not know too much about Persephone's feelings about or relation to her husband Pluto. What is known suggests a quietly implacable disinterest and sense of utter strangeness. Persephone is known to us through her identification with and love for her mother. Psyche, on the other hand, loves her husband Eros (Cupid), or loves the love of men. In the story, she is quite literally deserted by her mother and sisters and wedded in all darkness (ignorance).[4] Unlike Persephone, Psyche is happily and eternally reunited with her husband, and becomes the mother of a daughter called Pleasure. Psyche, an early prefiguration of the Catholic Madonna, embodies certain traits possessed by many women today. I am talking about female romanticism, tenderness, compassion, and altruism.** These traits are not devalued by either

‡ While I am opposed to assigning certain sex-typed characteristics at birth to either women or men, I am equally opposed to certain characteristics whether they are currently assigned to or encouraged in either sex. "Male" fear and hatred of women; "male" insecurity and bottomless emotional greediness; the "male" avoidance of emotional vulnerability are objectionable and inhuman characteristics.

** Studies and common sense suggest that personal "altruism" in our culture often stems from guilt, fear, and low self-esteem rather than from freedom or self-love. Margaret Adams[5] has discussed the crippling limitations and definite social function of what she calls "the Compassion Trap" in women.

men or women. However, men benefit from such traits, almost exclusively, and reward them rather poorly. A genuinely compassionate person would have a hard time participating in the spheres of public action. There is a ruthlessness that politics or science demands—but its devotees are never totally destroyed by this demand. The devotees are men, who expect to be revived each night by female compassion in the individual, private family unit.†† Apparently there is no place for "altruism" or "compassion" in political and military places—be they traditional or revolutionary ventures. From the psychological point of view, traditional, overtly discriminatory practices are hardly needed to keep women out of public places. The kind of training women receive as "compassion"-givers effectively keeps them in the home, often by choice, or steers them to "compassionate" and "reformist" semipublic ventures. In the twentieth century, the wives of upper-class men organize charity benefits for the poor; the wives of middle-class men organize peace and ecology demonstrations and work as social workers, nurses, teachers, and psychologists; the wives of lower-class men take care of their children and husbands and of their children's children, and of other people's children and husbands, as secretaries, domestics, and prostitutes. And yet poverty does not disappear; neither war nor pollution nor racism is abolished; and the universal female tie to childbearing and rearing remains as constant as ever.

The composite psychological portrait of Persephone-Psyche is one of a naïve and heterosexually romantic victim, an unindividuated, fearful, and conservative being, whose greatest pride

†† This revival doesn't always take place—and women are always blamed as nags and bitches, as ungrateful and manipulative albatrosses around their suffering husbands' necks. This may even be true. However, it is time to "blame" or examine the public sphere that has exiled "compassion or decency into private isolated places—and the ruthlessness involved in enforcing full-time "compassion"-service upon women.

lies in either childbearing and compassion or in a return to the ways of the Mother. The Maiden as Cinderella retains most of these traits, but with less pride and glory, with no place to return to, and with no princely or maternal "rescue."

Cinderella-Persephone-Psyche also embodies certain other unmistakably "female" traits which many women still possess. I am thinking of traits that men—and therefore women—either devalue or consider unimportant. For example, a certain type of "mindlessness" or "superficiality" (as men see it) exists among many women—which is neither mindless nor superficial. For example, many dialogues between women seem "senseless" or "mindless" to men. Two women talking often seem to be reciting monologues at each other, neither really listening to (or "judging") what the other is saying. Two personal confessions, two sets of feelings, seem to be paralleling one another, rather "mindlessly," and without "going anywhere." In fact, what the women are doing—or where they are "going"—is toward some kind of emotional resolution and comfort. Each woman comments upon the other's feelings by reflecting them in a very sensitive matching process. The two women share their feelings by alternating the retelling of the entire experience in which their feelings are embedded and from which they cannot be "abstracted" or "summarized." Their theme, method, and goal are non-verbal and/or non-verbalized. Facial expressions, pauses, sighs, and seemingly unrelated (or "non-abstract") responses to statements are crucial to such dialogue. A very special prescience is at work here. On its most ordinary level, it affords women a measure of emotional reality and a kind of comfort that they cannot find with men.‡‡ On its highest level, it constitutes the basic tools of art and psychic awareness.

Thus the psychological portrait of the individual and powerless woman consists of naïveté, compulsive heterosexuality, pro-

‡‡ And that men do not have with each other.

creative "pride," fearfulness, self-hatred, mistrust of other women —and of compassion, passion, and idealism. Let us look at such women in groups to see what happens to these individual themes in a social context.

FEMALE PSYCHOLOGY IN OUR CULTURE: WOMEN IN GROUPS

> Every effort for progress, for enlightenment, for science, for religious, political and economic liberty, emanates from the minority, and not from the mass. Today as ever, the few are misunderstood, hounded, imprisoned, tortured and killed. . . . The majority, that compact, immobile, drowsy mass, the Russian peasant, after a century of struggle, of sacrifice, of untold misery, still believes that the rope which strangles "the man with the white hands" [the intellectual] brings luck. . . . Not that I do not feel with the oppressed, the disinherited of the earth; not because I do not know the shame, the horror, the indignity of the lives the people lead, do I repudiate the majority as a creative force for justice or equality. . . . I wish not to concede anything to them [the masses] but to drill, divide and break them up, and draw individuals out of them.
>
> Emma Goldman[6]

> The aim of political action and social thought of all kinds is to create a tolerable background and leave people alone. The only tolerable background is an austerely simple one. The important parts of life will always be the things we do in our own small groups and on our own. They are art and science and sex and

God and compassion and romantic love. These should be rich and complex. There isn't one damned thing that society can do to help you with any of these. All society can do is to make sure that it doesn't prevent them.

Paul Goodman[7]

I learned 3½ years ago that women had always been divided against one another, were self-destructive and filled with impotent rage. I thought the movement would change all that. I never dreamed that I would see the day when this rage, masquerading as a pseudo-egalitarian radicalism under the "pro-woman" banner, would turn into a frighteningly vicious anti-intellectual fascism of the left, and used within the movement to strike down sisters. . . . I am referring, of course, to the personal attacks . . . to which women in the movement, who have painfully managed any degree of achievement, have been subjected. . . .

If you are in the first category (an achiever) you are immediately labelled a thrill-seeking opportunist, a ruthless mercenary, out to get her fame and fortune over the dead bodies of selfless sisters who have buried their abilities and sacrificed their ambitions for the greater glory of Feminism. Productivity seems to be the major crime—but if you have the misfortune of being outspoken and articulate, you are accused of being power-mad, elitist, fascist, and finally, the worst epithet of all: A MALE IDENTIFIER, AARRGGG!!! . . .

To emerge unscathed from this kind of assault is impossible. The effects I have observed, to name just a few, are: gradual or immediate decrease in productivity; an upsurge of self-doubt; depletion of whatever ego-strength had been salvaged from our pasts or recovered during the early stages of the movement; an increase in impotence and passivity, coupled with a rampant paranoia (completely justified); a severe dropping off of self-confidence and faith in one's ability; a detailed and obsessive self-examination for real or imagined sins which is

> completely useless since the mind-fucking has destroyed objectivity. . . .
>
> One last plea: If we women are ever to pull ourselves out of the morass of self-pity, self-destruction and impotence which has been our heritage for so long as we can remember, then it is perhaps even more important that we be supportive of each other's achievements and successes and strengths, than it is for us to be compassionate and understanding of each other's failures and weaknesses."
>
> Anselma dell'Olio[8]

Human group or social behavior either refers to *male* group behavior or to female group behavior in a male-dominated culture.* As such, it is hard to know whether "masses" must necessarily oppose justice, equality, or individual achievement; or whether "society" can't really do more for love, work, and art than simply not to outlaw them when they infrequently occur.

American children are reared to be exceptionally competitive and aggressive but increasingly are expected to "get along" with or be "liked" by others *in order* to "get ahead." More and more, people of all generations tend to "look alike" and, despite a potentially destructive and superficial individualism, conform rather than commit individual acts. "Individuals" in America, as elsewhere, risk ostracism, loneliness, grave self-doubt, and perhaps incarceration.†

Women, although similar to each other in many ways, are more isolated from each other *in terms of groups* than men are.

---

* Most of my discussion about women in groups concerns lower- and middle-class women and not the organizations founded by the wives of upper-class men.

† Juliet Mitchell makes a brilliant point in her analysis of the ideological function of the family in capitalist society. She says that "the family is a stronghold of what capitalism needs to preserve but actually destroys: private property and individualism." I don't think, however, that individualism was exactly permitted, especially to women, in a precapitalist era.[9]

Women are not consolidated into either public or powerful groups. Women as mothers are "grouped" with their children (who grow up and leave them), and only temporarily and superficially with other women: for example, in parks, at women's auxiliary functions, and at heterosexual parties. Such women only keep each other company as they fulfill what they feel are "freely" chosen private lives rather than necessary public labor. There is no need to organize for better working conditions if you don't feel you're "working," or if you feel the definition of work for women is and should be different from that of men. Women as secretaries, domestics, waitresses, prostitutes, and factory workers are not well unionized. These are mainly female jobs and as such are not easy to 'organize" for many reasons. (For example: female fatigue because of holding another job at home; female lack of skills and encouragement and consequently of optimism; female fear of male opposition; and, in the case of prostitution, fear of legal as well as physical reprisal, *plus* the knowledge that it is difficult if not impossible to earn as much money in any other job.)

Professional or middle-income "career" women are neither leaders nor "brothers" within the professional male organizations. For example, as a professional woman I cannot continue either an important or a casual conversation with a male colleague in the bathroom; I *can* with a female colleague and it makes an extraordinary difference. As a business woman, I cannot "do business" with a male colleague or client at an athletic or faculty club, or at a whorehouse or stag party. I have too few female colleagues to similarly indulge and in any event, as women, we have not been socialized to enjoy such institutions—even or especially if they were geared to our advancement. As a "career" woman I am less likely than a man is to take a sports trip or vacation with a male colleague: what would our spouses say? Without a wife, how could I afford the time away from my children and home? How can I risk being approached as a "mistress" and losing a "professional" or human contact? And if I must worry and stumble over each of these things, how can I have access to support and information that my male colleagues naturally share? If my chances of achieving real power are so slender compared to those of my male counterparts, no wonder my colleagues have no burning desire to cultivate my friendship or encourage my growth. Of course, I can be "cultivated"—as an assistant, confidante, mistress, or wife. I will not be experienced as a rival or as a protégé. I will be a weapon to be used against other men (real rivals). I will gain a token position by helping some male colleague become stronger or maintain his position. (Professional marriages are a common way for women to survive outside the home.)

It is only since the women's liberation movement that some American professional women (especially within the universities) have begun to organize as women. It is only recently that a woman professional, particularly in a non-female profession, may have some women as colleagues, clients, or employers. It is only recently that women, as feminists, have grouped together for intellectual, economic, emotional, political, and social purposes. As I noted in Chapter Nine, the various feminist groups constituted novel experiments in human female society, especially for those women whose experience of extended families or kinship systems was very limited; or whose female group experience was primarily as wives and mothers rather than as citizens, artists, business women, or human beings.‡ Consciousness-raising groups offered women female approval for their anger and for their desire for sexual and economic advancement and liberation.

‡ I do not mean that the act of mothering is not a human act. On the contrary. What I mean is that it is considered as something *other* than human by those who control the means of production and reproduction, i.e., by men. If mothering is a valuable human act it should be performed by both men and women.

In feminist groups, many women experienced temporary and isolated refuge from hostile or indifferent family, school, and wage-labor environments. The feminist group experience was an attempt to institutionalize the ideology of sisterhood and, hopefully, not a sisterhood of powerlessness and discontent.

Because of the revolutionary nature and vision of feminism, and woman's basic naïveté, many women suffered their first defeats with surprise. They were not yet aware of the enormity of the task being undertaken.** In American groups women were very critical of the "female" rules of handling conflict, such as politeness, tears, and evasion. They were equally critical of the "male" rules of handling conflict, such as logical or "objective" arbitration, compromise, or violence. When conflicts arose, the confrontations were raw and purposefully resisted either "male" or "female" interpretations or resolutions. Such heroic purism often led to the same bitterness and paranoia that have characterized many male groups, such as "revolutionary" political groups and nuclear family units—groups that feminists wanted to change or leave altogether.†† Unfortunately, one's psychology is no easier to change or escape from than is one's national and biological history. Any attempt to "revolutionize" any of these phenomena usually involves

---

** Juliet Mitchell has noted that "just as, on the one hand, it is crucial that we are never guilty of underestimating the potential of women, so we must never neglect to be aware of the difficulties of our position. In a different context (that of military struggle), Mao called going it alone and underestimating the difficulties "Left Sectarianism" and underestimating one's potential and fearing to struggle "Right Opportunism" . . . the conditions of our oppression *do* condition us. And we have to assess the weakness of women as a political force in order *not* to succumb to it.[10]

†† "Middle-class" work-oriented groups suffered these events somewhat less. They had specific tasks and goals and were not averse to exercising "male" rules of organization or conflict resolution. Their work is invaluable for women: like their counterpart male groups, their visions are not puristically romantic, and they can function with some success within our present culture. Medical, legal, economic, and political reform for women is not to be lightly tossed off as "reformist" and, therefore, useless. Some reforms are crucial and, depending on the total biosocial context in which they occur, can also be revolutionary.

some strict continuation or some modified reappearance of old myths, values, and structures. The blinding recognition of a common plight (oppression) does not immediately do away with that plight: it is only the first of many painful steps.

Thus, the American feminist movement has conformed to as many intrinsically valueless conditioned female traits as it has recognized those conditioned female traits which are valuable, and as it has explored new ways for women to "be" in the universe. For example, many women have not been able to avoid the female experience of disliking, competing with, and feeling betrayed by other women. And the reasons given are as varied as they are endless: economically and professionally successful women are aggressive elitists; heterosexually committed women are cowards and deserters; happy mothers and Marxist women are fools and fifth columnists; lesbians are sick; white women are racists; black women can't wait to walk behind their men; middle-aged women wear hats and gloves; young women carry spears and throw bombs. These divisions certainly have valid political and economic bases. However, what is being psychologically satisfied is the female belief that she cannot be enhanced or protected by the success or power of any other woman. Psychologically, what is also at work here is an absolute terror of differences.

We may remember (from Chapter One) that Demeter, the Earth Mother, incorporates her daughter, Persephone, into her own image. The sacrifice of "differences," of uniqueness, is deeply tied to the female's endless cycle of biological reproduction and cultural impotence. This is the mythological stratum of the "policing" of women by women, both within families and within feminist groups. Mothers initiate daughters into the sacred sisterhood of discontent not only in order that daughters survive. Mothers are lonely and need nurturance—something they did not receive from their own mothers or husbands, something, like Demeter, they may hope to receive from their daughters. Thus, "rebellious" daughters are treated harshly by their mothers as the deserting lovers and companions they are meant to be. The female "policing" phenomena is rooted in an anguish of powerlessness.

Mythologically then, a mother's (or adult woman's) success or power has meant a loss of freedom or uniqueness for her daughter. Psychologically and politically in male society, one woman's token or temporary "success" is usually purchased at another woman's expense. The "successful" woman today cannot protect (or instruct or "incorporate") other women into a non-biologically based image of power or individuality.‡‡ There are too few "successful" women to accomplish this by impersonal social example. On a personal level, the extraordinary demands placed on the "successful" woman either keep her from being a biological mother or make her allegiance to individual men (as husbands, sons, employers, or colleagues) nearly as necessary as her isolation from other women.

I may note that "differences" among men certainly exist and are both experienced and resolved, or not resolved, differently. For men, being incorporated or initiated into the male role (or god-figure, or Oedipal father) ideally demands the development of some kind of public strength, mobility, and perhaps even a touch of uniqueness. (It also means renouncing heterosexuality except under certain "safe" conditions.) Male conformity, as I have already noted, implies conformity to action, struggle, thought, mobility, and pleasure; female conformity implies conformity to inaction, resignation, emotionality, and unhappiness. Naturally, incorporation into the Oedipal father is purchased at great emotional ex-

‡‡ It seems to me that this dynamic of either female incorporation into the mother or doomed desertion of her will remain true as long as women bear the burden of motherhood within a patriarchal family. Also, the complicated Mother-Daughter interaction is a hard and tenacious model to shatter. The Feminist language of "sisterhood," rather than "motherhood" and "daughterhood" reflects both the painfulness of the female-role model problem, as well as an attempt to break down corrupt hierarchal barriers between women.

pense. The male "policing" of other men is rooted in an anguish of power, and it is a more literal, physical, and public policing than female policing is. (Men police both men and women. Adult women cannot police adult men in quite this way.)

Women alone and in groups, including feminist groups, are finding it hard to abandon the virulent double standard of male-female behavior. Paradoxically, while women must not "succeed," when they *do* succeed at anything, they have still failed if they're not successful at *everything*. Women must be perfect (goddesses) or they're failures (whores). (The violent conditioning of "spotlessness," coupled with a deep sense of "dirtiness," in female children runs deep indeed.) If a woman accomplishes a valuable task she, unlike men (who after all, are mortal), *still* has failed if she has, for example, abandoned the daily care of her children or her looks in order to do so. A woman has failed if she succeeds at winning a legal or intellectual battle and has hurt another woman's (or man's) feelings in the process.* Another example: mothers are praised for child rearing but severely condemned, by others, by psychiatrists, and by themselves for anything that goes "wrong" with either their children or their marriages. Ironically, mothers are often seen as "failures"—by their husbands, by "career" women, and by some feminists—because they haven't also achieved careers or independence from their families.†

Traditionally, women as well as men expect or demand another woman's help or sacrifice more quickly and easily than they demand a man's sacrifice or even his cooperation. Objectively, such

---

* Men have wives and female secretaries both to "mother" them and to smooth the ruffled feelings of others for them, to serve dinners, buy gifts, and answer the phone for them when they are in "bad" or "busy" tempers. Women don't. Men are also somewhat protected by the universal expectation that they don't have to be so "nice."

† Husbands may want their wives to "get out" of the house after they have done twenty years of domestic service and are no longer "young" or "interesting." Feminists want both nurturance and comradeship from women whose relationship to the family makes this difficult.

behavior is safer and is more potentially successful. Psychologically, it represents our culture's higher valuation of men, as well as the assigned female role of "policing" other women in the service of male supremacy. Even within the feminist movement, women do not demand or force certain support from men—either from men whom they know, or from public male sources such as philanthropic foundations, private industries, or government. Beyond a certain point, women are not able to force men to do anything. Fear of male reprisal in terms of physical violence or further economic abandonment is very great. Also, since women are conditioned to inhabit only the "private" and personal realms, they are genuinely confused about public action and the nature of power. Thus, in America, Betty Freidan's or Gloria Steinem's or Kate Millett's "contributions" to a particular woman's cause are more actively expected and sought after than are Governor Rockefeller's, President Nixon's, the Ford Foundation's, the U. S. Army's, General Motors', or the Vatican's—all institutions which have far greater resources than those of any individual woman or any individual woman's group. (Mommy is still safer to milk, blame, and hate than Daddy is. Daddy is feared and addressed in "good girl" tones, or not addressed at all.) Another example: most traditional and feminist child care centers or cooperatives are staffed with women, not men. Babysitting is usually expected of mothers, not fathers, by daughter-mothers. Never has a woman's group been able to succeed in having their employed husbands collectively assume responsibility for the duties of domesticity, child rearing, and compassion within a marriage.‡

Women, as well as men, are deeply threatened by a female who does not smile often enough and, paradoxically, who is not

‡ There are many reasons why a woman's group wouldn't want this to happen: loss of their own identity and source of employment plus a legitimate mistrust of male competence in these areas are the two most obvious reasons.

very unhappy. Women mistrust and men destroy those women who are not interested in *sacrificing* at least something for someone for some reason. Rather than achieve at least half or all of Caesar's power, many women, including some feminists, would prefer to leave it in Caesar's hands altogether and, in a misguidedly "noble" gesture, sacrifice their individual advancement for the sake of less fortunate women, Third World people, one's biological children, one's weary husband, etc. In other words, it is still difficult for most women to stop sacrificing themselves (or saying that they want to) for specific other people, or in personal and private acts.** It is still difficult for most women to consider political or technological power as a potentially valid means of alleviating at least *some* of the human misery and inequality, including their own, that surrounds them.

> The women say that, with the world full of noise they see themselves as already in possession of the industrial complexes. They are in the factories aerodromes radio stations. They have control of communications. They have taken possession of aeronautical electronic ballistic data-processing factories. They are in the foundries tall furnaces navy yards arsenals refineries distilleries. They have taken possession of pumps presses levers rolling-mills winches pullies cranes turbines pneumatic drills arcs blow-lamps. They say that they envisage themselves acting with strength and happiness.
>
> Monique Wittig[11]

** I'm not convinced that ultimately more than this can or should ever be done—but I would prefer a social order that maximizes such a personal mode *publicly* and also abolishes an individual's reliance on personal intervention in certain crucial areas, e.g., in the matters of economic survival, sexual freedom, early education, etc.

For example, women who eschew "leadership" and/or power are probably doing so because their valueless conditioning forces them to, rather than because they recognize the ruthless aspects of "leadership" in our culture. As we shall see, this is similar to women eschewing violence or self-defense on "principle"—when they can't perform such acts anyway. Such avoidance is not based on choice or morality but on necessity. Women are no more to be congratulated on their "pacifism" than men are to be congratulated for their "violence."

Women, even more than men, seem to be threatened by those personal traits *in a woman* which are original or "male"-like. (Men can afford to be less threatened because so few women manifest such traits and, when they do, can easily be checked or adopted into male service.) For example, women, including many feminists, respond more positively to those projects which *ease* the burdens of the female status quo rather than to those projects which attempt to redefine or abolish the status quo. Easing the burdens of motherhood and supporting abortion reform are essential tasks, yet they both imply a continuation of a powerless female responsibility for children and for birth control. Women in the public labor force, whether as factory workers or professionals, want more wages and better working conditions (for themselves or their husbands), and more public child care centers. Most women are not yet able to sever their ties to biological reproduction or to the family.††

For example, most women experience the male's physical or emotional abandonment of his family or children as either cruel or cruelly necessary. He is a "louse"—or a "victim" of harsh job realities. His behavior is human. However, the female's similar

†† As I've noted elsewhere, the female tie to biological reproduction will gradually change as a function of the population explosion crisis, advances in technology, and because of those factors that have shortened the child-rearing period and lengthened life expectancy.

abandonment of her family—for any purpose—is viewed as "unnatural" and "tragic." The female's social role is still a biological one: as such she is seen as transgressing against nature when she attempts to change her social role. It is important to note that men are allowed more leeway in social-role failure than are women. For example, although men are expected to achieve publicly or economically, when they fail or refuse to do so, they are not necessarily seen as "unnatural," but as either heroes or victims, deserving of our sympathy, understanding, and support.

Conformity, inflexibility, and a tendency to romanticize the emotional infantilism and unrealistic dependencies of the powerless woman (and to confuse it with a form of wisdom or power) still exist among many women and men, whether they are feminists or not. Women have had almost no collective experience of public problem-solving and no valuable female role-models. "Power" and "public action" are indeed male, and foreign to them. To the extent to which women in groups dwell more or only on personal feeling than on personal and group action, more on "process" than on "product," they are remaining victims of female biology *and* sex-role conditioning. As long as women remain more comfortable with decisions or analyses made by others, or by groups, than with an individually made decision, they are remaining comfortably "female."‡‡

Woman as Persephone-Psyche-Cinderella cannot accomplish certain things. It is absurd to expect that women, qua women, can any more easily or quickly than men achieve goals such as international peace or universal personal happiness. On the contrary, women, as *powerless* human beings, may have an even harder time than men—especially since men, who are powerful, are opposed

‡‡ This does not mean that no one but a "leader" has legitimacy or authority; it does mean that, ideally, each person should feel "legitimate" and should change an opinion or let someone else speak "for them" only if the listener agrees with her through understanding and not out of ignorance or fear.

both to absorbing "feminine" traits into the public sphere and to encouraging women to develop "masculine" traits for participation or domination in the public sphere. Certainly, women's first successful organized accomplishments will concern issues such as child care, abortion, and birth control—"female"-sphere issues. Women, as a group, as an interest group, or as individuals, will have a longer wait before they can *afford* to address themselves to scientific research, artistic production, economic advancement, and political decision-making.

What would an "ideal" group be? As a feminist and anarchist, I can only answer for myself and, unfortunately, in somewhat vague generalities. To me, the only acceptable groups are those that, unlike the family, can function as places of authentic responsibility and joy; as ways of supporting our deepest cravings for individual liberty, security, achievement, and love. Groups (ideologies, religions, "solutions") which in any way kill the individual spirit; which despise and crucify that which it longs for; which enforce conformity, mediocrity, and conservatism—*for any reason;* which seek to diminish each person to "manageable" and familiar levels rather than to enhance each person to "unmanageable" and unique levels which the group *supports*—such "groupings" are depressingly well known, such groupings are "male" and "female" rather than human groupings. They are doomed to spin out old patterns of martyrdom and oppression.* Such groupings cannot provide women with the strength to gain power and to redefine power, sexuality, and work.†

As a feminist and psychologist, I can discuss this question of

---

* Men are martyred or sacrificed when they preach or practice peace and love; women (and powerless men) when they preach or practice war. Even the mysterious and evil laws of martyrdom obey the laws of sex-role stereotyping.

† I honestly don't know exactly "how" such ideal groups would solve the problems of inequality and injustice. I do think that if such groups could really exist some of these problems would already have been better resolved.

"ideal groups" in quite another way. If women have been rendered culturally impotent because of their biology, it might be useful to discuss those societies in which women reigned culturally supreme *because* of their biology; that is Amazon societies.

AMAZON SOCIETIES:
VISIONS AND POSSIBILITIES

Were there actually such things as the fabulous nations of maidens, the mounted demons, galloping from the edges of the world to make ice and golden sand splash to all sides? Was there ever a "man-hating army" with clanging tresses and awesome customs? . . . In time and reality the Amazon kingdoms not only comprise an extremist end of matriarchy but also are a beginning and a purpose in themselves. Roaming daughter realms . . . they markedly differ from the serenely tolerant mother clan as old as mankind, which pacifically exiled a young upstart manhood by exogamy. The Amazon does not mime the male principle but denies it in order to unite the two fundamental forms of life in paradisaical harmony which had been divided by the great mother. . . . In the mother clan, there was a constant progression of great mothers begetting more great mothers. Amazons however, reproduced the daughter type, which practically skips a generation and is something altogether different. They were conquerers, horse tamers, and huntresses who gave birth to children but did not nurse or rear them. They were an extreme, feminist wing of a young human race, whose other extreme wing consisted of the stringent patriarchies.

Helen Diner[12]

The whole idea of the Amazon is the cancellation of the first, parthenogenetic female action, the separation and formation of the active principle and its shaping into a male. Amazons concede no separate existence to the active principle, reabsorb it, and develop it themselves in androgynous fashion: female on the left, male on the right. Their dematernalization begins with the shrinking or the removal of the right breast as a symbolic action of bold style. . . . All varieties of Amazon society share the characteristic that they reared only the girls into fullfledged specimens of mankind. . . .

Helen Diner[13]

Amazon society, as both mythology, history, and universal male nightmare, represents a culture in which women reign culturally supreme *because* of their sexual identity.‡ (Just as men have reigned culturally supreme because of *their* sexual identity.) Female sacrifice or self-sacrifice as we know it could not have existed in Amazon societies. For example, to be an Amazon mother does not imply *cultural* behavior in which constant interaction between a woman and her biological child is necessary. Despite many odes to child rearing, the fact remains that the child-rearing assignment (with whatever tediousness or immobility a particular class or technological level imposes) has traditionally been drawn by the relatively powerless sex.

In Amazon societies, women were mothers and their society's *only* warriors; mothers and their society's *only* hunters; mothers and their society's *only* political and religious leaders. No division of labor based on sex seems to have existed in all-female societies.**
Although Amazon leaders existed and queens were elected, the

‡ Amazon societies are also important because women were trained to be warriors—militarily and, presumably, in other ways as well. Amazons also owned their own land and lived on it together. This is very different from our only examples of women living together: in jails, in ghettos, in Islamic purdah, or in schools while still "growing up." Women live together only in states of shameful default or absolute necessity.

** In matriarchies, the fact that men were present *and* in positions of power led to some division of labor based on sex. It is certainly possible that divisions of labor based on other factors—such as physical strength or intelligence—could have existed in an all-female society. Perhaps some Amazons never biologically reproduced at all.

societies seem to have been classless ones, or at least ones in which any *woman* could aspire to and achieve full human expression.

In Amazon society, only *men*, when they were allowed to remain, were, in widely differing degrees, powerless and oppressed.††

> The mildest form of Amazon aversion [to men] caused them to engage in a quick assignation with their male neighbors, totally indiscriminate as a matter of principle, every spring. Female offspring was retained, the male was sent to its distant fathers. The more radical kind of administration did not send any babies away but crippled the newly born boys and rendered them innocuous for life through the twisting of one hand and one hip out of their sockets. Despised slave cripples, never touched erotically by the Amazons, they were used by them for the rearing of children, the spinning of wool, and domestic service. In the most extreme anti-male society, the male offspring was always killed, and sometimes the fathers were too.
>
> Of all the African Amazons, only the Gorgons seem to have maintained a pure Amazon state; the others, though keeping the army purely feminine, maintained some men in their camps. The Libyan Amazons, who removed their right breasts, had compulsory military service for all girls for a number of years, during which they had to refrain from marriage. After that, they became a part of the reserves and were allowed to take a mate and reproduce their kind. The women monopolized government and other influential positions. In contrast to the later Thermodontines, however, they lived in a permanent relationship with their sex partners, even though the men led a retiring life, could not hold public office, and had no right to interfere in the government of the state or society. Children, who were brought up on mare's milk, were given to the men to rear, just as among the Egyptians, Kamtchatkans, and some of the North American Indians.[14]

†† Diner notes that "the tyranny of woman over man (in the sexual realm) is never as complete as the converse sometimes is: there are only a few instances of anything like male prostitution, if for no other reason than because the male organ limits this possibility, for women."

Residents of Haverhill, Mass. take the game [Little League Baseball] so solemnly that the town was thrown into a tizzy when the coach of the local Rotary Club-sponsored team allowed Sharon Poole, a red-haired, freckle-faced girl of twelve, to don uniform No. 9 and fill a vacancy in the otherwise all-boys group. Batting cleanup, she drove in a run in her first game went hitless in her second, and earned her teammates' respect with her agility in center field as the team won both games. But Coach Donald Sciuto kept getting complaints from parents about allowing Sharon to play.

Time Magazine, 1971

Billie Jean King, the country's most successful woman athletic star, says she is never offended by people who tell her she plays tennis just like a man. But she has become increasingly irritated by people who ask her when she's going to settle down and attend to a home and family.

New York *Times*, 1971

Amazon society was *probably* better for the development of women's bodies and emotions than any male-dominated society has ever been. It may have been better for the development of women's intellect and art—although this remains a totally conjectural matter. Amazon society probably did not value modern or male-originated types of competitive art and intellect, any more than did other early or "primitive" societies.‡‡ However, Diner

‡‡ I really wonder what a group of Amazon women would make of my *writing* about them. And I wonder how much or how long I'd be able to accept a disinterested, indulgent, or negative response. I also wonder how "right" I'd be in steadfastly refusing to relinquish a truly barbarous culture—our own—because of certain of its "advantages."

notes that the entire Ionian tradition refers to the Thermodon Amazons as the founders of cities and sanctuaries.

> Though bestial until victory, they later like the Romans, became conciliatory. Gentleness and foresight earned them the adoration of the vanquished . . . their tradition was maintained uninterruptedly by temples, graves, cities, and whole countries. A large number of important cities boasted an Amazon as founder and godmother; Smyrna, Sinope, Cyme, Gryne, Pitania, Magnesia, Clete, Mytilene and Amastris.[15]

Earlier, the Libyan (Moroccan and African) Amazons rode through Egypt "peacefully," but conquered.

> Syria, Phrygia, and all the lands along the seacoast to the Caicus River. . . . The islands of Samos, Lesbos, Pathmos and Samothrace [were conquered and inhabited] by "Myrine," a Libyan Amazon Queen.[16]

If women take their bodies seriously—and ideally we should—then its *full* expression, in terms of pleasure, maternity, and physical strength, seems to fare better when *women* control the means of production and reproduction. From this point of view, it is simply not in women's interest to support patriarchy or even a fabled "equality" with men. That women do so is more a sign of powerlessness than of any biologically based "superior" wisdom.

Female sacrifice—either self-sacrifice, ritual virgin sacrifice, prostitution, or the sacrifice of self that women make in order to be mothers—is perhaps not unalterably rooted in our biological condition.

I am not saying that a female-dominated or Amazon society based on the oppression of men is any more "just" than is a male-dominated society based on the oppression of women. I am merely pointing out in what ways, *in terms of the body* (and the body

contains and expresses everything else), it is better for women.* To
the extent to which American or Western women desire a more
harmonious, tribal, collective, spiritual, and ritual existence, and
*are willing to forgo certain modern values and technologies to
achieve it*, then Amazon societies are probably better models for
women than are male-initiated models of "primitive" societies.†

> Dropping out is not the answer; . . . Most women are already
> dropped out; they were never in. . . . Dropping out, however, is
> an excellent policy for men, and *SCUM* will enthusiastically
> encourage it. . . .
>
> Valerie Solanas

> Last spring I sat through three hours of the film 'Woodstock'
> alternating between feelings of enchantment and repulsion. . . .
> For one thing, with the exception of a pregnant Joan Baez
> who couldn't seem to stop talking about her husband, all the

* Perhaps someday a choice between *forms* of injustice will not be necessary. Also, I don't know whether it is in women's interest to forgo the act of
childbirth—simply because men have enforced such an unfair price on it. I
don't know whether birth control technology in a male-dominated society is
particulary good for women. Being freed from multiple enforced maternity or
pregnancy fears does not necessarily or easily lead to the abolition of female
sexual "frigidity," or to the abolition of female prostitution. Birth control
"technology," by itself, like free twenty-four hour child care center "technology," will not necessarily lead to the abolition of sexism, any more than it
will usher in an era of non-alienated labor or alternative family forms. It may,
in fact, lead to male-dominated totalitarian decisions regarding sexual activity
and maternity—decisions over which the individual woman has as little to say
as she did about her enforced maternity.

† We must not forget that many primitive cultures feared the female
body and exercised strong taboos against menstruation, puberty, and deflora-
tion.[17]

musicians were men. Sweaty, bearded men were busy building the stage, directing traffic, shooting the film, and running the festival. *Brotherhood* was repeatedly proclaimed, both on stage and off. . . . The clearest indication of how rock music views womankind is in its lyrics. Women certainly can't complain that the image presented there is one-dimensional. On the contrary, the put-downs are remarkably multifaceted, ranging from open contempt to sugar-coated condescension. Above all, however, women are always available sexual objects whose chief function is to happily accommodate any man that comes along.

Marion Meade

New York *Times*, 1971

Amazon societies compose an early and little-explored culture,[18] one in which women dominated all areas of conceivable or necessary life—i.e., what was necessary included more than just the enforced bearing and rearing of a single man's children. The fact of women fully engaged in the task of humanity—at any technological level—is practically visionary. It produces fear and disbelief—together with an overwhelming sense of pride and excitement.

Of course, it is unrealistic and perhaps dangerous to take visions too seriously. Perhaps we must respect them as difficult truths with which to inform our lives—in some way. Perhaps we cannot go "backward" too longingly in time. (We can, of course, realize how little or badly "forward" we've come.) Despite the importance of knowing about goddesses and Amazons, I certainly believe that mass female liberation lies more in the technological future than in the biological past. The earth's female population is no longer small nor is the habit of warfare a desirable one. In general, hand-to-hand combat is anachronistic and militarily ineffective—for women as well as for men. Men in advanced countries possess the nuclear and chemical power to destroy the planet and/or redefine our ways of life.‡ Weaponry and military skills will ultimately prevail over any biologically muscled battle just as science will ultimately lead to more revolutionary victories than will apocalyptic military heroism. And yet I don't think that physical prowess and discipline are totally anachronistic for women. Women are raped because we cannot defend ourselves "like men." Much of our submissive, conciliatory, compassionate, and seductive behaviors have been cultivated in order to avoid either the fact or the onus of rape. Rape existed long before modern industrial capitalism, yet it seems an appropriate metaphor for that behavior (or social system) in which one man's pleasure or profit occurs only when someone else directly experiences physical pain and psychological humiliation (and who, of course, either "survives" or even "profits" from his or her pain).** I believe that the biological fact and significance of heterosexual rape and pregnancy were primary factors in the formation of the patriarchal family. Of course, the need for social efficiency and for a certain kind of group survival were also crucial: especially that form of survival that satisfied the male need for proof of his personal biological immortality by allowing him to "own" the "products" of his own sperm.

For women not to fear rape because we can successfully defend ourselves against it is not anachronistic but revolutionary. For women to be considered as potential warriors (in every sense of the word, *including* its physical representation) is not anachronistic but revolutionary. If realized, it would imply a radical change in

‡ However, total nuclear power has not been used since Nagasaki. I wonder how "anachronistic" military-physical skills have been in China, Cuba, Algeria, and Vietnam—all countries that were and are being opposed by superior military *technology*.

** I sometimes wonder how much certain biological as well as economic conditions led to our psychological acceptance of capitalism.

modern family and city life and, therefore, in our socialization, sexuality, and economic life. No one, neither man nor woman, can be a warrior in thought or action if he/she is enthralled by the family unit.†† What would it mean for a woman to be a warrior today? How could modern women control the means of production and reproduction?

THE PROBLEM OF SURVIVAL: POWER AND VIOLENCE

> Green as eunuchs, your wishes
> Hiss at my sins.
> Off, off, eely tentacle!
>
> There is nothing between us.
>
> Sylvia Plath
> *Medusa*[19]

> A time came when some of the people allowed doubt to enter their minds, and they began to wonder whether it was really possible, quantitatively and qualitatively, to resist the occupant's offensives. Was freedom worth the consequences of penetrating into that enormous circuit of terrorism and counter-terrorism? Did this disproportion not express the impossibility of escaping oppression?
>
> Frantz Fanon
> *A Dying Colonialism*[20]

†† I may note that men are often allowed more "warriorship" than women, and *without* having to renounce the comforts of companionship, progeny, domesticity, and sexual "affection." Still it is hard for men to develop the self or perform political service while they must economically support families.

One out of every five American men questioned in a nationwide survey said he believed some degree of violence was necessary to produce needed social change in this country. . . . The sample of 1,374 was selected to represent all men in the United States between the ages of 16 and 54, and to represent all races, regions, economic and social classes.

New York *Times*
May 26, 1971

A good revolutionary will never be effective unless he has a perfect balance of both physical and mental attributes.

George Jackson

Miracles of consciousness aside, I see no way for women to defeat the rule of violence without achieving power, and without doing whatever is necessary in order to survive. Unlike more powerful groups (in terms of either immediate physical strength or the implied threat of physical, military, or economic strength, i.e., "political" power), women have little power with which to either avoid or commit violence. Women traditionally are physically weak and politically powerless in a culture that values physical strength and its extended representation in the form of weaponry and money. Women, like men, must be capable of violence or self-defense before their refusal to use violence constitutes a free and moral choice, rather than "making the best of a bad bargain."

Survival is the characteristic property of power. Idealism may or may not, but often does, exist as a luxury for the powerful and a necessity for the (female) powerless. Powerless or relatively powerless men are not necessarily idealistic, nor are they physically helpless or pacifists. On the contrary. But they *are* forced to perform the male rites of violence against each other, against their will, or at least to their detriment, by more powerful men. They do not survive. Old, wealthy, white American men have not been dying in Vietnam. They survive—and some of these men also retain their ideals of "honor" or "pacifism." When *powerless* male groups begin to use "violence" to gain "power," since they are still powerless, most do not *survive* the early battle stages.

However, their violence is often viewed as heroic and courageous by other men and, of course, by many women. Twentieth-century women have personally nurtured, approved of, and impersonally obeyed male nationalist and/or Communist leaders: the reverse has been minimally if ever true. Just as the Catholic Pope, the Islamic mullah, the Jewish rabbi, and the European dictator cannot be women, so it would seem neither can a woman achieve the power and success of a Lenin, Stalin, Ho Chi Minh, Fidel Castro, Mao Tse-tung, or Ahmed Ben Bella.‡‡ In America, it is often said that poor and Third World women are physically and mentally "tougher" than middle-class white women. However, they have not assumed *political leadership* within the middle-class *or* liberation-oriented Third World communities. Neither have Third World women been able to successfully protect themselves or their daughters from the crimes committed against them by both Third World and white men.

While equality, justice, and peace are more "ethical" than their opposites, such concepts constitute male (or power) ideals,

‡‡ In Soviet Russia women comprised less than 1 per cent of the executive Communist leadership from 1958 to 1962. Specifically, of the 306 top Soviet party executives, all but two were women.[21] Krupskaya, Lenin's *wife,* was the Minister of Education, and the novelist Alexandra Kollantai was allowed no more than the ambassadorship to Sweden. (Stalin's wife was allowed to kill herself.) In China it was *Mrs.* Mao and *Mrs.* Chou who occupied relatively powerful positions: Mrs. Chou, or Ting-Ying Chao, was the vice president of the All-China Democratic Women's Federation. Despite *Mrs.* Allende's talents, it was her husband who was elected President of Chile. I wonder what position Leila Khaled will occupy *after* a successful Palestinian revolution? Will she and other women like her suffer the fate of the Algerian women revolutionaries?

and not male (or power) practices.* The ideal woman avoids committing direct physical violence—and avoids her own self-preservation. Psychologically, self-preservation is precisely what patriarchal society forbids women. Traditionally, the ideal female is trained to "lose" and the ideal male is trained to "win" (i.e., psychologically, females are trained to die, males to survive). And women are trained to mount the sacrificial altar willingly. For example, most mother-women give up whatever ghost of a unique and human self they may have when they "marry" and rear children. Most children in contemporary American culture invade their mothers' privacy, life space, sanity, and selves to such an extent that she must give up these things in order not to commit violence. (Invasion of a boundary into deserted territory is perhaps less painful than one into occupied and functional territory. Of course, such invasion is practiced by mothers against children. Fathers invade children too, but not as frequently. They don't have to: they already own the entire territory and need only make occasional forays to check on their holdings.)

> Dr. Christiaan Barnard, South African heart transplant pioneer says he's a swinger. Here on a honeymoon trip with his 19-year-old bride, the 47-year-old Barnard described himself to reporters at Kennedy Airport last night as a "doctor who is more open, swinging, and can enjoy life, not that sad-looking professor type the public has been used to." . . . "I don't know what's going on," Mrs. Barnard told reporters when they questioned her.
>
> New York *Post*, 1971

* Men are generally more verbal about "justice" and "equality" when it applies to abstract or public, global issues (*Their* reference sphere); they do not apply such concepts to their personal or family lives—woman's reference sphere. Unfortunately, women have no say in public areas, and only feminists have begun to look for "equality" in personal relationships. As a group, many feminists are still as removed from the public reference sphere as are non-feminist women.

> Once Lola Pierotti earned $24,000 a year and worked long hours as an administrative assistant on Capitol Hill. Now she works longer hours and has even more responsibility—but no pay. What happened? Was she demoted? No, she just married the boss. Her bridegroom, of four years this month, was the senior Republican Senator from Vermont—George D. Aiken. "All he expects of me is that I drive his car, cook his meals, do his laundry and run his office," she enumerated, with a grin.
>
> New York *Times*
> June 20, 1971

Women have fewer and fewer sexual, "romantic," and in-cestuous alternatives as they grow older.† They have never had access to direct political and economic power at any age. The older a woman is, the more at a "loss" she is. Our culture does not re-ward enslavement to "others" as well as it does enslavement to "self" and to "action." Ideally, male enslavement produces male "win-ners," whose prize is survival as we define it: money, sex, and maternal-like nurturance. Ideally, female enslavement produces fe-male "losers," whose prize of survival is a short-lived one, based on "allowance" money and some limited sex, received indirectly through a husband-man—from whom maternal-like nurturance is hardly ever received.

It is not that women "need" men more than men "need" women‡; on the contrary, men need women very much, but as

† Their "fathers" want younger and younger women
‡ However, perhaps they do. In 1971 I asked a group of black and white high school students what they wanted to do when they "grew up"; all females answered in terms of "marriage"; all males answered in terms of achieving some skill, trade, or adventure. I turned to the women and asked them who they had in mind when they thought of "marriage"—each other?

relatively interchangeable servants.** Women are conditioned to "need" one man as "irreplaceable." We may recall Farberow's statistics[22] about how many more widows than widowers commit suicide in America. Women are so trained to "need" a man that even male "losers" can find some woman to take care of them, certainly far more easily than female "winners" can find men or women to care for them. (In this respect they are really no better off than female "losers.") Women have learned to live without being nurtured for so long that when they experience it they grow guilty, uncomfortable, and frightened.

I suspect that wives are more willing to keep relatively non-violent "mentally ill" husbands at home with them, certainly more than husbands are willing to keep "mentally ill" wives. Wives can still serve and nurture a "lost" husband; "lost" wives cannot or will not serve their husbands and, as such, are annoying, inconvenient, threatening, and expendable.

Ideally, men become bigger and better "winners" as they grow older. Their alternatives and choices widen—or are supposed to—as a function of the increase in wealth, wisdom, and power that male aging denotes. Male power, which is based on the oppression of some men and all women, belongs to older men in patriarchal culture. Faced with these circumstances, "good" women destroy themselves gracefully, i.e., they get depressed and stay at home, or go "mad" and stay in asylums. In either case, they remove themselves from the path of adult male mobility and renewal. "Bad" women aren't good losers; they destroy, or rather attempt to de-

** Of course, poor American men "serve" in factories and in armies. They directly "serve" other men and indirectly the female *property* of those men. When poor men fight for wage increases or class revolution, their demands rarely include a doubling of their salary and a new method of payment, one that would reflect the importance of their wives' housework and childrearing. When poor men fight for wage increases it is to equalize some more power among men, and to allow more men to protect and own "their" women and children in better ways.

stroy, others. Ophelia in *Hamlet* is a "good" loser; Medea in *Medea* is a "bad" loser.

To those who think I am suggesting that we have a war between the sexes, I say: but we've always had one—and women have always lost it. Women hardly notice this fact because they take "losing" for granted just as men take "winning" for granted. When women question or change what they take for granted, the vision of the sex war we are *already* waging will become clearer. Similarly, it is not a "generation gap" that exists today, so much as a generation war, and one that has always existed. Parents sacrifice their own growth and pleasure for their children's sake: the parental casualties in terms of psychological and physical death are many. The children's casualties are also great: young men are sent by their parents to die in war, young women are sent to die in marriage, motherhood, and madness. Child abuse, child molestation, the stifling of creativity and individuality are all generation war statistics. Like the sex war, it is an ancient battle. What is new, however, is the desire to either end the war or turn the "losers" into "winners."

SOME PSYCHOLOGICAL PRESCRIPTIONS
FOR THE FUTURE

> The women say, truly is this not magnificent? The vessels are upright, the vessels have acquired legs. The sacred vessels are on the move. . . . The women say, this is a sacrilege, a violation of all the rules . . . must they not hold violence in abhorrence? Is not their structure fragile and will they not shatter at the first onslaught if they are not already in pieces from collision with each other? . . . Stamping the earth, they speed their movements.
>
> Monique Wittig[23]

How can women learn to survive—and learn to value survival? How can women banish self-sacrifice, guilt, naïveté, helplessness, madness, and sorrow from the female condition? How—or should —women sever their ties to childbearing and rearing? Should women *stop* being compassionate? Should or can there be a single standard of behavior for both sexes? Is there such a thing as a biologically rooted female culture that should remain separate from male culture, partly because it is "better" than male culture?

Women must convert their "love" for and reliance on strength and skill in others to a love for all manner of strength and skill in themselves. Women must be able to go as directly to the "heart" of physical, technological, and intellectual reality as they presumably do to the "heart" of emotional reality. This requires discipline, courage, confidence, anger, the ability to act, and an overwhelming sense of joy and urgency. Only resourceful women, women with resources, can either share them with other women or use them to accumulate more resources (skills or goods), for both themselves and others. Other things being equal, a group composed of re-sourceful *individuals* who are also pledged, through self-interest, to various ideals or goals is a potentially more powerful group than one composed of less resourceful members with similar ideals. The centuries of female spiritual, political, and sexual sacrifice will be better redeemed by the female entry into humanity and public institutions than by rejecting them because they are not perfect— or because the efforts to integrate them are difficult and heart-breaking—or because they have traditionally been based on the oppression of women. For example, science, religion, language, and psychoanalysis have as often as not been used against women. This does not mean that these modes and institutions—and their "prizes" —must necessarily be sacrificed or discarded as hopelessly tainted. We do not know if women would discover a completely different and better sort of science or language. However, it is clear that women who are feminists must gradually and ultimately *dominate* public social institutions—in order to insure that they are not used against women. I say "dominate" because I don't think that "equality" or "individuality" will be possible for women who have never experienced full participation or supremacy in public institutions as men have. For example, I happen to think that science must be used to either release women from biological reproduction—or to allow men to experience the process also. However, women who are feminists, just like men who are black liberationists, will not be able to quickly escort us all into the paradise of our choosing. Feminists, like black liberationists, may be: Communists, socialists, Marxists, anarchists, capitalists, Democrats, Republicans, artists, scientists, nationalists, separatists, integrationists, violently revolutionary, non-violently revolutionary, etc., etc. The point is to have our *entire* social drama played out as fully by women as by men. And it *is* revolutionary by definition to have women "out of the biological home," both psychologically and actually. Whatever happens *after* that is then a matter for . . . everyone.††

But how to do it? What will be necessary psychologically in order for women to finally enter the mainstream of *human* action, to finally have *social* rather than, or other than, biological roles?

Woman's primary ego-identity is rooted in a concern for limited and specific "others," and for what pleases a few men. Woman's ego-identity must somehow shift and be moored upon what is necessary for her own survival as a strong individual. Women must somehow free themselves to be concerned with many things and ideas, and with many people. Such a radical shift in

†† I am, of course, implying that child care is a public and crucial concern. I am not implying that any public state method in either capitalist or Communist countries has done very well by children; nor am I implying that specific individuals cannot, under certain conditions, be personal and nurturant to specific children—or people.

ego-focus is extremely difficult and very frightening. It grates and screeches against the grain of all "feminine" nerves and feelings, and implies grave retribution. Some women go "mad" when they make such a shift in focus, or when it occurs within them.

Such a shift in the basic female ego (or in the interpretation of female gender identity) implies a frank passion for achieving the power necessary to define oneself—a power which is always predicated on the direct control of worldly realities. Such a passion would do away with such common female behaviors as apologizing for, or disguising to oneself and to others, the concern with one's own survival and growth. From a psychological point of view, as I have noted, it is somewhat irrelevant whether a woman achieves this ego-shift as a "Communist" or as a "capitalist"; as a liberal reformer or as a guerrilla in training; as an "individualist" or as a "collectivist"; as a lesbian, as a heterosexual, or as a bisexual woman; as a biological or non-biological mother or not as a mother. Any woman who successfully becomes interested in and begins to achieve various powers directly, and not through or for a "man" or a "family," is, within the psychological kingdom of patriarchy, committing a radical act, i.e., an act that risks "winning." Only such a radical psychological act will make it possible for women to begin to try their hands at solving the issues of divisions among women based on class, race, and age.‡‡ Only such a radical psychological act will make it possible for women to tolerate and develop many individual differences, and to follow other sexual models than that of rape-incest-procreation.

Those women involved in such an ego-transformation would, by necessity, withdraw from all human interactions which are not extremely supportive of their survival and achievement of individual power. Other ways of saying this might be: the growth in women

‡‡ Female children are as oppressed as their aging and "useless" grandmothers. Both are denied sex and work.

of a greater psychological investment in female rather than in male survival, power, and pleasure; a withdrawal from the conditioned female addiction to masochism; a withdrawal from the female readiness to make painful and unnecessary compromises. Such a withdrawal would imply a rejection of many Judeo-Christian and liberal values. For example: the glorification of martyrdom, asceticism, helplessness, the devaluing of the body, an acceptance of Cartesian dualism or Platonism, etc.

Women whose psychological identities are forged out of concern for their own survival and self-definition, and who withdraw from or avoid any interactions which do not support this formidable endeavor, need not "give up" their capacity for warmth, emotionality, and nurturance. They do not have to forsake the "wisdom of the heart" and become "men." They need only transfer the primary force of their "supportiveness" to themselves and to each other—and never to the point of self-sacrifice. Women need not stop being tender, compassionate, or concerned with the feelings of others. They must start being tender and compassionate with themselves and with other women. Women must begin to "save" themselves and their daughters before they "save" their husbands and their sons; before they "save" the whole world. Women must try to convert the single-minded ruthlessness with which they yearn for, serve, and protect a mate or biological child into the "ruthlessness" of self-preservation and self-development. Perhaps one of the effects of this "transfer of affections" might be an increase in the male capacity to "nurture": themelves, each other, children, and hopefully women. Another effect would be the creation of a secure and revolutionary source of emotional and domestic nurturance for women, without which the courage for survival might falter and which, at this point in history, only biological females seem to know how or are willing to provide.

Women need not reject their (usually unsatisfied) need for

emotional comfort and affection. They must, in fact, find ways of satisfying these needs without losing their freedom or dignity. The female desire for love should be satisfied in a number of new ways, and as a counterpoint to or respite from events other than those dictated by powerlessness. Affection and sexuality among women must mingle with and mark the events of action and victory, of thought and wisdom.

It is important to realize that the kinds of changes in the female ego I am talking about are *psychological* changes. I am not "prescribing" or predicting any one economic or social form, or any one form of sexual behavior, to insure such psychological changes. New forms must and will occur—but only as enough women challenge or alter their relation to the means of production and reproduction. Perhaps the majority of women in America will be able to effect such psychological changes only after crucial changes in their economic and reproductive lives have already occurred. Perhaps only some young women, perhaps only a minority of all women, will be able to effect such changes through consciousness alone, through the strength of understanding, which, if transformed into wisdom, always means the performance of personally necessary actions.

THIRTEEN QUESTIONS

What to say to young girls who listen raptly and confidently to the most extreme feminist visions—and laugh, so happily, about them? What odes to write them? What deeds to teach them? What to learn from them? How can the creative impulse be nurtured in women—we, who have forgotten our myths, who have no rituals from which to proceed?

Who will our goddesses and heroines be? In what language shall we address them? How shall we experience divinity as residing in the female body? When shall we rejoice in the birth of "divine" daughters, when shall we respect and trust older women? How can we be sexual with our daughters? When will all foolish lies cease between mothers and daughters? How shall we celebrate that day?

Must we choose between the way of the spirit and the way of the sword? Must body and soul remain divided? Are murder and childbirth necessary? How closely are they related? Do women need a women's army? Or do we need an army of wise women? Or both? How shall we, as feminists, practice patience and collective loyalty—precisely when we must practice action and individuality?

Would intense maternal and paternal mothering in childhood lead to wisdom and strength among women? Amazons were probably not "smother-mothered"—or sexually seduced by fathers —as much as they were collectively reared, in peer groups, by *many* powerful adult women to face human necessity with efficiency and honor.

Are the helplessness and prolonged dependence of human children the models for all *culturally* oppressive relations? Can new methods of childbearing and rearing banish the human tendency to arbitrarily interpret biological differences in oppressive ways?

How can we dismiss all "men" as "hopeless"—when some of the by-products of power are knowledge, generosity, and likableness? How can we come to terms with this fact? Is it possible for socialized "women" ever to experience sexual freedom with socialized "men"? Isn't this a contradiction in terms—if public power is still unequally distributed between the sexes?

Must women sever their Maiden's marriage bonds with Eros —until all men have married with Her? Will lesbianism, bisexuality, and homosexuality occur more and more naturally among young people? What will this mean? Will men be able to become *more* heterosexual just as women are able to become *less* heterosexual? How much will adults already socialized into rigid sex roles be able to partake of such changes? What will happen to us if they can't?

How shall women learn to go beyond an incestuous and procreative model of sexuality?

What does it mean to use or to have one's body, time, and mind used solely for economic profit? Out of necessity or through conditioning or through lack of other alternatives? How different in meaning is the Nazi use of the human body for industrial purposes, for "profit," for the "future"—from most labor in capitalist and Communist societies? How does this Nazi practice as metaphor differ from female—or male—prostitution? How shall we redefine "work" and "human need" in industrial-technological times?

How can we rear male infants to bisexuality—to respect, trust, fear, and love women and men equally? How rear female infants to do the same?

When can we stop assigning any significance to biological differences? And if biological differences remain, despite true cultural neutrality, shall we, can we, use science to achieve a single standard of human behavior? Who shall decide what the standards shall be? Who shall teach them, who enforce them? And for what purpose? And can a single standard of behavior ever constitute anything more than a background against which more unique or dramatic behaviors can occur?

How shall we come to terms with our bodies and with the natural universe? Many "natural" events—like early death, disease, hardship—are neither desirable nor necessary. (Many "unnatural" events like slavery, monogamy, and pollution are not desirable either.) If "male" violence and "female" domesticity is indeed "natural," then is it in humanity's interest to channel or banish these predispositions, just as we wish to banish or protect ourselves from disease, poverty, earthquakes, floods, ecological disaster—and biological reproduction? Who shall decide which of these "natural" or historico-natural disasters are to be banished first, and for which people, and in what way? What familiar demonic price will be exacted from us as we move ever further from nature to civilization? Is a tragic price inevitable—whether we exist "naturally" or "unnaturally"?

How shall we rid ourselves of our ignorance and paranoia about scientific skills? How shall we create a climate in which neither Prometheus nor Christ is punished for his gifts of knowledge—a climate in which many female givers of knowledge can flourish?

Appendix

THE FEMALE CAREER AS A PSYCHIATRIC PATIENT:
The Sex, Class, Race, and Marital Status of America's Psychiatrically Involved Population, 1950–1969*

The statistical method is only one way, and an exceedingly troublesome way at that, of investigating a phenomenon. The initial criterion for a statistic often determines what "truth" it will lead to. National "mental illness" statistics prove no exception to this rule. For example, the National Institute of Mental Health has annually reported data for the predominantly male Veterans Administration psychiatric hospitals. The data represents a 100 per cent projection based on a 30 per cent random sampling of VA hospitals. This is a different method of deriving data than the one NIMH uses for other psychiatric facilities. The number of people in general or private hospitals are presented as raw data, based on the number of hospitals reporting for a given year. But not every hospital turns in a report every year to NIMH. In 1968, for example, 799 of the 1917 *known* psychiatric outpatient facilities

* As of the spring of 1972, NIMH had not yet fully tabulated the mental health statistics for 1969, 1970 and 1971. Some data exists for outpatient clinics, general psychiatric wards, community mental health centers, and State and County hospitals for 1969, and I have indicated the trends where possible.

reported no patient data; 263 of the *known* 1122 general psychiatric wards reported no data; 14 of the *known* 150 private hospitals reported no data; and 55 of the *known* 312 state hospitals reported no patient data.† Although there are more female than male patients in each of the reporting hospitals, particularly in the private, general, and outpatient facilities, there is no way of checking the sex-ratios in the non-reporting hospitals.

Further difficulties involve the fact that the criteria for certain of the statistics, such as "first admissions" or "residence at years end" may

(1) count the same patient twice in a given year;
(2) exclude some patients altogether who have already left (as well as the "invisible" patients who have never been there, e.g., the invisible housewife-alcoholic or prostitute-drug addict;)

† For state hospitals, I was able to use a statistic that takes this fact into consideration.

(3) not adequately reflect the phenomena of frequent short- or long-term readmissions and long-term stays that characterize female patients;

(4) not be based on the sex ratio in the American population at large for the given year;

(5) or, more important, not be based on the "real" population the particular patient derived from, e.g., the "population" of white divorced working women with children, or of foreign or native-born migrants, etc.

In other words, relevant demographic characteristics such as age, race, marital status, birthplace, social class, and education are usually not taken into account when researchers *do* present a breakdown by "per 100,000" population (except in smaller studies which attempt to do just this). Without such demographic variables we cannot answer such questions as: What is the probability of a black working mother's admission to a psychiatric facility compared with that of a black working father's? Or with that of a white non-working mother's? Or with that of a black non-working father's?‡

It is for just such reasons that I reviewed numerous small-sample studies and chose very carefully which of several NIMH statistics I would use. For example, many studies published by NIMH and elsewhere, have used statistics based on a "first admission" criterion to state and county psychiatric hospitals. Or they have not distinguished between those people who come once and those who remain for years in outpatient psychiatric facilities.**

‡ Pollack (1964) has shown that both black and white female heads of households in Maryland and Louisiana had a significantly higher admission rate to psychiatric facilities than did their male counterparts.[1]

** For political and economic reasons alone, even a five-minute phone call for information to a community mental health center is recorded as a "contact"; a single visit is regarded as a "first admission" or an "addition" on the statistical rolls.

Perhaps this is one of the reasons that sex-ratio differences in "mental illness" have been seen as negligible or, traditionally, as favoring a greater male than female psychiatric involvement.

The data presented in Tables 4 through 7 are based on the following statistics:

(1) For state and county hospitals the "residence at year's end" rather than the "first admission" statistic was used. The former statistic gives a better "prevalence" rate; the latter a better "incidence" rate, i.e., the "residence" statistic includes the total number of people committed for the first or for the tenth time, who are actually in the asylum on a given day. (Of course, this statistic excludes those who have died or been released on the day before the patient head count.††) I thought it a better way of "picking up" female patients, whose pattern of hospitalization is characterized by both frequency and lengthiness. (The "first admission" statistic only tells us how many new cases have occurred during a given period.) NIMH has recently indicated that in 1971, women were *detained* for longer time-periods than men in state and county hospitals (*Provisional Data on Length of Stay of Admissions to State and County Mental Hospitals, 1971*).

(2) For outpatient facilities the statistic based on those patients who are listed as having been "treated," was used, as opposed to the statistic based on the "untreated" population. The "treated" statistic gives a relatively truer picture of who remains in treatment,

†† Of course, a statistic based on "residence at year's end" will probably involve us in counting the same person twice—if we "collapse" over all psychiatric facilities for a given year. For example, a woman who enters a general psychiatric ward and is then committed to a state hospital where she is "resident" at year's end will be counted twice in any attempt to total the entire population for that year. This fact is a good argument for not "collapsing" over-all facilities for a given year. We can, however, "collapse" as long as we keep the above fact in mind—and accordingly, proceed with great caution. Perhaps it would make more sense to look at each kind of facility over a period of time: what is the sex ratio in private hospitals from 1961 to 1968 for example? This is shown in Table 5.

i.e., women. The "untreated" statistic reveals that people who are seen, momentarily, by themselves, or by law courts, as in need of treatment, have both been conditioned against seeking help and/or have other resources or outlets, i.e., men.

(3) For private hospitals and general psychiatric wards, NIMH usually presents only one statistic, based on "first admission" or "total addition." Having no choice, I used this statistic. Many women are probably admitted to general psychiatric wards for three-week stays, or to private hospitals, more than once a year; the "first admission" statistic would not include the "repeaters." Even so, there are still more women than men in both these facilities. Only a single statistic or patient head count is presented for community mental health facilities. This was reviewed, but as NIMH has not yet included it in either their in- or outpatient statistics, will be discussed separately here. It is not represented in the Tables.

Tables 4, 5, 6, and 7 present NIMH statistics from 1960 to 1968. As we have seen in Chapter Four, it is clear that more women than men have been involved in a dramatically increasing way, in the following forms of psychiatric treatment facilities in America from 1964 through 1968: Private psychiatric hospitals, state and county psychiatric hospitals, inpatient psychiatric wards in general and Veterans Administration hospitals, and general and Veterans Administration outpatient psychiatric facilities. In 1968, for example, 50,363 more women than men were psychiatrically hospitalized and treated. This number excludes the number of women involved in both private treatment and as in- or outpatients in community mental health centers.

Before discussing these tables in greater depth, let me make some comments about some general statistical trends in "mental illness" in America. The number of people (both male and female) seeking psychiatric help on an outpatient basis and being committed as inpatients to private and public facilities has increased enormously during the last fifteen years. NIMH has estimated that the total number of psychiatric "episodes"‡‡ of care has more than doubled since 1955, "increasing from 1.7 million to 3.4 million in 1968."[2] According to my own statistics, the total "psychiatrically involved" population increased from 957,255 (nearly a million) in 1964 to 1,179,861 (nearly 2 million) in 1968 (Table 4). As of 1970, NIMH has estimated that one out of every three hospital beds in America is a psychiatric bed, and that the ratio by geographic division is considerable, "ranging from a low of 1 out of 5 beds in the Mountain States to a high of 2 out of 5 beds in the Middle Atlantic states."[3] NIMH has also estimated the "cost" of mental illness to have been 21 billion dollars in 1968.[4]

Although the total number of "residents" in state and county asylums has decreased over the last decade,* the number of first admissions and readmissions has been steadily increasing, as has the number of people being serviced by community mental health centers.[5] It is important to realize that there are more people confined to institutions because of mental illness than because of criminal conviction.[6] In 1960, 630,046 of the population institutionalized in America were in mental asylums; 469,717 were in homes for the aged; 174,727 were institutionalized as being mentally handicapped; and 346,015 were inmates of correctional institutions.[7] In 1964, the average daily census of mental asylums was 563,354; of institutions for the mentally retarded, 186,735; and of federal and state prisons, 214,356.†[8]

---

‡‡ They are referring to "patient care episodes," a statistic based on criteria other than what I could use. According to my statistics, for example, the total number of people involved in all of the psychiatric facilities shown in Table 4 comprise 2 per cent of the total American population (190 million people), from 1966 through 1968.

* Due to the use of tranquilizers and the (minimal) construction of community mental health centers.

† As of this writing, the comparable figures for 1970 are unavailable.

TABLE 4:
INSTITUTIONAL POPULATION BY SEX IN EACH OF SIX

YEAR	1964		1965	
TYPE OF HOSPITAL	WOMEN	MEN	WOMEN	MEN
General	146,632	108,518	179,348	126,394
State and county	248,815	241,634	241,244	233,958
Outpatient	58,179	50,000	78,191	71,963
Private	24,003	14,741	43,099	27,822
V. A. Inpatient	1,438	57,687	1,409	56,545
V. A. Outpatient	100	5,508	447	17,423
Total	479,167	478,088	543,738	534,105

Table Description: This table shows a dramatic increase in the number of public psychiatric patients in America within a five-year period. The number of female patients increased from 479,167 in 1964 to 615,112 in 1968. In 1964 there were 1,079 more women than men in the various psychiatric facilities. By 1968, 50,363 more women than men were psychiatrically hospitalized and treated in public facilities.

While there are many more men than women in prison, there are many more people, the majority of whom are women, involved in the female-culture of "psychiatric careers." (As I suggested in Chapter Two, the kinds of behaviors considered "criminal" and "mentally ill" are sex-typed, and each sex is conditioned accordingly.) While the total number of psychiatrically

SYCHIATRIC FACILITIES: 1964–1968 (INCLUSIVE)

1966		1967		1968	
WOMEN	MEN	WOMEN	MEN	WOMEN	MEN
172,231	115,127	227,258	153,664	219,950	150,630
229,899	222,190	214,894	211,415	199,635	199,517
107,501	94,103	122,955	104,166	143,638	120,433
27,244	16,560	27,474	17,716	49,669	32,676
1,465	55,655	1,265	51,830	1,110	46,590
342	13,034	379	14,811	1,110	14,903
538,682	516,669	594,225	553,602	615,112	564,749

SOURCE: Reference Tables on Patients in Mental Health Facilities. U. S. Department of Health, Education and Welfare. Public Health Services. Health Services and Mental Health Administration. National Institute of Mental Health: 1964–1968.

"involved" men has increased by 71,443 (from 493,306 in 1963 to 564,749 in 1968)‡ the total number of women similarly involved increased more dramatically, from 488,961 in 1963 to 615,112 in 1968 (Table 5). There were 4345 *more* men than

‡ The majority of whom, we must remember, are diagnosed as alcoholics, drug addicts, psychophysiologically disturbed, or sociopathic personalities.

TABLE 5:
INSTITUTIONAL POPULATION BY SEX IN EACH

TYPE OF HOSPITAL	GENERAL		STATE AND COUNTY	
	WOMEN	MEN	WOMEN	MEN
1960	116,930 (54%)	98,492 (46%)	273,211 (51%)	262,329 (49%)
1961	120,472 (55%)	96,597 (45%)	268,377 (51%)	259,079 (49%)
1962	127,461 (57%)	97,236 (43%)	261,986 (51%)	253,672 (49%)
1963	136,423 (57%)	103,400 (43%)	256,240 (51%)	248,364 (49%)
1964	146,632 (57%)	108,518 (43%)	248,815 (51%)	241,634 (49%)
1965	179,348 (59%)	126,394 (41%)	241,244 (51%)	233,958 (49%)
1966	172,231 (60%)	115,127 (40%)	229,899 (51%)	222,190 (49%)
1967	227,258 (60%)	153,664 (40%)	214,894 (50%)	211,415 (50%)
1968	219,950 (59%)	150,630 (41%)	199,635 (50%)	199,517 (50%)
TOTAL	1,446,705	1,050,058	2,194,301	2,132,158

Table Description: The majority of psychiatric patients in General Psychiatric Wards, Private Hospitals, Outpatient Clinics, and State and County Hospitals have been women. For example, in 1968, women comprised 59% of the population in General Wards, 60% in Private Hospitals, 50% in State and County Hospitals and 54% in Outpatient Clinics.

OF SIX PSYCHIATRIC FACILITIES: 1960–1968.

OUTPATIENT		PRIVATE		V.A. INPATIENT		V.A. OUTPATIENT	
WOMEN	MEN	WOMEN	MEN	WOMEN	MEN	WOMEN	MEN
*	*	25,301 (61%)	15,876 (39%)	1,398 (2%)	58,816 (98%)	*	*
*	*	21,842 (62%)	13,509 (38%)	1,467 (2%)	59,206 (98%)	*	*
*	*	25,090 (63%)	15,039 (37%)	1,366 (2%)	58,669 (98%)	*	*
68,601 (52%)	63,139 (48%)	26,087 (63%)	15,266 (37%)	1,488 (3%)	57,985 (97%)	122 (2%)	5,152 (98%)
58,179 (54%)	50,000 (46%)	24,003 (62%)	14,741 (38%)	1,438 (2%)	57,687 (98%)	100 (2%)	5,508 (98%)
78,191 (52%)	71,963 (48%)	43,099 (61%)	27,822 (39%)	1,409 (2%)	56,545 (98%)	447 (3%)	17,423 (97%)
107,501 (53%)	94,103 (47%)	27,244 (62%)	16,560 (38%)	1,465 (3%)	55,655 (97%)	342 (3%)	13,034 (97%)
122,955 (54%)	104,166 (46%)	27,474 (61%)	17,716 (39%)	1,265 (2%)	51,830 (98%)	379 (2%)	14,811 (98%)
143,638 (54%)	120,433 (46%)	49,669 (60%)	32,676 (40%)	1,110 (2%)	46,590 (98%)	1,110 (7%)	14,903 (93%)
579,065	503.804	269,809	169,205	12,406	502,983	2,500	70,831

Source: Reference Tables on Patients in Mental Health Facilities. U. S. Department of Health, Education and Welfare. Public Health Services. Health Services and Mental Health Administration. National Institute of Mental Health: 1960–1968.

TABLE 6:
INSTITUTIONAL POPULATION BY SEX AND AGE (18–64)

TYPE OF HOSPITAL	GENERAL		STATE AND COUNTY	
	WOMEN	MEN	WOMEN	MEN
1966	142,599 (60%)	93,318 (40%)	123,638 (47%)	137,012 (53%)
1967	184,954 (60%)	123,488 (40%)	124,224 (47%)	139,930 (53%)
1968	177,103 (60%)	119,443 (40%)	105,195 (46%)	121,903 (54%)
TOTAL	504,656 (60%)	336,249 (40%)	353,102 (47%)	398,845 (53%)

Table Description: In the years from 1966 to 1968 adult women comprised at least 60% of the adult patient population in General Psychiatric Wards and Outpatient Clinics. The same was true in Private Psychiatric Hospitals except for 1967. Women over 65 comprise nearly a third of all female patients in State and County Hospitals. It is important to note that in 1968 women of all ages comprised 54% of the patients in Outpatient Clinics (Table 5), and 62% of the Outpatient Clinic population when male children and adolescents (under 18) are excluded from the population.

IN EACH OF SIX PSYCHIATRIC FACILITES: 1966–1968.

OUTPATIENT		PRIVATE		V.A. INPATIENT		V.A. OUTPATIENT	
WOMEN	MEN	WOMEN	MEN	WOMEN	MEN	WOMEN	MEN
84,507 (61%)	54,378 (39%)	22,984 (63%)	13,353 (37%)	1,260 (3%)	41,355 (97%)	324 (3%)	12,588 (97%)
96,182 (61%)	60,327 (39%)	22,559 (56%)	17,660 (44%)	1,110 (3%)	39,265 (97%)	365 (2%)	14,380 (98%)
113,392 (62%)	70,470 (38%)	40,965 (61%)	26,673 (39%)	950 (3%)	35,690 (97%)	1,098 (7%)	14,438 (93%)
294,081 (61%)	185,175 (39%)	86,508 (60%)	57,686 (40%)	3,320 (3%)	116,310 (97%)	1,787 (4%)	41,406 (96%)

SOURCE: Reference Tables on Patients in Mental Health Facilities. U. S. Department of Health, Education and Welfare. Public Health Services. Health Services and Mental Health Administration. National Institute of Mental Health: 1966–1968.

women psychiatrically involved in 1963; by 1968, there were 50,363 more women than men similarly involved (Tables 4 and 5).**

Tables 4 and 5 indicate that the majority of the "psychiatrically involved" are concentrated, first, in general psychiatric wards. From 1960 to 1968, women comprised approximately 58 per cent of the psychiatric population in general hospitals. Where age-adjusted figures could be obtained (for 1966, 1967, and 1968), women comprised 60 per cent of the psychiatric population in general hospitals between the ages of eighteen and sixty-four (see Table 6). Both percentages are higher than the percentage of women in the population at large (which was 51 per cent in 1960 and 53 per cent in 1970.) (According to data just received from NIMH, the number of women in general psychiatric wards increased from 219,950 in 1968 to 259,701 in 1969; the male increase was from 150,630 to 160,535).

The second greatest concentration of the "psychiatrically involved" are in state and county psychiatric hospitals. From 1960 to 1968, women comprised approximately 51 per cent of this population—an adequate representation of their percentage in the population at large. Where age-adjusted figures could be obtained (for 1966, 1967, and 1968), women comprised 47 per cent of the state and county inmates between the ages of eighteen and sixty-four. This suggests the extent to which state and county asylums

** There is some unexplained and fascinating phenomenon afoot here. From 1961 through 1963, more men than women were psychiatrically involved —i.e., as based on statistics which are different from those available beginning in 1964. For example, no distinction between people who were "treated" or "untreated" in outpatient facilities was made by NIMH for these years. Nevertheless, it is possible that the dramatic increase in the female psychiatric population is a true phenomenon of the 1960s. The trend of increase in fact suggests an epidemic-like occurrence, one that is similar to other social trends in the '60s, such as certain forms of drug addiction, political assassination, city crime, and the growth of liberation movements.

TABLE 7: PATIENT POPULATION BY SEX AND AGE IN
AMERICAN STATE AND COUNTY HOSPITALS: 1950–1968.

	NUMBER OF WOMEN	NUMBER OF MEN	NUMBER OF WOMEN OVER 65	PERCENTAGE OF TOTAL FEMALE POPULATION OVER 65	NUMBER OF MEN OVER 65	PERCENTAGE OF TOTAL MALE POPULATION OVER 65
1950	262,063	250,438	69,916	27%	59,985	24%
1951	266,718	253,608	69,452	26%	59,064	23%
1952	273,999	257,982	74,613	27%	62,938	24%
1953	280,998	264,047	78,447	28%	65,577	25%
1954	286,877	267,102	83,244	29%	68,249	26%
1955	289,517	269,405	88,153	30%	70,132	26%
1956	285,437	265,953	89,629	31%	70,217	26%
1957	282,430	266,196	92,045	33%	71,059	27%
1958	280,018	265,164	94,161	34%	71,220	27%
1959	277,432	264,451	92,235	33%	68,541	26%
1960	273,211	262,329	92,647	34%	68,059	26%
1961	268,377	259,079	91,669	34%	65,868	.25%
1962	261,968	253,672	90,030	34%	63,279	25%
1963	256,240	248,364	88,120	34%	60,722	24%
1964	248,815	241,634	85,841	34%	57,992	24%
1965	241,244	233,958	83,712	35%	56,618	24%
1966	229,899	222,190	81,018	35%	53,962	24%
1967	214,894	211,415	76,453	36%	51,884	25%
1968	199,635	199.517	72,046	36%	48,094	24%
TOTAL	4,979,772	4,756,536	1,593,431	32%	1,193,460	25%

SOURCE: Trends in Resident Patients. State and County Mental Hospitals
1950–1968. Biometry Branch. National Institute of Mental Health: April 1970.

function as custodial old-age homes for women.†† As Table 7 indicates, 36 per cent of all women (and 24 per cent of all men) hospitalized in state and county asylums in 1968 were over sixty-five.

The third largest concentration of the "psychiatrically involved" is in outpatient facilities. From 1963 to 1968 women comprised approximately 53 per cent of the outpatient population.‡‡ Where age-adjusted figures were obtainable (from 1966 through 1968), women comprised approximately 61 per cent of the outpatient population between the ages of eighteen and sixty-four (Table 6). Both percentages are in excess of the percentage of females in the general population.*

Let me note several things here: (1) a large number of under-eighteen males are brought by their parents for "outpatient" treatment and swell the male patient ranks; adult men are not similarly coerced or involved in these facilities; (2) 57 per cent of people who have been listed as "untreated" in general and VA outpatient facilities combined, from 1963 to 1968, are adult men who simply don't return to the "female psychiatric life"; (3) NIMH reports, small-sample studies, and an unpublished survey of my own, all document the fact that women comprise two thirds of the adult population in general and community mental health outpatient facilities. NIMH has recently reported that 542 adult women per 100,000 adult women, compared with 444 adult men per 100,000 adult men, were involved in outpatient services in 1969.[9] Seventy-two per cent of the people serviced by the Massachusetts Mental Health Center during its first twenty-seven months (1957–59) were women, 61 per cent of whom were unmarried.[10] Women comprised from 60 to 73 per cent of the long-term patients

†† As well as a detention camp for both male and female poor and black people.
‡‡ And 51 per cent of the outpatient population involved in general and VA outpatient facilities combined.
* We must not forget that these percentages are based on the number of outpatient facilities reported for a given year: from 1961 to 1968, 26 per cent of the known outpatient facilities did not report to NIMH; and community mental health centers have not yet been included in the annual NIMH reports.

involved in the Fort Logan Community Mental Health Center from 1961 to 1968.[11] Two thirds of the adult outpatients in 1963 in Southern and Northeastern clinics in twelve American states were women[12]; 65 to 70 per cent of the outpatients in public hospital clinics in New York City between 1958 and 1960 were women.[13] Women comprised two thirds of all adult outpatient admissions from 1968 to 1970 at a Brooklyn community mental health center.[14] In 1970, NIMH, based on 1968 reports from fifty-four community mental health centers, documented a greater "number of female than male additions" in all three types of care services—twenty-four hour, partial, and outpatient.[15] (4) In a recent NIMH report on CMHC populations in 1969 this trend increased, especially in the partial hospitalization facilities, where there were only "seventy male additions for every one hundred females." More women than men are involved in private therapy— a population that NIMH doesn't analyze. However, several investigators have tried to do this. Dr. William Ryan has documented that two thirds of the patients in treatment with psychiatrists in Boston from 1960 through 1962 were women.[16] Dr. Anita K. Bahn et al. have documented that women outnumbered men by three to two in private psychiatric treatment from 1963 to 1964 in New York, Washington, D.C., Wisconsin, Kentucky, and California.[17] Dr. William Schofield found that the average psychiatrist sees more female than male patients.[18] While Dr. Charles Kadushin does not find more women than men involved in private therapy in New York City—in comparison to their existence in the population in New York City—he does note that women comprise 72 per cent of the patients at "St. Matthew" clinic; 64 per cent of the patients at "St. Francis" clinic; 59 per cent of the patients in "religious and psychiatry institutes"; and in "interpersonal psychiatry clinics"; 57 per cent of the patients in "advanced psychotherapy clinics" and in "personal psychology clinics"; and 54 per cent of the patients in "psychoanalytic clinics."[19] Women are certainly not *underrepresented* as private patients. Dr. Olle Hagnell, in a study of the Swedish population, found that women consulted psychiatrists twice as often as men, at all age groups, and that more women than men who have consulted psychiatrists have been admitted to a psychiatric hospital.[20]

Returning to Tables 5 and 6, we see that the fourth largest concentration of "psychiatrically involved" people is in private hospitals. From 1960 to 1968, women have comprised approximately 61 per cent of this population at all ages, and 60 per cent of this population between the ages of eighteen and sixty-four (Table 6). Both these percentages are in excess of the percentage of women in the American population at large. The fifth and sixth largest concentrations of "psychiatrically involved" patients are in Veterans Administration psychiatric wards. Both in- and outpatients are nearly all men.

RACE AND "MENTAL ILLNESS"

Racism, like sexism in America, cuts deep and tragically complicated wounds through our "body politic." Statistics or a choice of statistics on race and "mental illness" are as hard to find (and as problematic) as statistics on rape or child molestation—and for similar reasons. Where statistics do exist regarding race and "mental illness" they are not necessarily broken down in terms of social class, specific race, marital status, diagnostic category, or per 100,000 of the population, nor do they exist for all psychiatric facilities, for all years during the last decade. NIMH has published data recently, based on a "first admission" statistic† to outpatient and state and county hospitals for 1969.

† A statistic that is insensitive to the characteristics of the female "psychiatric career."

The NIMH report shows that in outpatient services the number of female admissions exceeded the number of male admissions in each age/color group with two exceptions[21]:

> for the under 18 years of age, male admissions exceeded female admissions for both whites and non-whites; for non-white admissions in the age group 35–44, the number of male and female admissions was about equal.

Table 8 shows that adult white men have much lower admission rates at all ages to outpatient facilities than do white women, non-white women, and non-white men.‡

Graph I demonstrates, more than anything else, the operation of racism and sexism in diagnosis in 1969. Graph II shows the higher rates of admission to state hospitals in 1969 for non-whites, of both sexes, than for whites of both sexes.[22] Dr. Herbert Gross studied the diagnosis and treatment of 2279 voluntary patients in a Baltimore psychiatric emergency service over a two-year period, from 1964 to 1966.[23] He found that a diagnosis of "schizophrenia" was made precipitously and as a function of either sex, race, or class misunderstanding. Women were diagnosed as "psychotic" more than men, black women especially so. (Black women tended to be referred for hospitalization more than white women with the same diagnosis.) He also found that black male alcoholics tended to be hospitalized more than white male alcoholics. There is no question that psychiatric hospitalization, with all its attendant cruelties, is both racist in its practices and in its meaning. However, I would like to continue reviewing the relationship between race and "mental illness" within the statistical perspective of sex, marital status,

---

‡ If we excluded non-white adult males for a moment, it is easy to see that white males seek (or "need") help far less than do white or black women; and that women of all races seek help more than men of all races. However, we also see here the extent to which outpatient statistics are swelled by non-white adult males. Whether the non-white males get equally involved in "psychiatric careers" as do white or non-white females is, of course, unclear.

TABLE 8: ADMISSION RATE BY AGE, SEX AND RACE IN AMERICAN OUTPATIENT PSYCHIATRIC FACILITIES: 1969

RATE PER 100,000 POPULATION

| | WOMEN | | MEN | |
AGES	NONWHITE	WHITE	NONWHITE	WHITE
18–24	571	718	572	650
25–34	1,041	851	844	578
35–44	853	594	1,058	503
45–64	823	331	593	264
AVERAGE	822	623.5	766.7	498.7

Table Description: Adult white men have lower admission rates at all ages than do white women, non-white men and non-white women.

SOURCE: Carl A. Taube. *Statistical Note 36.* Survey and Reports Section. Biometry Branch. Office of Program Planning and Evaluation. National Institute of Mental Health: December 1970.

and social class, mainly because more information is available, and partly because it is difficult for me to view these factors separately.

Sex, Race, and Marital Status

As I have noted earlier, "marital status" is a difficult factor to assess in terms of perceived "impairment" and psychiatric incarceration. While single white women may be seen as psychologically "healthier" than their married counterparts,[24] this does

GRAPH I
DIFFERENTIAL UTILIZATION OF
AMERICAN OUTPATIENT PSYCHIATRIC FACILITIES
BY WHITES AND NON-WHITES, 1969.

Admissions diagnosed as schizophrenic, rate per 100,000
population, outpatient psychiatric services, United States, 1969

SOURCE: Carl A. Taube. *Statistical Note 36.* Survey and Reports Section. Biometry Branch. Office of Program Planning and Evaluation. National Institute of Mental Health: December 1970.

GRAPH II
ADMISSION RATES TO AMERICAN STATE AND COUNTY MENTAL HOSPITALS BY AGE, SEX AND RACE, 1969.

SOURCE: Carl A. Taube. *Statistical Note 41.* Survey and Reports Section. Biometry Branch. National Institute of Mental Health: February 1971.

not mean that the eventual stress of being female and single (or divorced) will not lead to seeking treatment[25] or to being psychiatrically hospitalized. Since the male model of mental health involves a man's ability to "own" or be "serviced by" a woman, men who will not or cannot do this (male homosexuals, male "schizophrenics," *some* male alcoholics and drug addicts,) will be labeled as "neurotic" or "psychotic," and often hospitalized. Also, the absence of a woman (or mother) to take care of them, despite their lack of "masculinity," will be associated with longer psychiatric hospital stays. It has been noted that married men who are psychiatrically hospitalized have shorter stays than single men.[26] For women, the matter is more complicated. Table 9 is a condensation of an NIMH Statistical Note concerning the relationship between outpatient services and marital status.[27] The age-adjusted admission rate to outpatient services for the separated and divorced is over five times as high as the rate for the married. However, many more women than men are admitted to outpatient facilities—regardless of their marital status. Many more married women than married men are admitted**; many more widows than widowers are admitted. (We may remember Dr. Norman Farberow's finding that 50 per cent of all women who commit suicide and 45 per cent of all women who attempt suicide are "housewives"; and that about five times as many widows *commit* suicide as attempt suicide, compared with the twice as many widowers who commit rather than attempt suicide.[29])

Dr. Earl Pollack has shown that, among both black and white women, those with more children have a higher incidence of psychiatric hospitalization than do women with fewer children —and than do their husbands.[30] Pollack also showed that both

** This supports Dr. Jessie Bernard's findings in "The Paradox of the Happy Marriage" in which marriage "means more" to women than to men, but they are less "happy" with it.[28]

TABLE 9: PATIENT ADMISSION RATES BY MARITAL STATUS AND AGE IN AMERICAN OUTPATIENT PSYCHIATRIC FACILITIES: 1969.

MARITAL STATUS	BOTH SEXES	MEN	WOMEN
All Admissions	494.4	444.3	542.3
Married	325.0	374.2	344.6
Never Married	755.8	770.9	764.6
Widowed	913.3	757.7	945.4
Separated/Divorced	1,799.1	1,884.4	1,701.0

ADMISSION RATES BY AGE

AGES	WOMEN	MEN
18–24	706	620
25–34	883	592
35–44	623	548
45–64	382	296

ADMISSION RATES OF MARRIED PEOPLE BY AGE

AGES	WOMEN	MEN
18–24	531	403
25–34	600	387
35–44	433	347
45–64	253	189

Table Description: Divorced and separated people of both sexes have an admission rate that is nearly five times as high as that of the married population. However, many more women than men are admitted regardless of their marital status.

SOURCE: Carl A. Taube. *Statistical Note 35*. Survey and Reports Section. Biometry Branch. Office of Program Planning and Evaluation. National Institute of Mental Health: December 1970.

black and white female heads of households have a higher rate of psychiatric admission than do their male counterparts. Dr. Olle Hagnell, in his study of the Swedish population, found a higher probability of mental disorder and hospitalization among married than among single women.[81] Certainly Dr. Pauline Bart's portrait of the classic "depressive" is that of a married woman and mother —and not of a single woman.[82] Nevertheless, women who are single because they never married, or are divorced or widowed, do comprise a substantial portion of psychiatric inmates. This is because sex and age are probably more important predictors of psychiatric hospitalization for women than is their marital status. Marital status is probably a more important predictor of psychiatric hospitalization for men.††

Sex, Race, and Social Class

The classic post-World War II studies of social class and mental illness never considered women as constituting either a caste or class of their own. Women were assigned their fathers' or husbands'‡‡ social class and were viewed in terms of the "buying power" they were therefore entitled to or deprived of— regardless of their own education or lack of one, or their own income or lack of one. It is difficult to construct a female scale of class rank for many reasons. Since no one has ever done so, I would suspect that most of the findings regarding "class" and "mental illness" in America apply more to men than to women. For example, the usual inverse relationship between employment

†† Srole et al. found a particularly high prevalence or risk of "mental pathology" among single men and among the divorced of both sexes. They say: ". . . given the greater frequency of such pathology among the single men, the latter proportionately contribute the most to the patient loads of psychiatric hospitals and clinic facilities." The authors do not, however, offer any firm support for this.[83]

‡‡ Women on welfare are the "wives" of the father-state.

or educational level and psychiatric hospitalization or "involvement" is probably truer for men than for women—within both the black and the white populations. (Of course, this also reflects the greater economic "opportunities" offered to poor and black women at low-paying levels.) Evidence for this speculation is scanty: however, NIMH reported that in 1969 female admission rates to outpatient psychiatric services was generally higher than male rates—regardless of whether the women were well or poorly educated.[34] (For men, the inverse relationship still existed.) Unfortunately, there are no comparable statistics available for state and county hospital inmates. I would *guess* that the disproportionate number of black women in state hospitals[35] have a wider range of educational backgrounds or earning capacities than do their even more disproportionately numbered male counterparts.* Perhaps fewer well-educated or well-employed black men embark on "psychiatric careers" of any kind than do their female well-educated counterparts—i.e., perhaps the economics and psychology of "tokenism," combined with sex-role stereotyping and the masculine standard of mental health, make it *comparatively* easier for black middle-class men than for black middle-class women to assert their (masculine) mental health.

Traditionally, women are not listed as "heads of household" by the Census Bureau when a husband lives at home, even if the woman is the primary "breadwinner." This fact makes demographic studies of psychiatric populations, like Pollack's,[36] rather difficult. Another difficulty involved in assigning women a class rank of their own has to do with the fact that, even when women perform the same tasks as men, it means something entirely different. For example, most women within a profession not only earn less and have less mobility than professional men; unlike men, they also still have

* One we must remember that we are dealing with a "first admission" statistic here—one that is not sensitive to the characteristics of the female psychiatric "career."

female responsibilities, behave in "feminine" ways, subtly or overtly, on or off the job, and still view themselves as "feminine."†

Recently a number of feminists have argued, rather cogently, that women constitute a caste.[88] Essentially they are correct; sex, like race, is a condition you are born into and cannot change throughout life. However, the sheer insight that one belongs to a caste will not lead caste members, i.e., women, into behavioral or psychological denials of their class. Further, while women share many important economic, biological, and psychological facts of life with all other women, they also share important things with their male same-class or same-race counterparts; and do not share certain things with women of other classes or races. But from the psychological point of view, I would argue strongly for the hypothesis of a cross-class and cross-race female culture.

For example, all (married) women, except for the 1 per cent of the American female population *earning* $10,000 or more annually, are virtually penniless except for the "largesse" or court-imposed largesse of their husbands. Women are not paid direct wages for childbearing, child rearing, housework, and sexual or emotional "services." When married women are abandoned or divorced, they, like single women, have three direct sources of income —other than their husbands' support: futureless low-paying jobs, illegal prostitution, or state welfare. This is as true for the suburban wives of advertising executives as it is for the wives of construction workers or grocery clerks.

While some controversy exists, based, as usual, on different methods applied to different kinds of populations at different time periods, the "social class" theorists have traditionally either found no sex-ratio differences in psychiatric morbidity and/or hospitalization, or have seen class as a more important predictor than sex.[89]

† We may recall (Chapter Two) that in McClelland's study of sex-role alienation the control group of "employed women" were more "feminine" in their test responses than were the female schizophrenics.[37]

In general, several "social class" theorists have been aware of but have not tackled the ideological-methodological problems of sex as a class or caste. For example, in their study of "psychiatric morbidity" (in which they found no significant male-female differences) Dr. Leo Srole et al.[40] note that (their) research psychiatrists knew the sex of each respondent in formulating their preliminary classifications.

> Accordingly we are unable to assert with complete confidence that the known relationship just recorded does not reflect different preconceptions held by the psychiatrists about the sexes.

Dr. Dorothy Leighton,[41] who did find higher female rates of morbidity and hospitalization, notes this problem also.

The classic Hollingshead and Redlich study, *Social Class and Mental Illness*,[42] found a significant relationship between social class (poor or low) and mental hospitalization. However, 67 per cent of their entire pre-1950 New Haven sample was derived from state hospitals,‡ as compared with a 2 per cent sample involvement in private hospitals, and 8 per cent sample involvement in public clinics, a 4 per cent sample involvement in VA hospitals, and a 19 per cent sample involvement in private therapy. What this means is that the facilities in which women are concentrated most heavily (at least during the last decade) are underrepresented in this study—i.e., general psychiatric wards, private hospitals, outpatient clinics, and private therapy. Hollingshead and Redlich found that poor people, both male and female, are overrepresented as psychiatric patients. According to the authors' calculations, 18 per 100,000 Class Five men and 19 per 100,000 Class Five women (the "poorest" class) exist in the population at large; they *both* comprise 43 per 100,000 of the psychiatric population.

The various studies referred to in Chapter Four and in this

‡ Again, they used the "first admission" statistics.

Appendix suggest that women of all classes and races constitute the majority of the psychiatrically involved population in America, Britain, Sweden, and Canada. In order for Hollingshead and Redlich (or anyone) to further support, qualify, or refute such a suggestion, they would have to class-rank a psychiatric sample derived equally from *all* existing psychiatric facilities (rather than from a predominantly state hospital sample) and use a more sensitive statistic than that of a "first admission." Also, they would have to use a separate method for the class- or caste-ranking of women—no easy ideological or methodological task.

Footnotes

CHAPTER ONE

1. Adrienne Rich, "Snapshots of a Daughter-in-law," in *Snapshots of a Daughter-in-law: Poems 1954–1962* (New York: W. W. Norton, 1968).

2. Peter Weiss, *Marat/Sade: The Persecution and Assassination of Jean-Paul Marat As Performed by the Inmates of the Asylum of Charenton Under the Direction of the Marquis De Sade* (New York: Atheneum, 1965).

3. Anais Nin, *Cities of the Interior,* distributed by Phoenix Box Shop (New York, 1959).

4. C. Kerenyi, *Eleusis: Archetypal Images of Mother and Daughters,* translated from the German by Ralph Manheim; Bollingen Series LXV, Bollingen Foundation (New York: Pantheon Books, 1967).

5. Lara Jefferson, *These Are My Sisters* (Tulsa: Vickers Publishing Co., 1948).

6. Erich Neumann, *Amor and Psyche: The Psychic Development of the Feminine. A Commentary on the Tale by Apuleius,* translated from the German by Ralph Manheim; Bollingen Series LIV, Bollingen Foundation (New York: Pantheon Books, 1956).

7. Sylvia Plath, *The Bell Jar* (New York: Doubleday, 1971). (Originally published in 1963 by Faber and Faber.)

8. Ludwig Binswanger, "The Case of Ellen West," in Rollo May, ed., *Existence* (New York: Basic Books, 1958).

9. Ibid.

10. Nancy Milford, *Zelda* (New York: Harper & Row, 1970).

11. Jessie Bernard, "The Paradox of the Happy Marriage" in Vivian Gornick and Barbara K. Moran, eds., *Woman in Sexist Society: Studies in Power and Powerlessness* (New York: Basic Books, 1971).

12. Elizabeth P. Ware Packard, *Modern Persecution or Insane Asylums Unveiled* and *The Liabilities of the Married Woman* (New York: Pelletreau and Raynor, 1873). These two remarkable volumes were her only source of income after her "escape" from the asylum and during her legal battle for the rights of mental patients and married women.

13. Charles W. Ferguson, *The Male Attitude* (Boston: Little, Brown, 1966).

14. A. Alvarez, "Sylvia Plath: A Memoir" *New American Review* No. 12 (New York: Simon & Schuster, Inc., 1971).

15. I. J. Singer, "The Dead Fiddler" in *The Seance* (New York: Avon, 1964).

16. C. G. Jung and C. Kerenyi, *Essays on a Science of Mythology: The Myth of the Divine Child and the Mysteries of Eleusis,* translated by R. F. C. Hull, 1949 (New York: Bollingen Foundation. Princeton, N.J.: Princeton University Press, 1969); C. Kerenyi, *Eleusis: Archetypal Images of Mothers and Daughters,* translated from the German by Ralph Manheim; Bollingen Series LXV, Bollingen Foundation (New York: Pantheon Books, 1967); Sir James G. Frazier, *The Golden Bough* (New York: Macmillan, 1958).

17. Simon Dinitz, Russel Dynez, and Alfred Clarke, "Preferences for Male or Female Children: Traditional or Affectional," in *Marriage and Family Living,* Vol. 16, May 1954; Alfred Adler, *Understanding Human Nature,* translated by W. Beran Wolfe, copyright 1927 (New York: Fawcett World Library, 1969); Joan D. Mandle, "Women's Liberation: Humanizing Rather than Polarizing," *Annals of the American Academy of Political and Social Science,* September 1971. The history of many royal family "tragedies"

in Europe involves the hysterical need for a male rather than a female heir. The Tudor families of Henry VIII in England and the Romanov families of Nicholas in Russia are two well-known examples. I may note that Queen Hatshepsut of ancient Egypt wore male dress and a ceremonial false beard during her reign: royalty and/or divinity are somehow more associated with the male than the female sex. In non-Western and/or pre-Catholic cultures there are, of course, many goddesses. Many are treated by gods in depressingly familiar mortal ways: for example, Zeus's treatment of his wife Hera. Buddha, Shiva, Allah, and Jehovah are most often depicted or thought of as men. It is interesting that the Egyptian god Osiris is a Demeter-Persephone-like *male* god of earth, vegetation, and rebirth, and that the three most important Egyptian goddesses—Isis, Nephthys, and Hathor—are concerned with "female" provinces: the protection of children, the home, love, happiness, dance, and music.

18. Emma Goldman, "Marriage and Love," *Anarchism and Other Essays* (New York: Dover Publications, Inc., 1969).

19. Judith Bardwick, *The Psychology of Women: A Bio-cultural Conflict* (New York: Harper & Row, 1971).

20. Naomi Wesstein, "Psychology Constructs the Female," in Gornick and Moran, eds., *Woman in Sexist Society: Studies in Power and Powerlessness.*

21. Shulamith Firestone, *The Dialectic of Sex* (New York: William Morrow, 1971).

22. Neumann, op. cit.

23. These and other of the myths I've drawn upon are discussed in the following two books, as well as in the books referred to in footnote 16: Helen Diner, *Mothers and Amazons: The First Feminine History of Culture,* edited and translated by J. P. Lundin (New York: Julian Press, 1965). (First published in the 1930s under the pseudonym of "Sir Galahad"); Phillip E. Slater, *The Glory of Hera: Greek Mythology and the Greek Family* (Boston: Beacon Press, 1971).

24. Slater, op. cit.

25. Régine Pernoud, *Joan of Arc By Herself and Her Witnesses,* translated from the French by Edward Hyams (London: MacDonald, 1964).

26. Ibid.

27. Slater, op. cit.

28. Jung and Kerenyi, *Essays on a Science of Mythology.*

29. Ibid.

30. Virginia Woolf, *A Room of One's Own* (New York: Harcourt, Brace & World, 1929).

CHAPTER TWO

1. Michel Foucault, *Madness and Civilization: A History of Insanity in the Age of Reason* (1961), translated by Richard Howard (New York: Pantheon, 1965).

2. Allan M. Dershowitz, "Preventive Detention and the Prediction of Dangerousness. Some Fictions about Predictions," *Journal of Legal Education,* Vol. 23, 1969.

3. Foucault, op. cit. Thomas S. Szasz, *The Manufacture of Madness* (New York: Harper and Row, 1970); George Rosen, *Madness in Society: Chapters in the Historical Sociology of Mental Illness* (New York: Harper & Row, 1968).

4. Szasz, op. cit.

5. Foucault, op. cit.; Thomas S. Szasz, *The Myth of Mental Illness: Foundations of a Theory of Personal Conduct* (New York: Hoeber-Harper, 1961); Erving Goffman, *Asylums* (New York: Doubleday-Anchor, 1961); T. J. Scheff, *Being Mentally Ill: A Sociological Theory* (Chicago: Aldine Press, 1966).

6. Arnold Ludwig, Arnold J. Marx, Phillip A. Hill, and Robert M. Browning, "The Control of Violent Behavior Through Faradic Shock: A Case Study," *Journal of Nervous and Mental Diseases,* Vol. 148, 1969.

7. C. M. Wignall and C. E. Meredith, "Illegitimate Pregnancies in State Institutions," *Archives of General Psychiatry,* Vol. 18, 1968.

8. Bruce Dohrenwend and Barbara Dohrenwend, *Social Status and Psychological Disorders* (New York: John Wiley, 1969). Olle Hagnell quotes another theory of conditioned female "patient" behavior made by H. Holter in *A Prospective Study of the Incidence of Mental Disorders: The Lundby Project* (Sweden: Svenska Bokforlaget, 1966).

9. Jean MacFarlane et al., *A Developmental Study of the Behavior Problems of Normal Children Between Twenty-one Months and Thirteen Years* (Berkeley: University of California Press, 1954); L. Philips, "Cultural vs. Intra Psychic Factors in Childhood Behavior Problem Referrals," *Journal of Clinical Psychology,* Vol. 13, 1957; D. R. Peterson, "Behavior Problems of Middle Childhood," *Journal of Consulting Psychology,* Vol. 25, 1961; L. M. Terman and L. E. Tyler, "Psychological Sex Differences," ed. by L. Carmichael in *Manual of Child Psychology* (New York: John Wiley, 1954).

10. Leslie Phillips, "A Social View of Psychopathology," ed. by Perry London and David Rosenhan, *Abnormal Psychology* (New York: Holt, Rinehart and Winston, 1969).

11. E. Zigler and L. Phillips, "Social Effectiveness and Symptomatic Behaviors," *Journal of Abnormal and Social Psychology*, Vol. 61, 1960.

12. Szasz, *The Myth of Mental Illness*.

13. Frederick Engels, *The Origins of the Family, Private Property and the State* (New York: International Publishers, 1942).

14. Konrad Lorenz, a noted writer on animal behavior, has recently been quoted as saying, "There's only one kind of people at a social disadvantage nowadays—a whole class of people who are treated as slaves and exploited shamelessly—and that's the young wives. They are educated as well as men and the moment they give birth to a baby, they are slaves . . . they have a 22-hour workday, no holidays, and they can't even be ill." Interview, New York *Times*, July 5, 1970.

15. National Institute of Mental Health Statistics 1965–1968, U. S. Department of Health, Education and Welfare; Phyllis Chesler, "Patient and Patriarch: Women in Psychotherapeutic Relationship," in Gornick and Moran, eds., *Woman in Sexist Society: Studies in Power and Powerlessness* (New York: Basic Books, 1971); Judy Klemesrud, "When the Diagnosis Is Depression" (The Depression Research Unit in New Haven referred to treats mainly women between the ages of 21–65), New York *Times*, May 5, 1971; Lee Burke, E. Renkin, S. Jacobson, S. Haley, "The Depressed Woman Returns," *Archives of General Psychiatry*, Vol. 16, May 1967; Margaret M. Dewar and Iain MacCammend, "Depressive Breakdown in Women of the West Highlands," *American Journal of Psychiatry*, Vol. 119, 1962; Theodore Reich and George Winston, "Postpartum Psychoses in Patients with Manic Depressive Disease," *Journal of Nervous and Mental Disease*, Vol. 151, No. 1, 1970; Pauline Bart, "Portnoy's Mother's Complaint," in Gornick and Moran eds., *Woman in Sexist Society*.

16. Pauline Bart, op. cit.

17. Earl Pollack, Richard Redick, and Carl Taube, "The Application of Census Socioeconomic and Familial Data to the Study of Morbidity from Mental Disorders," *American Journal of Public Health*, Vol. 58, No. 1, January 1968.

18. Alfred L. Friedman, "Hostility Factors and Clinical Improvement in Depressed Patients," *Archives of General Psychiatry*, Vol. 23, 1970.

19. Joan Didion, *Play It As It Lays* (New York: Farrar, Straus & Giroux, 1970).

20. Alfred L. Kinsey, Wardell B. Pomeroy, Clyde E. Martin, and Paul H. Gebhard, *Sexual Behavior in the Human Female* (Philadelphia: Saunders, 1953); Sigmund Freud, *Female Sexuality* (1931) (New York: Basic Books, 1959); Wilhelm Stekel, *Frigidity in Woman in Relation to Her Love Life* (New York: Washington Square Press, 1954); Karen Horney, *The Neurotic Personality of Our Time* (New York: W. W. Norton, 1967);

William Masters and Virginia Johnson, *Human Sexual Response* (Boston: Little, Brown, 1966) and *Human Sexual Inadequacy* (Boston: Little, Brown, 1970).

21. Masters and Johnson, *Human Sexual Response* and *Human Sexual Inadequacy;* Jacob Sprenger and Heinrich Kramer, *Malleus Maleficarum,* cited by Thomas S. Szasz in *The Manufacture of Madness;* Mary Jane Sherfey, "The Evolution and Nature of Female Sexuality in Relation to Psychoanalytic Theory," *Journal of the American Psychoanalytical Association,* 1966.

22. Sylvia Plath, "Lady Lazarus" in *Ariel* (New York: Harper & Row, 1965).

23. Norman L. Farberow and Edwin F. Schneidman, "Statistical Comparisons Between Attempted and Committed Suicides," in *The Cry for Help* (New York: McGraw-Hill, 1965).

24. Richard H. Sieden, *Suicide Among Youth.* Prepared for the Joint Commission on Mental Health of Children, 1970.

25. Shirley Angrist, Simon Dinitz, Mark Lefton, Benjamin Pasamanick, "Rehospitalization of Female Mental Patients," *Archives of American Psychiatry,* Vol. 4, 1961. Her patient sample was drawn from state and private hospitals, and included people released after 1957. Her original intention was to compare the parents of "schizophrenics" with those of "normals."

26. Shirley Angrist, Simon Dinitz, Mark Lefton, Benjamin Pasamanick *Women After Treatment* (New York: Appleton-Century-Crofts, 1968).

27. Frances Cheek, "A Serendipitous Finding: Sex Role and Schizophrenia," *Journal of Abnormal and Social Psychology,* Vol. 69, No. 4, 1964.

28. M. Letailleur, J. Morin, and Y. Le Borgne, "Heautoscopie Hetersexuelle et Schizophrenie [The Self-Induced Heterosexual Image and Schizophrenia]," *Ann. Med. Psychology,* Vol. 2, 1958.

29. David C. McClelland and Norman F. Watt, "Sex Role Alienation in Schizophrenia," *Journal of Abnormal Psychology,* Vol. 73, No. 3, 1968. The sample was drawn from a Boston hospital, and involved people who were hospitalized from one to twenty years. All groups were matched for age, education, and class.

30. Ibid.

31. M. Lorr and C. J. Klett, "Constancy of Psychotic Syndromes in Men and Women," *Journal of Consulting Psychology,* Vol. 29, No. 5, 1969.

32. M. Lorr, J. P. O'Connor, and J. W. Stafford, "The Psychotic Reaction Profile," *Journal of Clinical Psychology,* Vol. 16, 1960.

33. Jonas Rappoport, *The Clinical Evaluation of the Dangerousness of the Mentally Ill,* (Charles Thomas: Springfield, Illinois, 1968.)

34. Alan M. Kraft, Paul R. Binner, Brenda Dickey, "The Community Mental Health Program and the Longer-Stay Patient," *Archives of General Psychiatry,* Vol. 6, January 1967.

35. Carl A. Taube, "Admission Rates by Marital Status: Outpatient Psychiatric Services," Statistical Note 35, Survey and Reports Section, National Institute of Mental Health, December 1970.

36. Marcel Saghir, Bonnie Walbran, Eli Robins, Kathy Gentry, "Psychiatric Disorders and Disability in the Female Homosexual," *American Journal of Psychiatry,* Vol. 27, 1970; Charlotte Wolff, *Love Between Women* (U.K.: St. Martins Press, 1971).

CHAPTER THREE

1. Ilse Ollendorff Reich, *Wilhelm Reich: A Personal Biography* (New York: St. Martins, 1969).

2. Paul Roazan, *Brother Animal* (New York: Knopf, 1969).

3. Shulamith Firestone, *The Dialectic of Sex, The Case for Feminist Revolution* (New York: William Morrow and Co., 1970).

4. Juliet Mitchell, *Woman's Estate* (New York: Pantheon Books, 1971).

5. Kate Millett, *Sexual Politics* (New York: Doubleday & Co., 1970).

6. Evelyn P. Ivey, "Significance of the Sex of the Psychiatrist," *Archives of General Psychiatry,* Vol. 2, 1960; William Schofield, *Psychotherapy: The Purchase of Friendship* (Englewood Cliffs, N.J.: Prentice-Hall, 1963); Phyllis Chesler, unpublished study, 1971.

7. Carl A. Taube, "Transitional Mental Health Facilities Staffing Patterns," *Statistical Note 28,* NIMH Survey and Reports Section, October 1970.

8. Carl A. Taube, "Consultation and Education Services in Community Mental Health Centers—January 1970," Statistical Note 3, NIMH Survey and Reports Section, February 1971.

9. Phyllis Chesler, "Patient and Patriarch: Women in the Psychotherapeutic Relationship," in Vivian Gornick and Barbara K. Moran, eds., *Woman in Sexist Society: Studies in Power and Powerlessness* (New York: Basic Books, 1971).

10. Schofield, op. cit.

11. Matina Horner, "Fail: Bright Women," *Psychology Today,* November 1969.

12. Maurice K. Temerlin, "Suggestion Effects in Psychiatric Diagnosis," *Journal of Nervous and Mental Disease,* Vol. 47, 1968.

13. Inge K. Broverman, Donald M. Broverman, Frank E. Clarkson, Paul S. Rosenkrantz, Susan R. Vogel, "Sex Role Stereotypes and Clinical

Judgements of Mental Health," *Journal of Consulting and Clinical Psychology*, Vol. 34, 1970.

14. W. R. Orr, Ruth Anderson, Margaret Martin Des. F. Philpot, "Factors Influencing Discharge of Female Patients from a State Mental Hospital," *American Journal of Psychiatry*, Vol. 3, 1954.

15. Nathan K. Rickel, "The Angry Woman Syndrome," *Archives of General Psychiatry*, Vol. 24, 1971.

16. Herbert C. Modlin, "Psychodynamics in the Management of Paranoid States in Women," *General Psychiatry*, 1963.

17. Judith Bardwick, *Psychology of Women: A Bio-cultural Conflict* (New York: Harper & Row, 1971).

18. Mary Jane Sherfey, "The Evolution and Nature of Female Sexuality in Relation to Psychoanalytic Theory," *Journal of the American Psychoanalytical Association*, 1966.

19. Judith Bardwick, *Psychology of Women: A Bio-cultural Conflict* (New York: Harper & Row, 1971).

20. Joseph Rheingold, *The Mother, Anxiety and Death* (Boston: Little, Brown, 1967).

21. Carl P. Malmquist, Thomas J. Kiresuk, Robert M. Spano, "Personality Characteristics of Women with Repeated Illegitimacies: Descriptive Aspects," *American Journal of Orthopsychiatry*, Vol. 35, 1966; Oscar B. Markey, "A Study of Aggressive Set Misbehavior in Adolescents Brought to Juvenile Court," *Journal of Orthopsychiatry*, Vol. 20, 1950; Kathryn M. Nielson, Rocco L. Motto, "Some Observations on Family Constellations and Personality Patterns of Young Unmarried Mothers," *American Journal of Orthopsychiatry*, Vol. 33, 1963; Irving Kaufman, Elizabeth S. Makkay, Joan Zilbach, "The Impact of Adolescence of Girls with Delinquent Character Formation," *Journal of Orthopsychiatry*, Vol. 29, 1959; Paul A. Walters, Jr., "Promiscuity in Adolescence," *American Journal of Orthopsychiatry*, 1965; Ames Robey, Richard J. Rosenwald, John E. Snell, and Rita E. Lee, "The Runaway Girl: A Reaction to Family Stress," *American Journal of Orthopsychiatry*, March 9, 1964.

22. Captain Noel Lustig, MC, USA; Captain John Dresser, MCS, USA; Major Seth W. Spellman, MCS, USA; Major Thomas B. Murray, MC, USA; "Incest," *Archives of General Psychiatry*, Vol. 14, January 1966; Irving Kaufman, Alice L. Peck, Consuelo K. Tagiuri, "The Family Constellation and Overt Incestuous Relations Between Father and Daugher," *Journal of Orthopsychiatry*, Vol. 24, 1954; Sol Chaneles, "Sexual Abuse of Children" (Denver: The American Humane Association, Children's Division, 1966); Vincent de Francis, "Protecting the Child Victim of Sex Crimes Committed by Adults" (Denver: The American Humane Association, Children's Division,

1966); Lindy Burton, *Vulnerable Children* (New York: Schocken Books, 1968); Yvonne Tormes, "Child Victim of Incest" (Denver: The American Humane Association, Children's Division, 1966); David Gil, *Violence Against Children* (Waltham: Harvard University Press, 1970); Florence Rush, "The Sexual Abuse of Children: A Feminist Point of View," New York Radical Feminists Conference on Rape, April 17, 1971; Harry Nelson, "Incest: 1 Family out of 10" New York *Post,* September 1971.

23. Charles William Wahl, "The Psychodynamics of Consummated Maternal Incest: A Report of Two Cases," *Archives of General Psychiatry,* Vol. 3, 1960.

24. Harold Greenwald, *The Elegant Prostitute* (New York: Ballantine Books, 1958).

25. Sigmund Freud, "Some Psychological Consequences of the Anatomical Distinction Between Sexes," *Collected Papers,* Vol. 5 (London: Hogarth Press, 1956).

26. Sigmund Freud, *New Introductory Lectures in Psychoanalysis* (New York: W. W. Norton, 1933).

27. Erik H. Erikson, "Inner and Outer Space: Reflections on Womanhood," *Daedalus,* Vol. 3, 1965.

28. Bruno Bettelheim, "The Commitment Required of a Woman Entering a Scientific Profession in Present Day American Society" in *Woman and the Scientific Professions,* M.I.T. Symposium on American Women in Science and Engineering, Cambridge, Mass., 1965.

29. Joseph Rheingold, *The Fear of Being a Woman* (New York: Grune and Stratton, 1964).

30. Carl G. Jung, *Contributions to Analytical Psychology* (New York: Harcourt, Brace, 1928).

31. M. Esther Harding, *The Way of All Women* (New York: Longmans, Green, 1933).

32. Sigmund Freud, *Case of Dora: An Analysis of a Case Hysteria* (New York: W. W. Norton, 1952).

33. Leonard Simon, "The Political Unconscious of Psychology: Clinical Psychology and Social Change," unpublished manuscript, 1970.

34. Felix Deutsch, "A Footnote to Freud's 'Fragment of an Analysis of a Case of Hysteria,'" *The Psychoanalytic Quarterly,* Vol. 25, 1957.

35. Thomas S. Szasz, *The Myth of Mental Illness: Foundations of a Theory of Personal Conduct* (New York: Hoeber-Harper, 1961).

36. Karen Horney, "The Flight from Womanhood" in *Feminine Psychology,* edited by H. Kelman (New York: W. W. Norton, 1967).

37. Sigmund Freud, "Female Sexuality" (1931) *Collected Papers,* Vol. 4 (New York: Basic Books, 1959).

38. Ilse Ollendorff Reich, *Wilhelm Reich: A Personal Biography* (New York: St. Martins, 1969).

39. Wilhelm Reich, *The Function of the Orgasm: The Discovery of the Orgone* (New York: Farrar, Straus & Giroux, 1942).

40. Ronald D. Laing and A. Esterson, *Sanity, Madness and the Family* (New York: Pelican Books, 1970).

41. David Cooper, *The Death of the Family* (New York: Pantheon Books, 1970).

42. Thomas S. Szasz, *The Manufacture of Madness* (New York: Harper & Row, 1970).

43. Jules Michelet, *Satanism and Witchcraft: A Study in Medieval Superstition* (Toronto: Citadel Press, 1939).

44. Una Stannard, "The Male Maternal Instinct," *Trans-action*, December 1970.

45. Sigmund Freud, "On the History of the Psychoanalytic Movement" in *Collected Papers* (1914) Vol. 1 (New York: Basic Books, 1959).

46. Thomas S. Szasz, *The Myth of Mental Illness: Foundations of a Theory of Personal Conduct* (New York: Hoeber-Harper, 1961).

47. William Schofield, *Psychotherapy: The Purchase of Friendship* (Englewood Cliffs, N.J.: Prentice-Hall, 1963).

CHAPTER FOUR

1. Judith Bardwick, *The Psychology of Women: A Bio-cultural Conflict* (New York: Harper & Row, 1971).

2. Dorothy C. Leighton, John S. Harding, David B. Machlin, Allister M. MacMillan, Alexander H. Leighton, *The Character of Danger: The Stirling County Study of Psychiatric Disorder and Sociocultural Environment*, Vol. III (New York-London: Basic Books, 1963).

3. "Selected Symptoms of Psychological Distress," U. S. Department of Health, Education and Welfare, Public Health Services and Mental Health Administration, 1970. This study is based on data collected in 1960–62 from a probability sample of 7710 persons selected to represent the 111 million adults in the U.S. non-institutional population, aged eighteen to seventy-nine.

4. Gerald Gurin, J. Veroff, and S. Feld, *Americans View Their Mental Health* (New York: Basic Books, 1960).

5. Leo Srole, Thomas S. Langner, Stanley T. Michael, Mervin K. Opler, and Thomas A. C. Rennie, *Mental Health in the Metropolis: Midtown Manhattan Study* (New York: McGraw-Hill, 1962).

6. Leighton et al., op. cit.

7. Olle Hagnell, *A Prospective Study of the Incidence of Mental Disorders: The Lundby Project* (Sweden: Svenska Bokforlaget, 1966).

8. NIMH Annual Reports on Patients in Mental Health Facilities, U. S. Department of Health, Education and Welfare, 1950–1969.

9. Phyllis Chesler, "Patient and Patriarch: Women in the Psychotherapeutic Relationship," in Vivian Gornick and Barbara K. Moran, eds., *Woman in Sexist Society: Studies in Power and Powerlessness* (New York: Basic Books, 1971); Hagnell, op. cit., Leighton, et al., op. cit.; Edwin Zolik, Edna Lantz, Richard Sommers, "Hospital Return Rates and Prerelease Referrals," *Archives of General Psychiatry*, Vol. 18, June 1968; "Chronic Illness in a Large City," *The Baltimore Study* (1957); Anita K. Bahn, Margaret Conwell, and Peter Hurley, "Survey of Psychiatric Practice: Report on a Field Test," *Archives of General Psychiatry*, Vol. 12, 1965; William Ryan, *Distress in the City Essay on the Design and Administration of Mental Health Services* (Cleveland: The Press of Case Western Reserve University, 1969); Charles Thrall, "Presenting Problems of Psychiatric Out-Patients: Out-Patient Studies Section," Biometrics Branch, NIMH 1963; Richard Redick, "Age-Sex Diagnostic Distribution of Additions to Community Mental Health Centers 1968," Statistical Note 13, NIMH Survey and Reports Section, January 1970; William Schofield, *Psychotherapy: The Purchase of Friendship* (Englewood Cliffs, N.J.: Prentice-Hall, 1963); Alan M. Kraft, Paul R. Binner, Brenda Dickey, "The Community Mental Health Program and the Longer-Stay Patient," *Archives of General Psychiatry*, Vol. 16, January 1967; Gerald Landsberg, David Cole, Eleanor Sabbagh, Rachel Deutsch, "Characteristics of Enrolled Patients as of September 1969," Maimonides Medical Center, Community Mental Health Center, December 1969; Rachel Deutsch, Gerald Landsberg, David Cole, "Report of a Survey of Patients: January 17, 1970–June 16, 1970," Maimonides Medical Center, Community Mental Health Center, June 1970; Phyllis Chesler, Janice Lasecki, Lucy DiPaola, unpublished manuscript, 1971.

10. Kraft et al., op. cit.; Hagnell, op. cit.; Charles Thrall, "Presenting Problems of Psychiatric Out-Patients," Out-Patients Studies Section, Biometrics Branch, NIMH 1963; Kurt Gurwitz, Anita Bahn, Gerald Klee, and Murray Solomon, "Release and Return Rates of Patients in State Mental Hospitals of Maryland," *Public Health Reports*, Vol. 1, 1966.

11. Kraft et al., op. cit.; *Provisional Data on Length of Stay of Admissions to State and County Mental Hospitals* U.S., 1971, NIMH.

12. Mildred S. Cannon, "Age-Sex Diagnostic Distribution of Additions to Community Mental Health Centers, 1969," Statistical Note 59, NIMH Survey and Reports Section, December 1970.

13. Charles Kadushin, *Why People Go to Psychiatrists* (New York: Atherton Press, 1969).

CHAPTER FIVE

1. Fernando Enriquez, *Prostitution and Society: Primitive, Classical and Oriental* (New York: Grove Press, 1962); Emma Goldman, "The Traffic in Women," reprinted in *Anarchism and Other Essays* (New York: Dover, 1969); Harold Greenwald, *The Elegant Prostitute: A Social and Psychoanalytic Study* (New York: Ballantine Books, 1958); Steven Marcus, *The Other Victorians* (New York: Basic Books, 1964); Kate Millett, *Sexual Politics* (New York: Doubleday, 1971); W. W. Sanger, *The History of Prostitution* (New York: Eugenics Publishing, 1937); Charles Winick and Paul M. Kinsie, *The Lively Commerce* (Chicago: Quadrangle Books, 1971); Eric Pace, "Feminists Halt Session on Prostitution, Demanding To Be Heard," New York *Times*, September 15, 1971; Robert Prosser, "The Speedy Call Girls in Formosa," San Francisco *Chronicle*, December 23, 1970; "Russia's Bedroom Blackmail," San Francisco *Chronicle*, December 28, 1970; Jim Brewer, "San Francisco Child Prostitutes," San Francisco *Chronicle*, May 9, 1970; David Sanford, "A Brothel in Curaçao," *Village Voice*, March 13, 1969; Ernest Lenn, "State Crackdown on B-Girls, Vice," San Francisco *Examiner and Chronicle*, July 13, 1969; "Aimed at Prostitutes, the Loitering Law Is Voided," New York *Post*, September 14, 1970; New Orleans, A.P., "Shaw Judge Is Ordered Ousted Over His Arrest in a Vice Raid," New York *Times*, November 24, 1970; "Prostitutes—Some New Tricks for the Oldest Profession," New York *Times*, March 28, 1971.

2. Uniform Crime Reports 1960–1970; Rosalyn Lacks, "The Politics of Rape—A Selective History," *Village Voice*, February 4, 1971; New York Radical Feminist Conference on Rape, April 17, 1971; Female Liberation Newsletter ¥8, April 16, 1971; "Women Who Are Tired of Being Harassed," New York *Times*, September 7, 1971; "The Civilized Rapist," *Village Voice*, September 9, 1971; "Cops Use TV to Trap Rape Suspect," New York *Daily News*, March 19, 1971; Gloria Emerson, "Vietnamese Voice Hostility to G.I.'s," New York *Times*, May 2, 1971; "Bronx School Posts 2 Guards after Attacks on Teachers," New York *Post*, May 6, 1971.

3. Captain Noel Lustig, MC, USA; Captain John Dresser, MCS, USA; Major Seth W. Spellman, MCS, USA; Major Thomas B. Murray, MC, USA; "Incest," *Archives of General Psychiatry*, Vol. 14, January 1966; Irving Kaufman, Alice L. Peck, Consuelo K. Tagiuri, "The Family Constellation and Overt Incestuous Relations Between Father and Daughter," *Journal of Orthopsychiatry*, Vol. 24, 1954; Sol Chaneles, "Sexual Abuse of Children" (Denver: The American Humane Association, Children's Division, 1966);

Vincent de Francis, "Protecting the Child Victim of Sex Crimes Committed by Adults" (Denver: The American Humane Association, Children's Division, 1966); Lindy Burton, *Vulnerable Children* (New York: Schocken Books, 1968); Yvonne Tormes, "Child Victim of Incest" (Denver: The American Humane Association, Children's Division, 1966); David Gil, *Violence Against Children* (Waltham: Harvard University Press, 1970); Florence Rush, "The Sexual Abuse of Children: A Feminist Point of View," New York Radical Feminist Conference on Rape, April 17, 1971; Harry Nelson, "Incest: 1 Family Out of 10," New York *Post*, September 1971; George Carpozi, Jr., "Seize Dad, Daughter in Nudie Case," New York *Post*, May 6, 1971.

4. Conrad Van Emde Boas in his article "The Doctor-Patient Relationship" (*Journal of Sex Research*, Vol. 2, No. 3, November 1966) says: "In my own practice—largely psycho-therapeutical and sexuological—I have noticed that the frequency of this kind of officially frowned upon relationship varies within the different branches of the medical profession. Gynecologists offer the most frequent targets. Second on the list are dentists and family doctors. But let me add immediately that psychotherapists, too, are not far behind, according to the 'statistics'—obviously limited and incomplete—which I have compiled from my own observations."

5. Boas, op. cit.; Charles C. Dahlberg, "Sexual Contact Between Patient and Therapist," *Contemporary Psychoanalysis*, Spring 1970; Judd Marmor, "The Seductive Therapist," *Psychiatry Digest*, October 1970; William Masters and Virginia Johnson, *Human Sexual Response* (Boston: Little, Brown, 1966); William Masters and Virginia Johnson, *Human Sexual Inadequacy* (Boston: Little, Brown, 1970); James L. McCartney, "Overt Transference," *Journal of Sexual Research*, Vol. 2, No. 3, November 1966; Leon J. Saul, "The Erotic Transference," *Psychoanalytic Quarterly*, Vol. 31, 1962; Martin Shepard, *The Love Treatment: Sexual Intimacy Between Patients and Psychotherapists* (New York: Peter H. Wyden, 1971); Arthur J. Snider, "One Analyst's Touching Tale," New York *Post*, November 17, 1969.

6. Louis Lewis, "Psychotherapeutic Malpractice," unpublished manuscript, 1971; William Greaves and Leo Standore, "Secretary Sues Analyst for Sexual Malpractice," New York *Post*, April 1971.

7. Paul Roazen, *Brother Animal* (New York: Knopf, 1969).

8. Marmor, op. cit.

9. McCartney, op. cit.

10. Marmor, op. cit.

11. Saul, op. cit.

12. Dahlberg, op. cit.; Marmor, op. cit.; McCartney, op. cit.

13. Dahlberg, op. cit.; Frieda Fromm-Reichman, *Principles of Intensive*

Psychotherapy (Chicago: University of Chicago Press, 1950); Clara Thompson, "A Critical Incident in Psychotherapy," *Interpersonal Psychoanalysis* (London: Basic Books, 1964).

14. Dahlberg, op. cit.
15. McCartney, op. cit.
16. Dahlberg, op. cit.
17. Roazen, op. cit.

CHAPTER SIX

1. $40,000 Damages Awarded Against Psychiatrist. Stowers *v.* Wolodzko. Supreme Court of Michigan, November 9, 1971. *The Mental Health Court Digest*, Vol. 15, No. 8, February 1972.
2. Allan M. Dershowitz, "Preventive Detention and the Prediction of Dangerousness. Some Fictions About Predictions." *Journal of Legal Education*, Vol. 23, 1969.

CHAPTER SEVEN

1. Jill Johnston, *The Village Voice*, March 25, 1971, and May 6, 1971.
2. J. J. Bachofen, *Myth, Religion and Mother Right*, translated by Ralph Manheim, 1926, Bollingen Series LXXXIV (Princeton, N.J.: Princeton University Press, 1967).
3. Gilbert D. Bartell, *Group Sex* (New York: Peter H. Wyden, 1971).
4. Charlotte Wolff, *Love Between Women* (New York: St. Martins, 1971).
5. Alfred C. Kinsey, Wardell B. Pomeroy, Clyde E. Martin, Paul H. Gebhard, *Sexual Behavior in the Female* (New York: Pocket Books, 1953).
6. Hubert Selby, Jr., "The Queen Is Dead," *Last Exit to Brooklyn* (New York: Grove Press, Inc., 1957).
7. Marcel Saghir, Eli Robins, Bonnie Walbran, and Kathy Gentry, "Homosexuality IV: Psychiatric Disorders and Disability in the Female Homosexual," *American Journal of Psychiatry*, Vol. 27, 1970; Wolff, op. cit.

CHAPTER EIGHT

1. Nancy Henley, "On Sexism and Racism: A resource paper published as part of the Report of the Sub-Committee on Women of the Committee on Equal Opportunity in Psychology, February 1971.

2. Toni Morrison, "What the Black Women Think About Women's Lib." New York *Times Magazine*, August 22, 1971.

3. Frances Beale, "Double Jeopardy: To Be Black and Female," in *The Black Woman: An Anthology*. Toni Cade, ed. (New York: New American Library, 1970).

4. Joanna Clark, "Motherhood" in *The Black Woman: An Anthology*, op. cit.

5. Barbara Burris in agreement with Kathy Barry, Terry Moon, Joann DeLor, Joann Parenti, Cate Stadelman, *The Fourth World Manifesto: An angry response to an imperialist venture against the women's liberation movement* (New Haven: Advocate Press, January 13, 1971).

6. Frantz Fanon, *A Dying Colonialism*, translated from the French by Haakon Chevalier (New York: Grove Press, 1965). Originally published in France as L'An Cinq de la Révolution Algérienne, 1959, by François Maspero.

7. Barbara Burris et al., op. cit.

8. Abram Kardiner, M.D., and Lionel Ovesey, M.D., *The Mark of Oppression* (Cleveland: Meridian Books, The World Publishing Co., May 1967).

9. Daniel P. Moynihan, "Moynihan Report and the Politics of Controversy," a Trans-action social science and Public Policy Report (Cambridge, Mass.: M.I.T. Press, 1967).

10. William H. Grier and Price M. Cobbs, *Black Rage* (New York: Basic Books, Inc., Publishers, 1968).

11. Nancy Henley, op. cit.

12. Herbert Gross, Myra Herbert, Genell Knatterud, Lawrence Donner, "The Effect of Race and Sex on the Variation of Diagnosis in a Psychiatric Emergency Room," *Journal of Nervous and Mental Disease*, Vol. 148, No. 6, 1969; Carl A. Taube, "Differential Utilization of Out-Patient Psychiatric Services by Whites and Nonwhites, 1969," Statistical Note 36, NIMH Survey and Reports Section, December 1970; Carl A. Taube, "Admission Rates to State and County Mental Hospitals by Age, Sex and Color, 1969," Statistical Note 41, NIMH Survey and Reports Section, February 1971; Earl S. Pollack, Richard Redick, Carl A. Taube, "The Application of Census Socioeconomic and Familial Data to the Study of Morbidity from Mental Disorders," *American Journal of Public Health*, Vol. 58, No. 1, 1968.

13. "Selected Symptoms of Psychological Distress," U. S. Department of Health, Education and Welfare, Public Health Services and Mental Health Administration, 1970.

14. Martha Weinman Lear, "Q: If You Rape a Woman and Steal Her TV, What Can They Get You for in NY? A: Stealing Her TV," New York *Times Magazine*, January 30, 1972.

CHAPTER NINE

1. Margaret Fuller, "The Great Lawsuit—Man versus Men; Woman versus Women, *The Dial,* July 1843. Reprinted in *Margaret Fuller: American Romantic. A Selection from Her Writings and Correspondence.* Edited by Perry Miller (Ithaca, N.Y.: Cornell University Press, 1963).

2. Ibid.

3. Emma Goldman, "The Traffic in Women," in *Anarchism and Other Essays.* Introduction by Richard Prinnon (New York: Dover Publications, 1970). Also reprinted in *Red Emma Speaks: Selected Writings and Speeches by Emma Goldman.* Compiled and edited (and beautifully introduced) by Alix Kates Shulman. (New York: Vintage Books, Random House, 1972).

4. Emma Goldman, "Woman Suffrage," in *Anarchism and Other Essays,* op. cit.

CHAPTER TEN

1. Monique Wittig, *Les Guérillères,* translated from the French by David Le Vay (New York: The Viking Press, 1971).

2. Ibid.

3. C. G. Jung and C. Kerenyi, *Essays on a Science of Mythology: The Myth of the Divine Child and the Mysteries of Eleusis,* Bollingen Series XXII, translated by R. F. C. Hull (Princeton, N.J.: Princeton University Press, 1949); Sir James Frazier, *The Golden Bough* (New York: Macmillan, 1958); C. Kerenyi, *Eleusis: Archetypal Image of Mother and Daughter,* translated from the German by Ralph Manheim, Bollingen Series LXV 4 (New York: Pantheon Books, Random House, 1967).

4. Erich Neumann, *Amor and Psyche: The Psychic Development of the Feminine. A Commentary on the Tale by Apuleius,* translated from, the German by Ralph Manheim, Bollingen Series LIV (New York: Pantheon Books, 1956).

5. Margaret Adams, "The Compassion Trap," *Psychology Today,* Vol. 5, No. 6, November 1971.

6. Emma Goldman, "Minorities versus Majorities," reprinted in *Anarchism and Other Essays,* introduction by Richard Drinnon (New York: Dover Publications, Inc., 1970).

7. Paul Goodman, "On Society, the Young, and Sex," *Psychology Today,* Vol. 5, No. 6, November 1971.

8. Anselma dell'Olio, unpublished manuscript.

9. Juliet Mitchell, *Woman's Estate* (New York: Pantheon Books, Random House, 1971).

10. Ibid.

11. Wittig, op. cit.

12. Helen Diner, *Mothers and Amazons: The First Feminine History of Culture,* edited and translated by J. P. Lundin (New York: Julian Press, 1965). (First published in the 1930's under the pseudonym of "Sir Galahad.")

13. Ibid.

14. Ibid.

15. Ibid.

16. Ibid.

17. Frazier, op. cit., 1958; Sigmund Freud, "Contributions to the Psychology of Love: The Taboo of Virginity," *Collected Papers,* Vol. 4 (1918) (New York, Basic Books, 1959).

18. Robert Briffault, *The Mothers* (New York: Grosset and Dunlap, 1927); Bachofen, *Das Mutteracht,* cited by Diner, op. cit.; Frazier, op. cit.; J. F. Lafitau, *Moeurs de Sauvages Américains Comparés aux Moeurs des Premiers Temps* (Paris: 1724); Matthew Paris, *Chronica Magna* (Chronicles and Memorials of Great Britain and Ireland), edited by S. Henry Richards Luard, 7 vols. (London: 1872–83); Nancy Reeves, *Womankind* (Chicago: Aldine, Atherton, 1971). Jesco von Puttkamer and Altair Sales have recently discovered caves in Brazil they believe were inhabited by Amazon warriors (*Time* magazine, December 27, 1971).

19. Sylvia Plath, "Medusa" in *Ariel* (New York: Harper & Row, 1965).

20. Frantz Fanon, *A Dying Colonialism,* translated by Haakon Chevalier (New York: Grove Press, Inc., 1965). Originally published in France as *L'An Cinq de la Révolution Algérienne,* 1959, by François Maspero.

21. George Fischer, *The Soviet System and Modern Society* (Chicago: Aldine-Atherton, 1968).

22. Norman L. Farberow and Edwin F. Schneidman, *The Cry for Help* (New York: McGraw-Hill, 1965).

23. Wittig, op. cit.

APPENDIX

1. Earl S. Pollack, Richard Redick, Carl A. Taube, "The Application of Census Socioeconomic and Familial Data to the Study of Morbidity from Mental Disorders," *American Journal of Public Health,* Vol. 58, No. 1, 1968.

2. Carl A. Taube, "Changes in the Distribution of Patient Care

Episodes, 1955–68 by Type of Facility," Statistical Note 23, NIMH Survey and Reports Section, April 1970.

3. Carl A. Taube, "Distribution of Psychiatric Beds by Geographic Division—1970," Statistical Note 45, NIMH Survey and Reports Section, April 1971.

4. Ronald Conley, Margaret Conwell, Shirley G. Willner, "The Cost of Mental Illness, 1968," Statistical Note 30, NIMH Survey and Reports Section, October 1970.

5. Shirley Angrist, Mark Lefton, Simon Dinitz, Benjamin Pasamanick, *Women After Treatment* (New York: Appleton-Century-Crofts, 1968); Taube, "Changes in the Distribution of Patient Care Episodes, 1955–1968 by Type of Facility."

6. Allan M. Dershowitz, "Two Models of Commitment: The Medical and the Legal," *The Humanist,* July/August 1971.

7. Inmates of Institutions, 1960 Bureau of the Census, U. S. Department of Commerce.

8. Thomas S. Szasz, *The Manufacture of Madness* (New York: Harper & Row, 1970).

9. Carl A. Taube, "Admission Rates by Marital Status, Outpatient Psychiatric Services," Statistical Note 35, NIMH Survey and Reports Section, December 1970.

10. M. Greenblatt, R. G. Moore, R. F. Albert, N. H. Solomon, *The Prevention of Hospitalization: Treatment Without Admission for Psychiatric Patients* (New York: Grune and Stratton, 1963).

11. Alan M. Kraft, Paul R. Binner, Brenda Dickey, "The Community Mental Health Program and the Longer-Stay Patient," *Archives of General Psychiatry,* Vol. 16, January 1967.

12. Charles Thrall, "Presenting Problems of Psychiatric Out-Patients," Out-Patient Studies Section, Biometrics Branch, NIMH, 1963.

13. Charles Kadushin, *Why People Go to Psychiatrists* (New York: Atherton Press, 1969).

14. Gerald Landsberg, David Cole, Eleanor Sabbagh, Rachel Deutsch, "Characteristics of Enrolled Patients as of September 1969," Maimonides Medical Center, Community Mental Health Center, December 1969; Rachel Deutsch, Gerald Landsberg, David Cole, "Reports of a Survey of Patients: January 17, 1970–June 16, 1970," Maimonides Medical Center, Community Mental Health Center, June 1970; Phyllis Chesler, Janice Lasecki, Lucy DiPaola, unpublished study, 1971.

15. Richard Redick, "Age-Sex Diagnostic Distribution of Additions to Community Mental Health Centers 1968," Statistical Note 13, NIMH Survey and Reports Section, January 1970.

16. William Ryan, *Distress in the City: Essays on the Design and Ad-*

ministration of Mental Health Services (Cleveland: The Press of Case Western Reserve University, 1969).

17. Anita K. Bahn, Margaret Conwell, Peter Hurley, "Survey of Psychiatric Practice: Report on a Field Test," *Archives of General Psychiatry,* Vol. 12, 1965.

18. William Schofield, *Psychotherapy: The Purchase of Friendship* (Englewood Cliffs, N.J.: Prentice-Hall, 1969).

19. Kadushin, op. cit.

20. Olle Hagnell, *A Prospective Study of the Incidence of Mental Disorders: The Lundby Project* (Sweden: Svenska Bokforlaget, 1966).

21. Carl A. Taube, "Differential Utilization of Out-Patient Psychiatric Services by Whites and Nonwhites, 1969," Statistical Note 36, NIMH Survey and Reports Section, December 1970.

22. Carl A. Taube, "Admission Rates to State and County Mental Hospitals by Age, Sex and Color, 1969," Statistical Note 41, NIMH Survey and Reports Section, February 1971.

23. Herbert Gross, Myra Herbert, Genell Knatterud, Lawrence Donner, "The Effect of Race and Sex on the Variation of Diagnosis in a Psychiatric Emergency Room," *Journal of Nervous and Mental Disease,* Vol. 148, No. 6, 1969.

24. Leo Srole, Thomas S. Langner, Stanley T. Michael, Mervin K. Opler, Thomas A. C. Rennie, *Mental Health in the Metropolis: Midtown Manhattan Study* (New York: McGraw-Hill, 1962).

25. Taube, "Admission Rates by Marital Status: Outpatient Psychiatric Services—1969."

26. Shirley Angrist, Mark Lefton, Simon Dinitz, Benjamin Pasamanick, *Women After Treatment* (New York: Appleton-Century-Crofts, 1968).

27. Taube, "Admission Rates by Martial Status: Outpatient Psychiatric Services—1969."

28. Jessie Bernard, "The Paradox of the Happy Marriage" in *Woman in Sexist Society: Studies in Power and Powerlessness,* edited by Vivian Gornick and Barbara K. Moran. (New York: Basic Books, 1971).

29. Norman L. Farberow and Edwin F. Schneidman, "Statistical Comparisons between Attempted and Committed Suicides," *The Cry for Help* (New York: McGraw-Hill, 1961).

30. Pollack et al., op. cit.

31. Hagnell, op. cit.

32. Pauline Bart, "Depression in Middleaged Women" in Vivian Gornick and Barbara K. Moran, eds., *Woman in Sexist Society: Studies in Power and Powerlessness* (New York: Basic Books, 1971).

33. Srole et al., op. cit.

34. Richard Redick, "Admission Rates by Highest Grade of School Completed: Out-Patient Psychiatric Services 1969," Statistical Note 45, NIMH Survey and Reports Section, 1970.

35. Taube, "Admission Rates to State and County Mental Hospitals by Age, Sex and Color, 1969."

36. Pollack et al., op. cit.

37. David C. McClelland and Norman F. Watt, "Sex Role Alienation in Schizophrenia," *Journal of Abnormal Psychology*, Vol. 73, No. 3, 1968.

38. Roxanne Dunbar, "Caste and Class," *No More Fun and Games: A Journal of Female Liberation*, Issue 3, November 1969; Barbara Burris in agreement with Kathy Barry, Terry Moon, Joann DeLor, Joann Parenti, Cate Stadelman, *The Fourth World Manifesto: An angry response to an imperialist venture against women's liberation movement.* New Haven: Advocate Press, January 13, 1971.

39. August B. Hollingshead and Frederick C. Redlich, *Social Class and Mental Illness* (New York: John Wiley, 1958); Bruce Dohrenwend and Barbara Dohrenwend, *Social Status and Psychological Disorders* (New York: John Wiley, 1969); Srole et al., op. cit.

40. Srole et al., op. cit.

41. Dorothy C. Leighton, John S. Harding, David B. Machlin, Allister M. MacMillan, Alexander Leighton, *The Character of Danger: The Stirling County Study of Psychiatric Disorder and Sociocultural Environment,* Vol. III (New York-London: Basic Books, 1963).

42. Hollingshead and Redlich, op. cit.

Index

Women After Treatment
Shirley Anquist p. 50

CREDITS